ANGLES OF ATLANTA

ANGLES OF ATLANTA

A Culture of Resilience and Soul

Desirée James

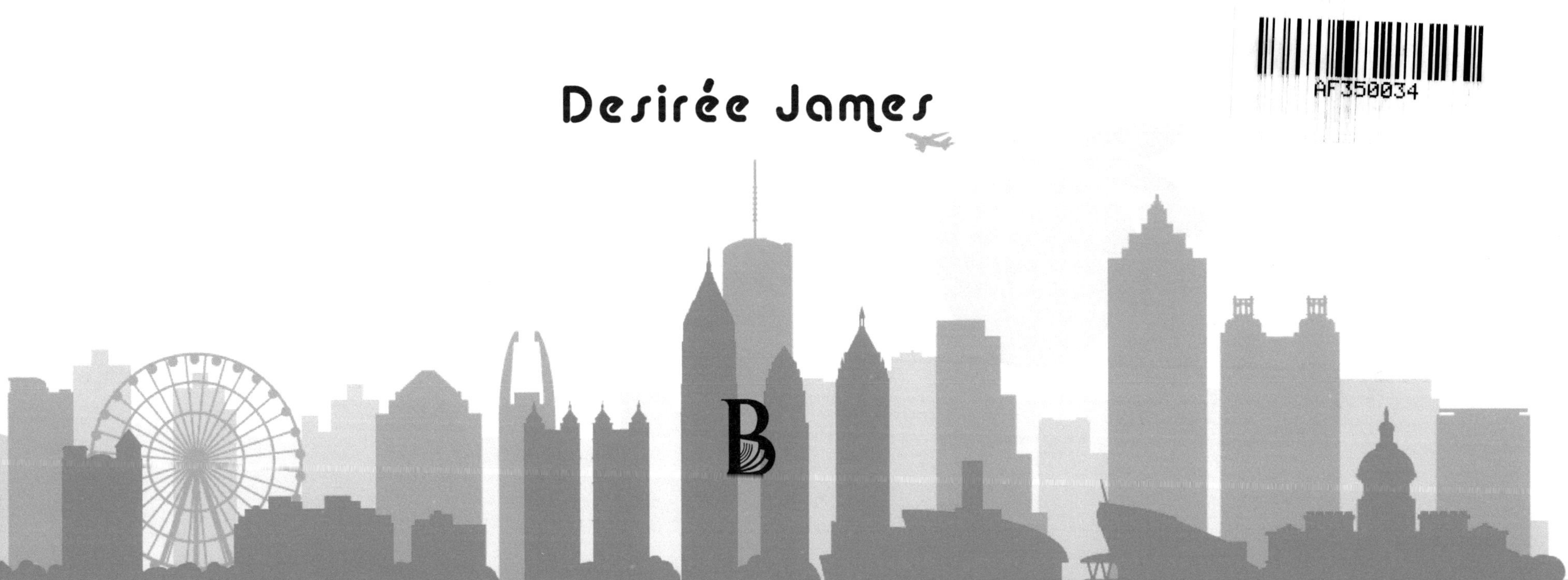

AF350034

Dedicated to the life and legacy and love of my dad and my brother,
the late Herman James Sr. and Herman James Jr. It's with heartfelt gratitude that
I thank my mom, Mattie James, my brother, Shannon James Sr., and my uncle, Bill Russell, Sr.

If you seek me and put me first and study my word,
you will not have to stress over your job or photography project . . .
I will give you innovative ideas that you know not of, says the Lord.
—Mattie James

BOOKLOGIX®
Alpharetta, Georgia

ISBN: 978-1-6653-0776-5

This ISBN is the property of BookLogix for the express purpose of sales and distribution of this title. The content of this book is the property of the copyright holder only. BookLogix does not hold any ownership of the content of this book and is not liable in any way for the materials contained within. The views and opinions expressed in this book are the property of the Author/Copyright holder, and do not necessarily reflect those of BookLogix.

Library of Congress Control Number: 2024915181

♾ This paper meets the requirements of ANSI/NISO Z39.48-1992 (Permanence of Paper)

1 0 1 5 2 4

Visit Desirée's website for more photos and purchasing options: dezsskyline.com

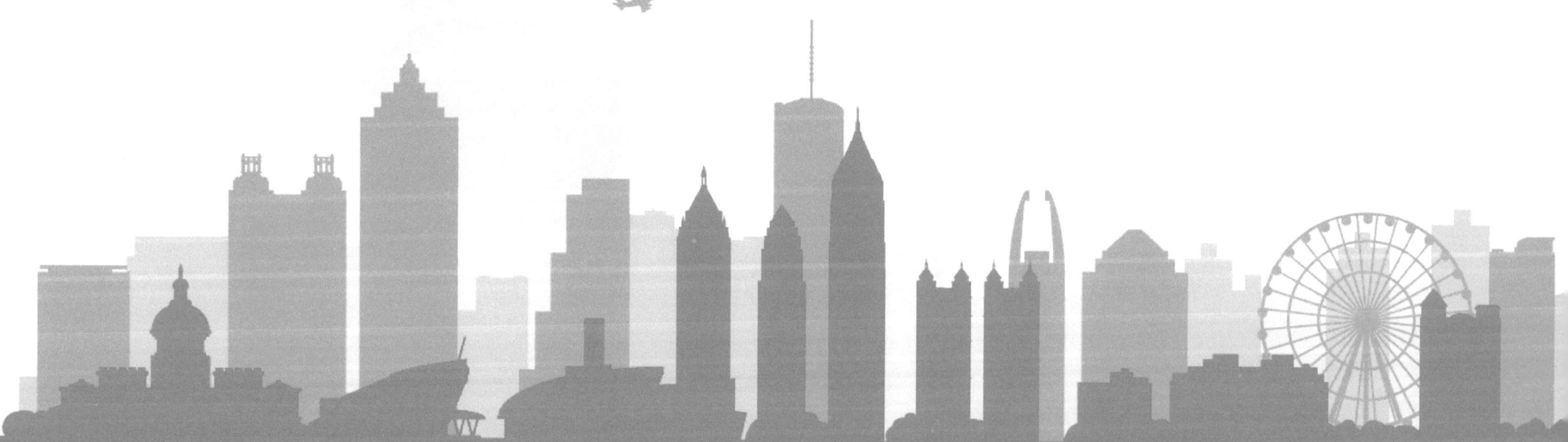

Introduction

Feast your eyes on *Angles of Atlanta*, a creation of collective moments in time.

Reflect on the past, bask in the South's hidden gems, and visually experience the magnificence of this mecca!

Magic often happens—even at the most inopportune times. In 2014, I can remember wanting to learn something new and turning it into something extraordinary. I began immersing myself in a couple of photography classes and discovering my knack for capturing special moments on camera. Things were going well in my life.

In the summer of 2015, I ventured to Louisiana to give my mom a much needed break from caring for my father, who was experiencing health challenges. That week was time well-spent. That Sunday, before heading to church with Mom, I ventured to Dad's bedroom to plant a goodbye kiss on his forehead. Next, it was time to fly home to Atlanta. After landing safely while the plane was still rolling, I phoned Mom to let her know I had made it. Mom hesitantly and gently shared some unexpected news. My dad had passed with no warning.

I was a daddy's girl. He was my rock and once represented great stability and strength in my life. Soon, my drive for photography began to dwindle. My very foundation was shaken, and the lack of vision in this area lasted for a few years.

Then, the pandemic became a reality. For some, it was doom and gloom. For me, it was an opportunity to grow.

While home for a few months, I was able to navigate around the city without the challenges of traffic congestion. I carved out the time I needed to experience the city more intimately—the homelessness, the amazing architecture, the rich history and evolution of our communities, hidden treasures, and so much more.

Friends played a special role in my journey. They saw my gifts,

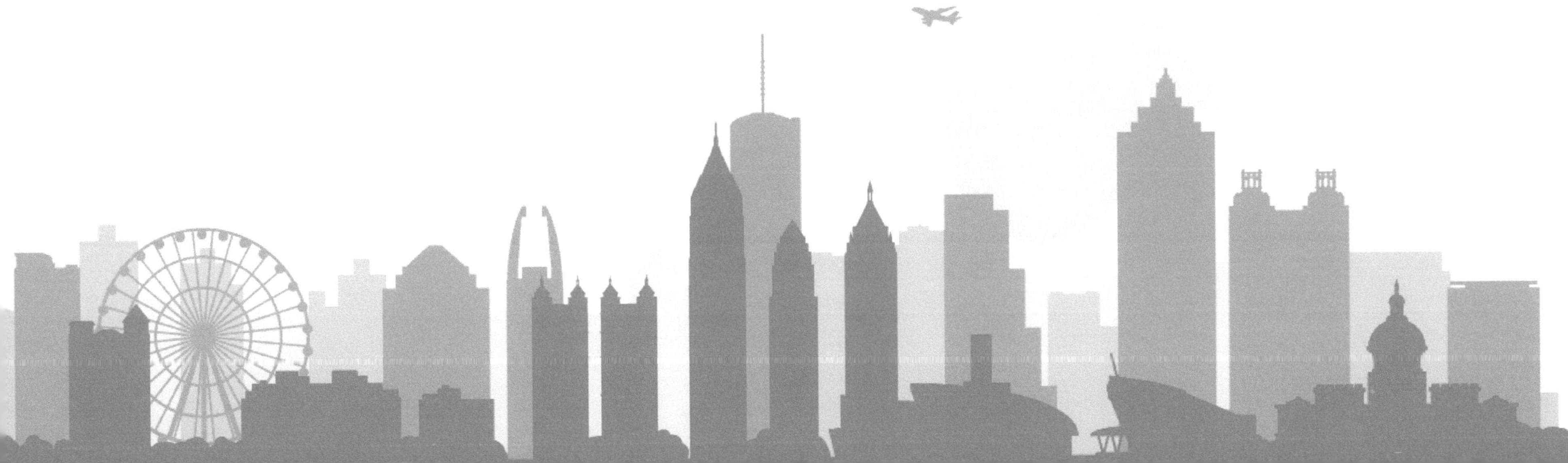

encouraged me, and inspired me to move to higher levels of fulfillment. My spark for photography began to blossom and come back to life. My desire to write this book was born.

My focus was on orange-tinged sunrises and wondrous city skylines. It was therapeutic, but often challenging and unpredictable. I felt that God Himself was painting a kaleidoscope of breathtaking hues just for me. Now, mornings are quite special—a fresh opportunity to discover a better me, to push harder, to seek clarity, and to hone my creativity. My passion grew and it birthed in me a desire to arise early, to exercise patience, and to capture the ultimate beauty I had been missing. Some scenes were framed in risky situations and in the fiery upheaval of protests. Anything short of excellence evoked short-lived moments of disappointment, but somehow, it was God's perfect timing, and it was all worthwhile.

Atlanta's eclectic vibe is a song of constant renewal. My camera lens often illuminates cultural aspects that educate and the ingenuity of young people that stimulates. This collection reflects a ray of hope—the vertex of the past, the present, and the future. A witness to the tenacity that's been bold for generations and bold enough to pave the future.

THESE ARE THE *ANGLES OF ATLANTA*!

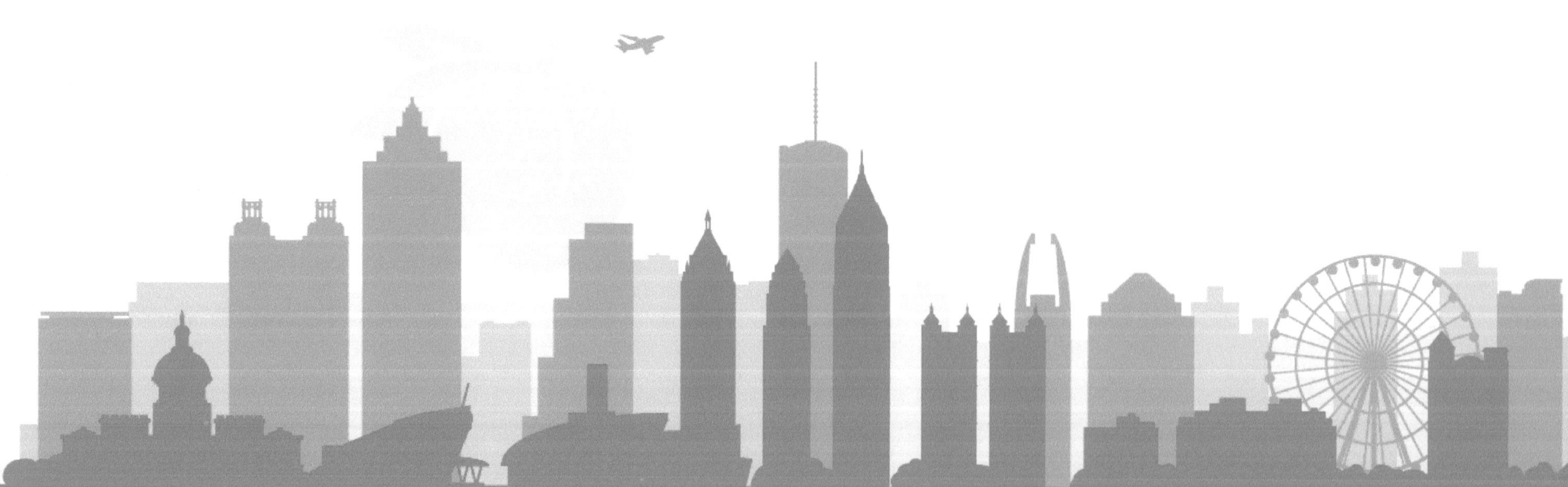

Atlanta's Sunrise

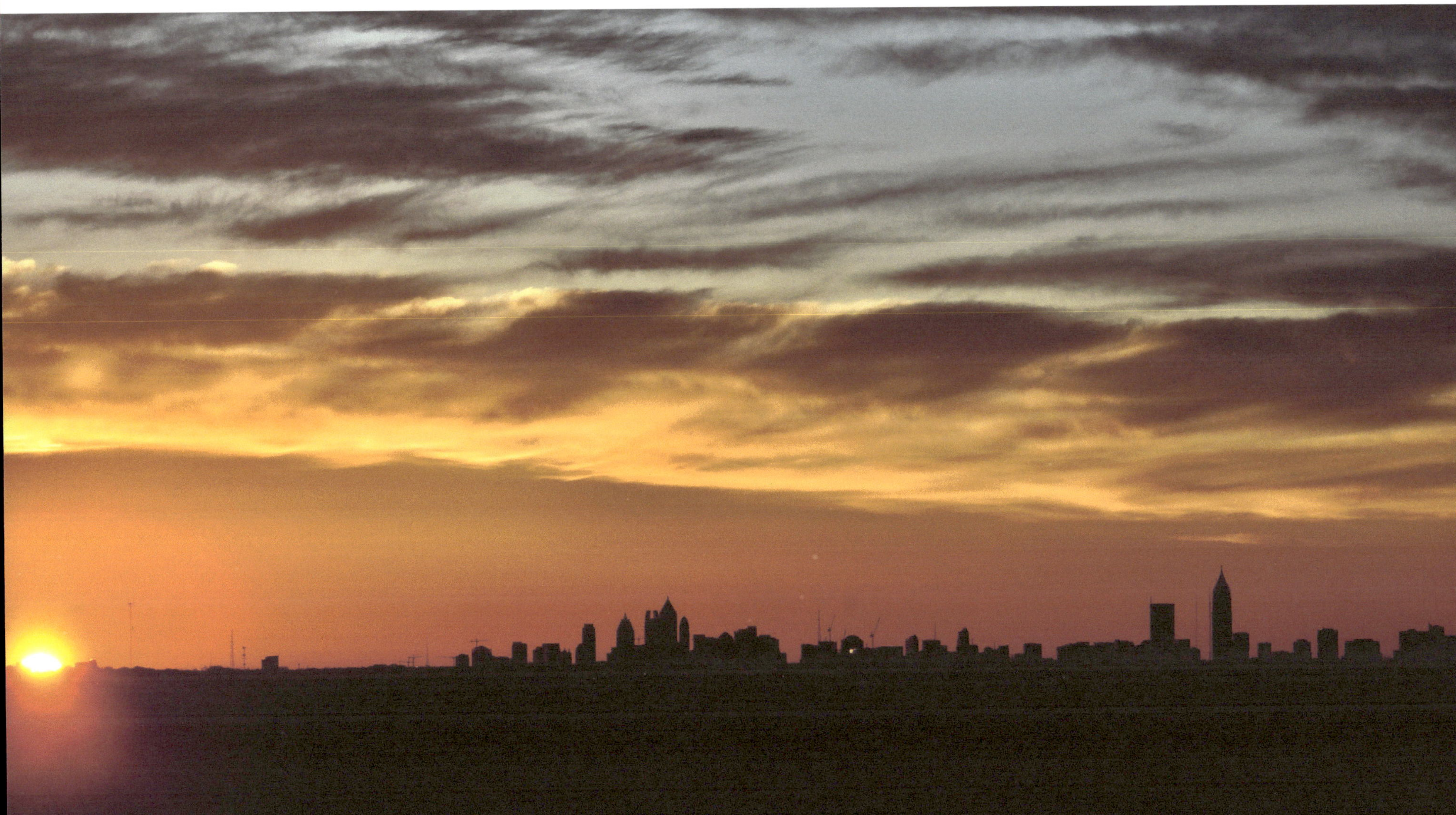

Traffic

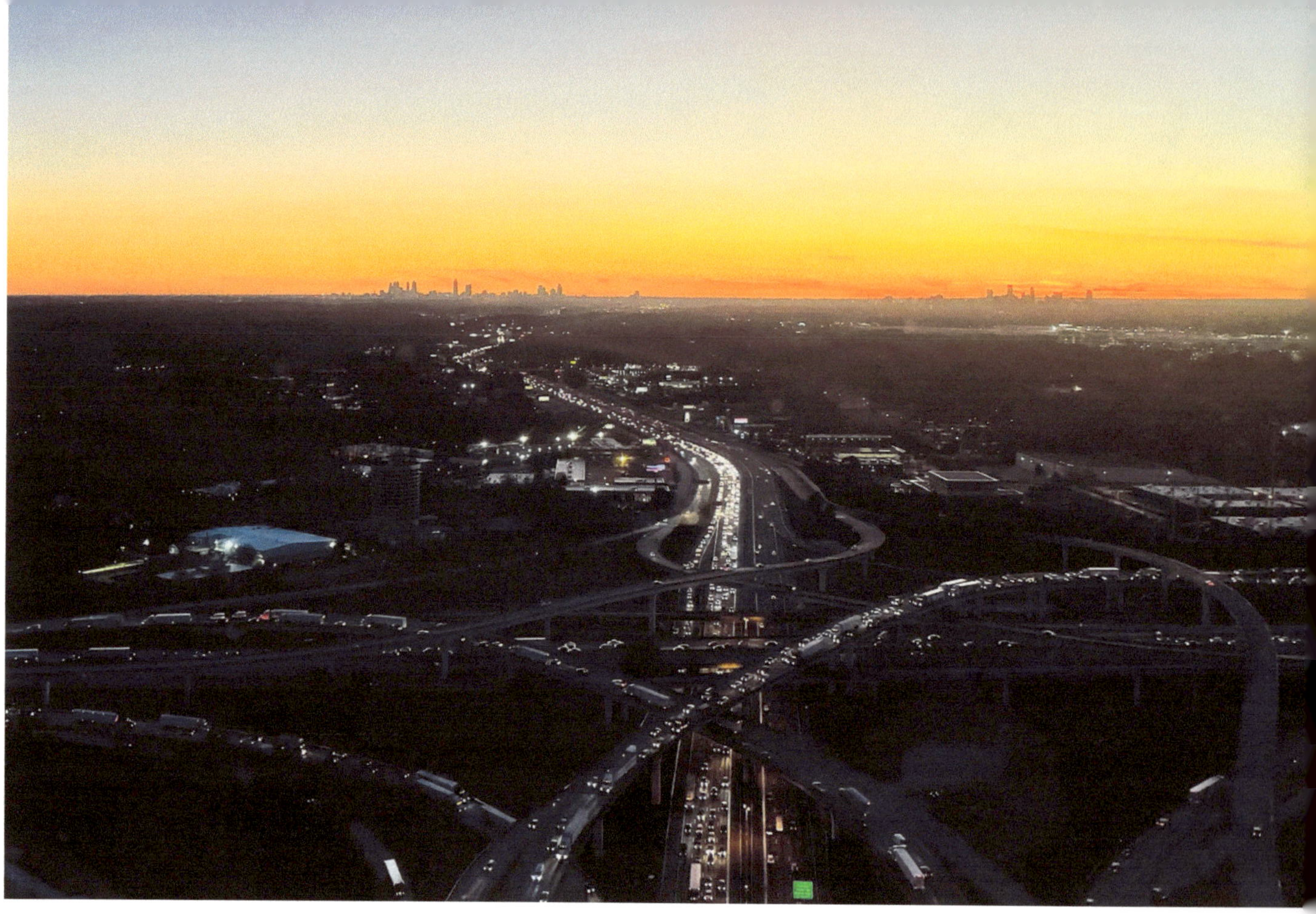

Spaghetti Junction

Spaghetti Junction at sunrise; photo courtesy of Smilin' Mark McKay. This junction intersects Interstates 85 and 285, along with lesser roads in Atlanta.

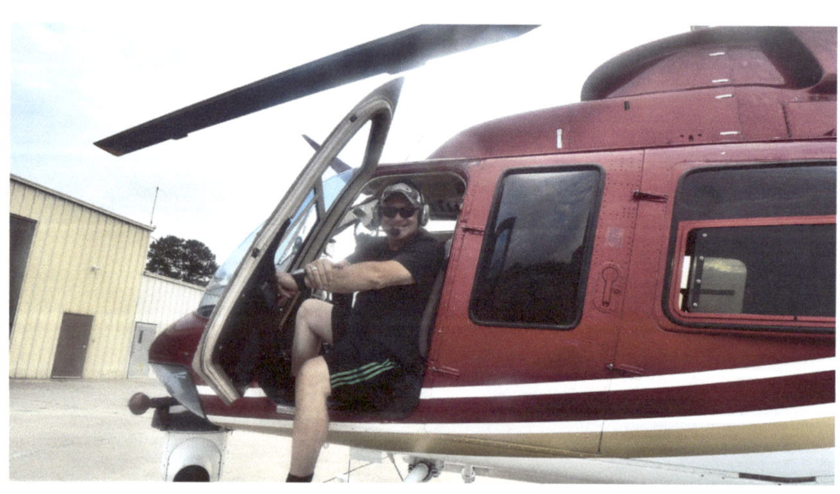

Smilin' Mark McKay

Atlanta's morning cup of coffee, Smilin' Mark McKay, is an airborne traffic anchor and reporter for 95.5 WSB Radio and WSB-TV Ch 2. Mark is also an Edward R. Murrow Award winner, as well as an Emmy award-winning former sports anchor/reporter at CNN.

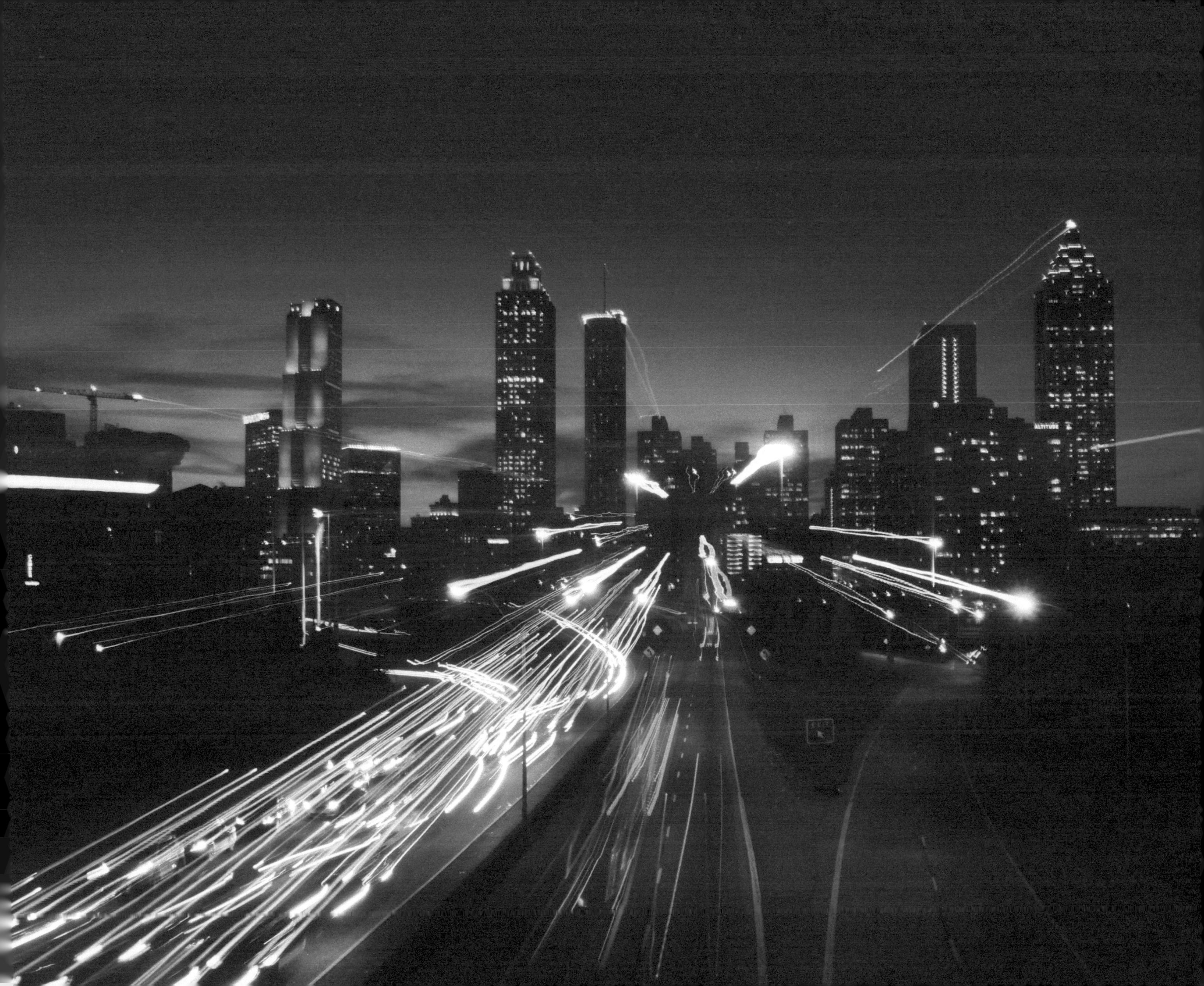

Atlanta's Hartsfield-Jackson Airport

During the pandemic, I spent many mornings in the airport's cell phone lot, determined to capture an image of an aircraft ascending out at sunrise. After about two weeks, it finally happened— THAT AHA MOMENT.

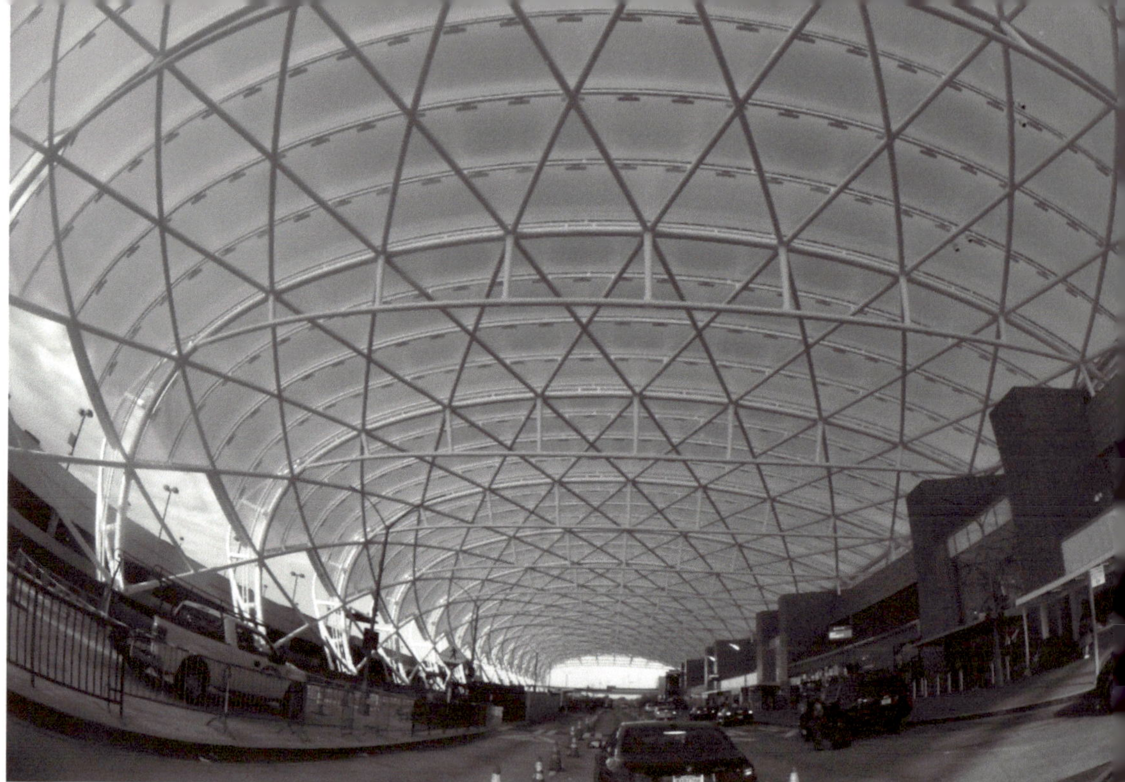

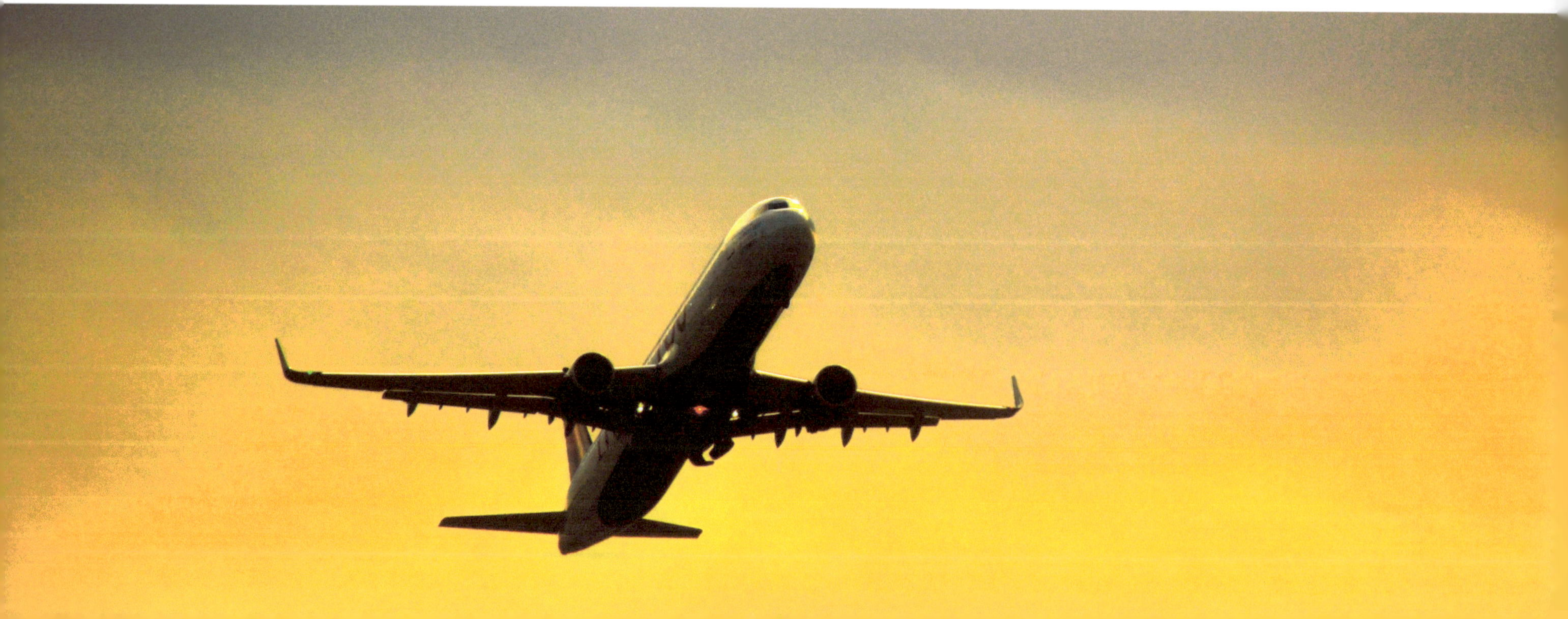

Atlanta City Skyline

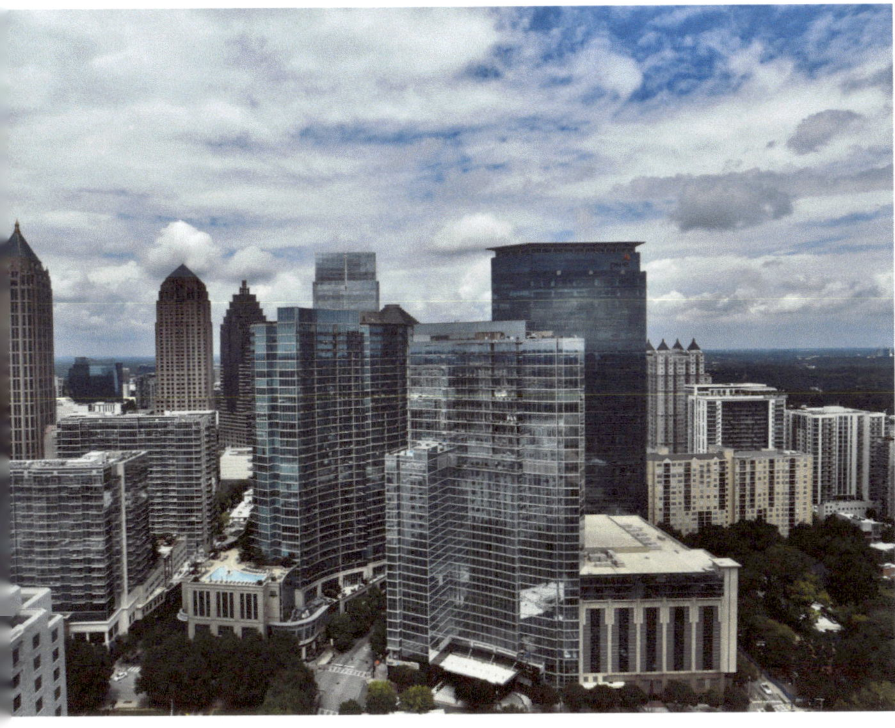

Midtown Atlanta

Downtown Atlanta

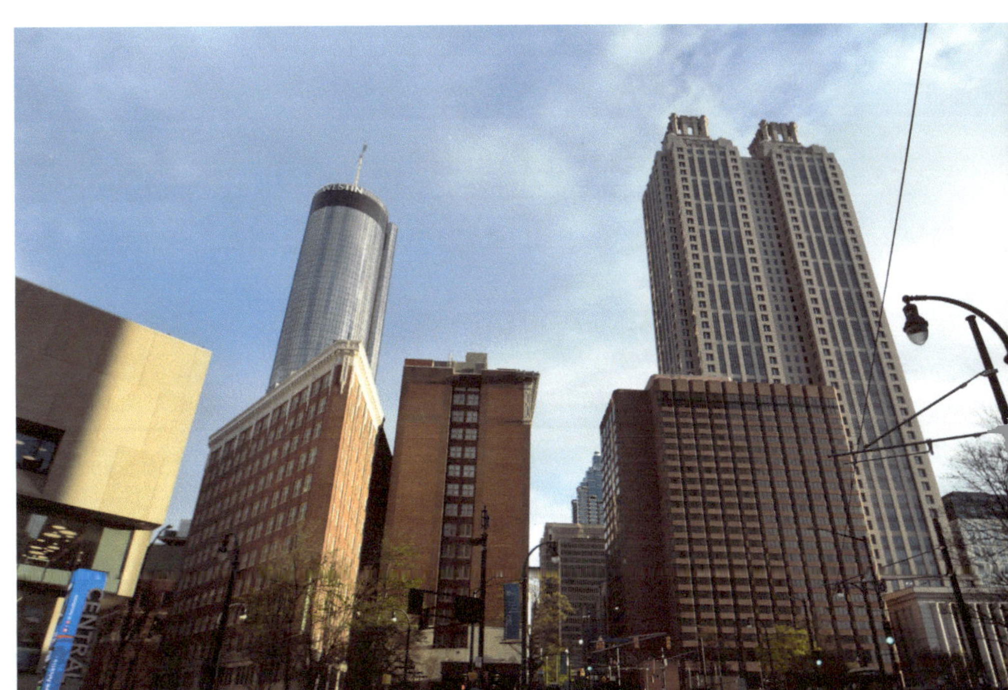

Iconic Atlanta Buildings

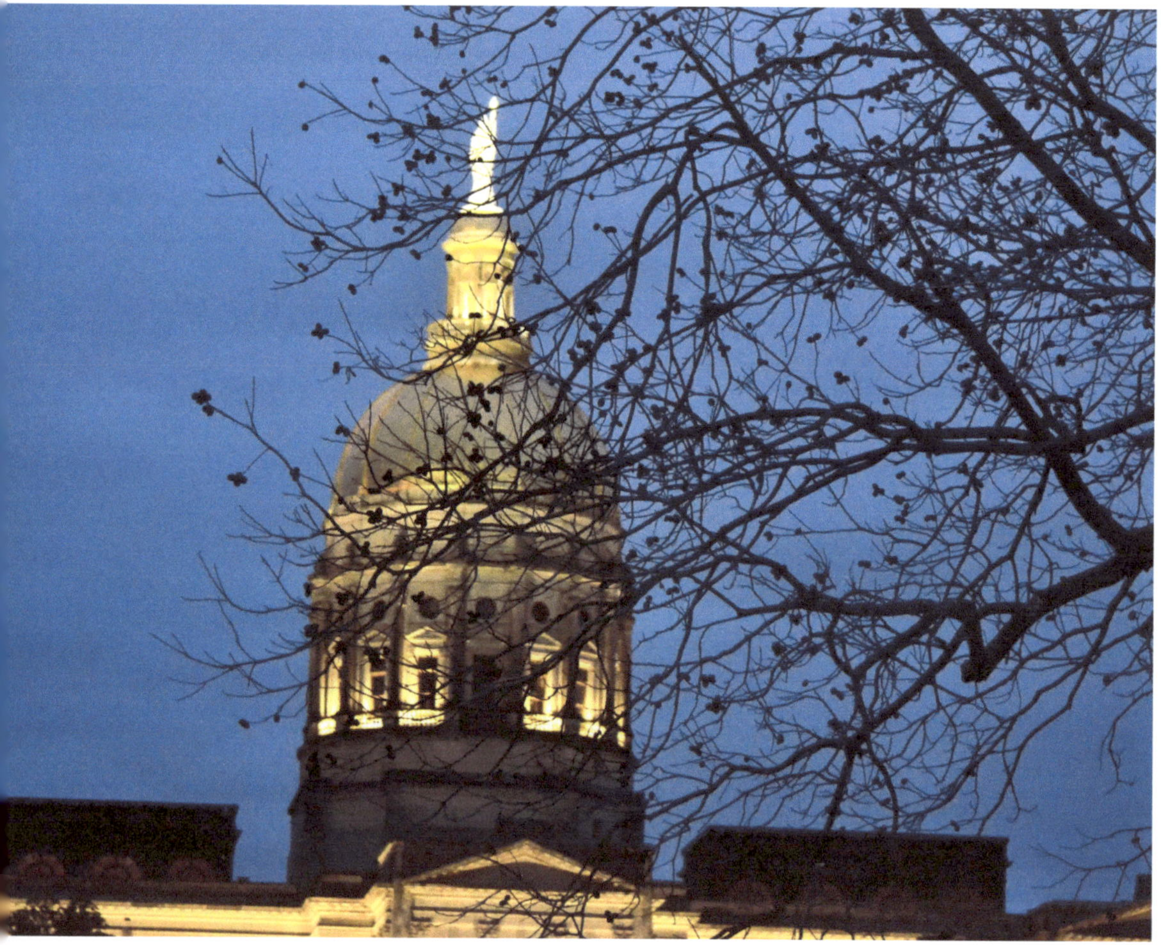

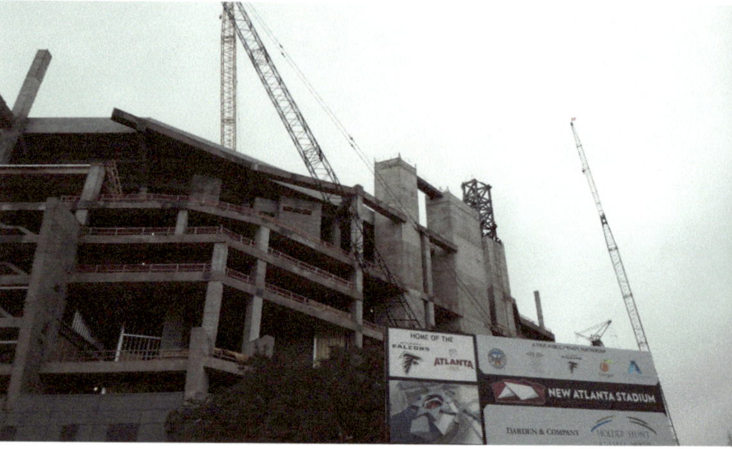

Atlanta's Mercedes-Benz Stadium under Construction in 2014

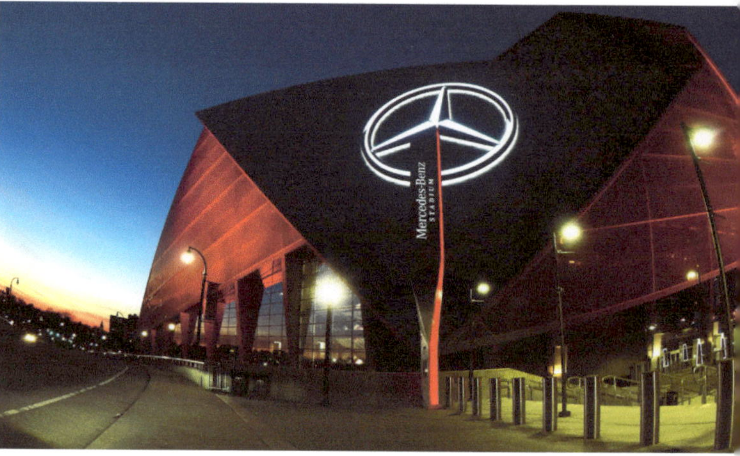

Georgia State Capitol

One of the most recognizable features of the Atlanta skyline, the Georgia State Capitol was completed in 1889. The gold for the dome was donated by the citizens of Dahlonega and Lumpkin County.

Atlanta's Mercedes-Benz Stadium—Now

This photo of Mercedes-Benz Stadium was worth the risks when I stepped out into the narrow margin of rush hour traffic. I captured it in the nick of time, catching an amazing sunset alongside the entertainment center that is home to both the Atlanta Falcons and Atlanta United.

The Promenade II at Dusk

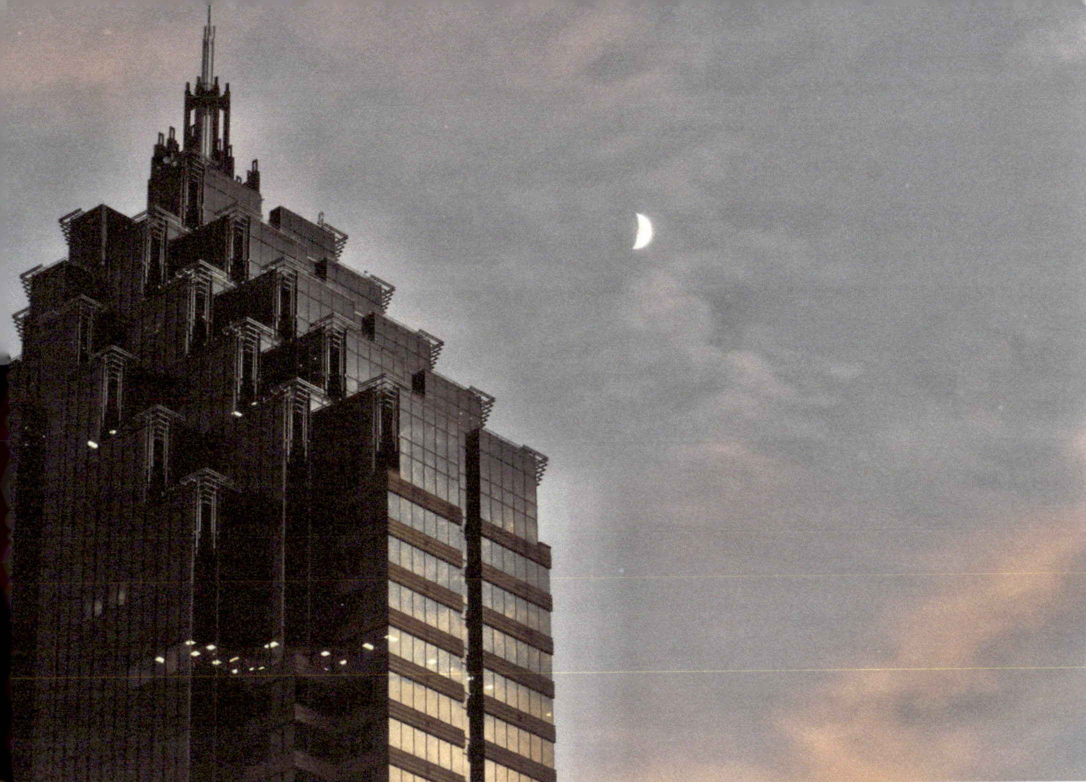

Atlanta's King and Queen Buildings

Named for their bedecked crowns, housed in the Perimeter Center are Atlanta's King and Queen Buildings, two of the tallest structures in the suburban United States. Fatigued by conditions and ebbed by time, with a steadied balance, I captured this magnificent photo at sunrise.

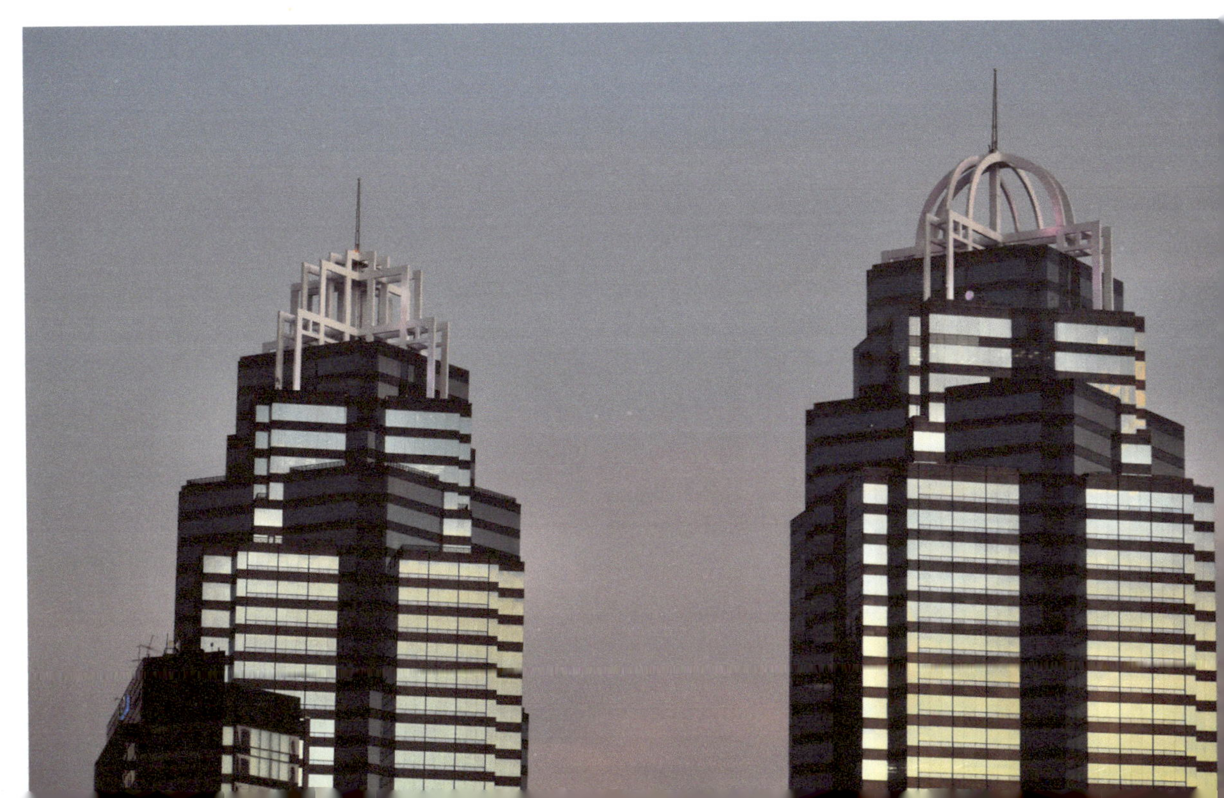

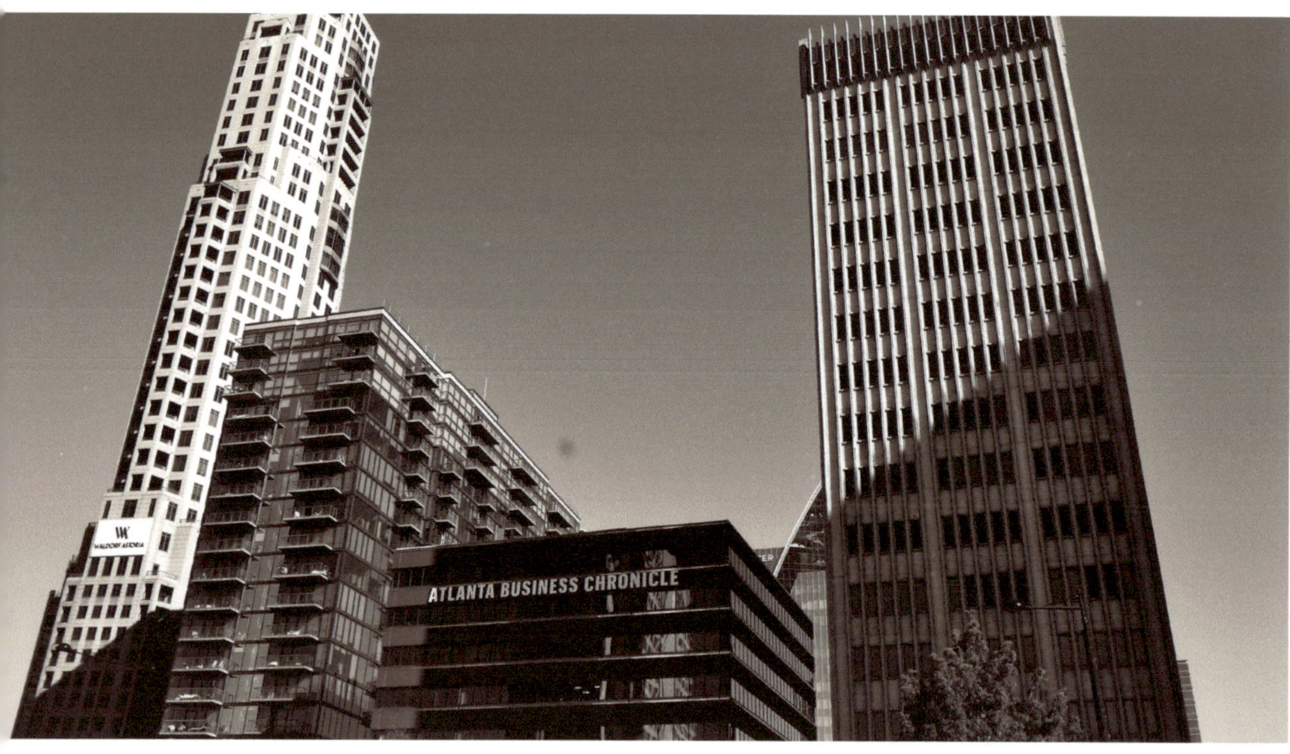

The *Atlanta Business Chronicle*
The Atlanta Business Chronicle, *with its inception in 1978, continues to serve the Atlanta community with local business news.*

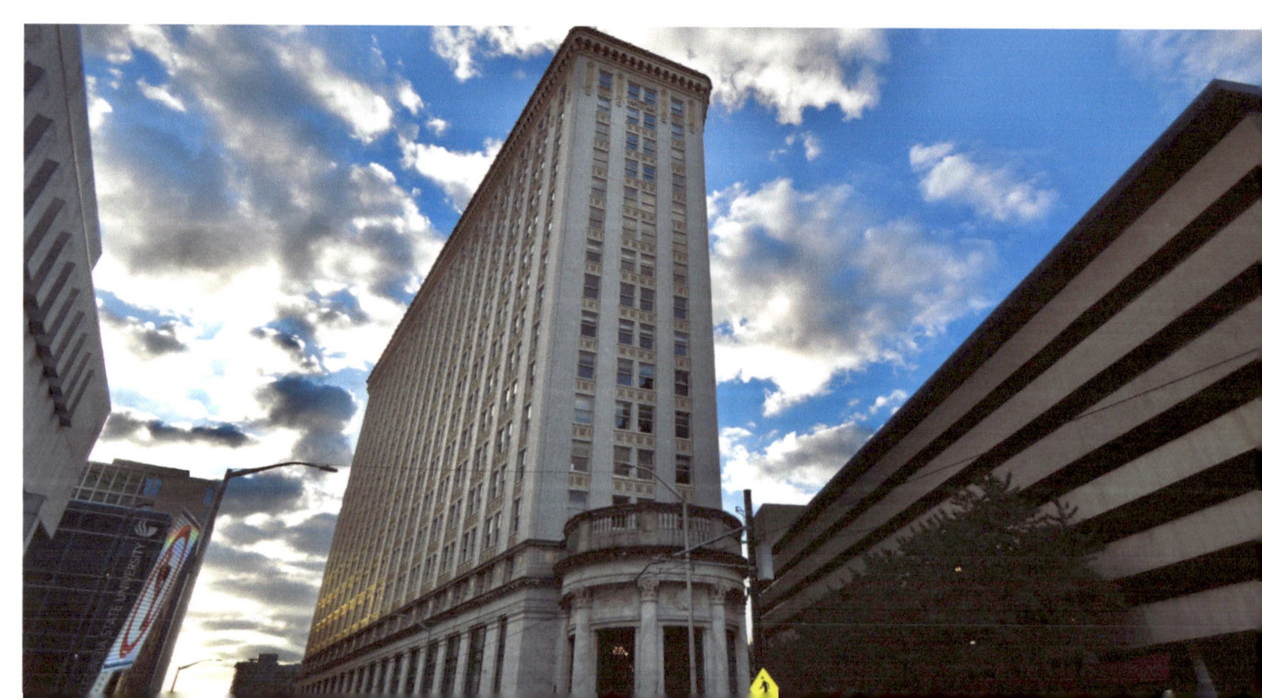

The Hurt Building
This triangular-shaped structure located in downtown Atlanta was once home to the Federal Reserve Bank of Atlanta.

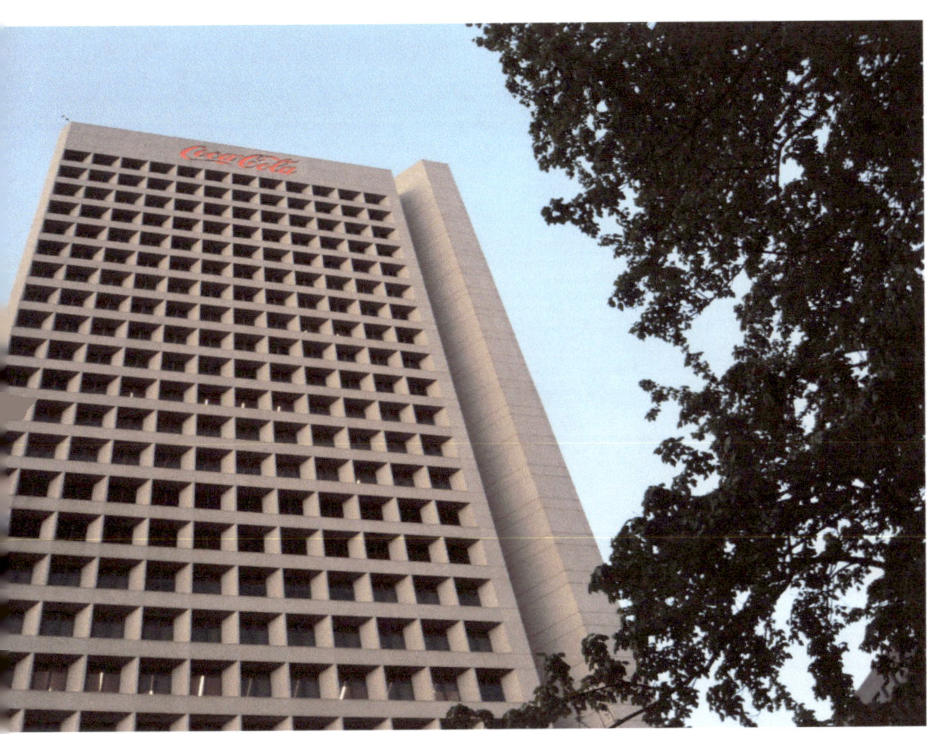

The Coca-Cola Company Headquarters

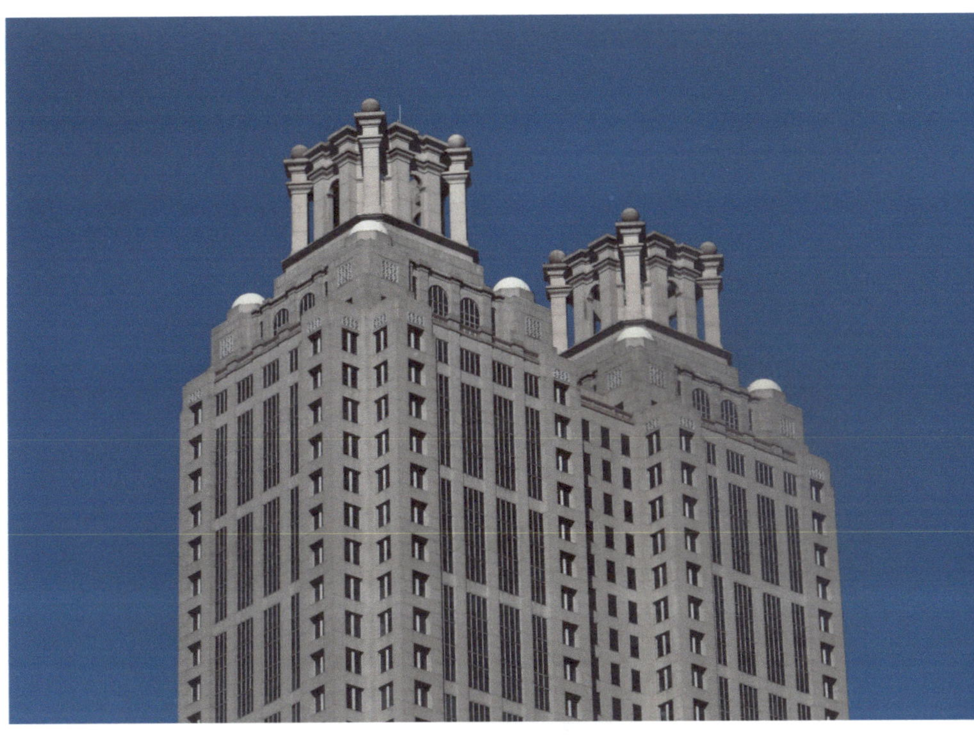

191 Peachtree Tower

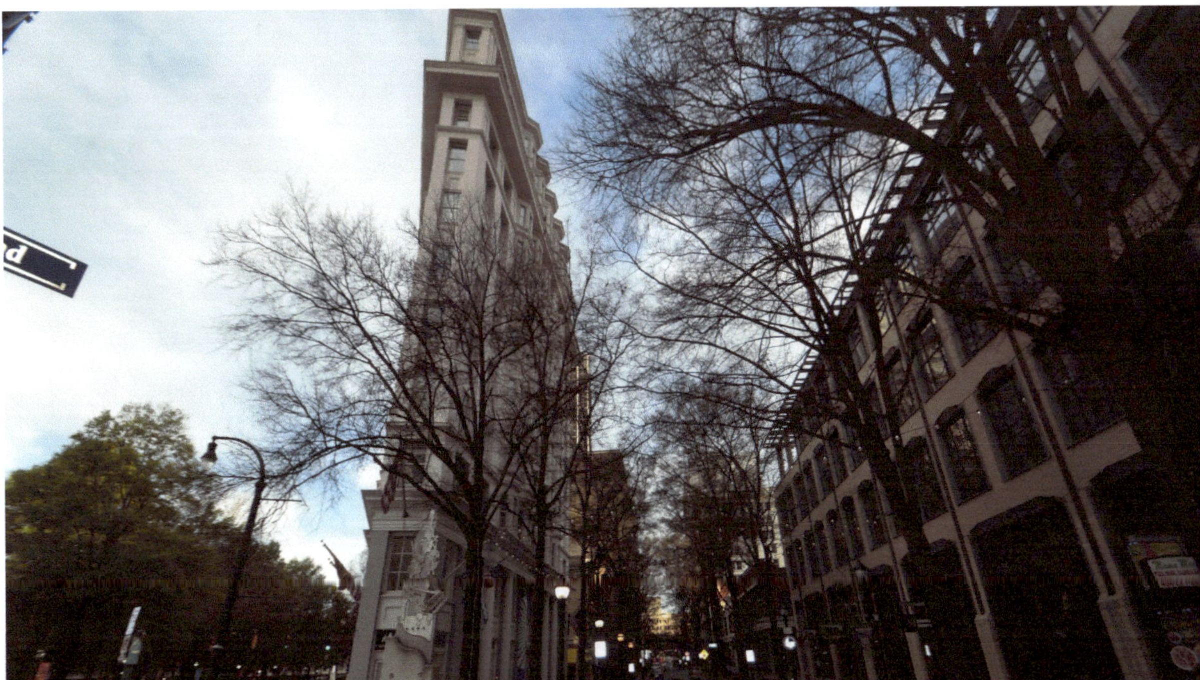

Flatiron Building
Built in 1897, the Flatiron Building is Atlanta's oldest Skyscraper.

Bank of America Plaza

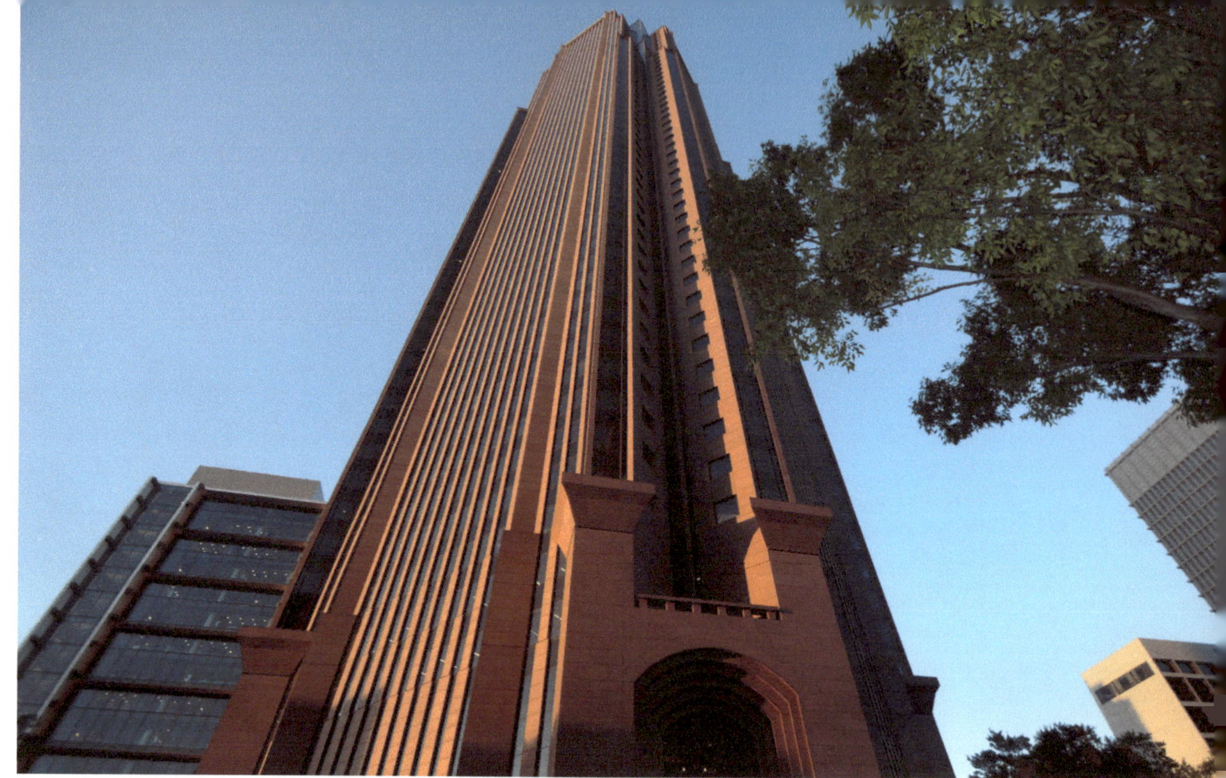

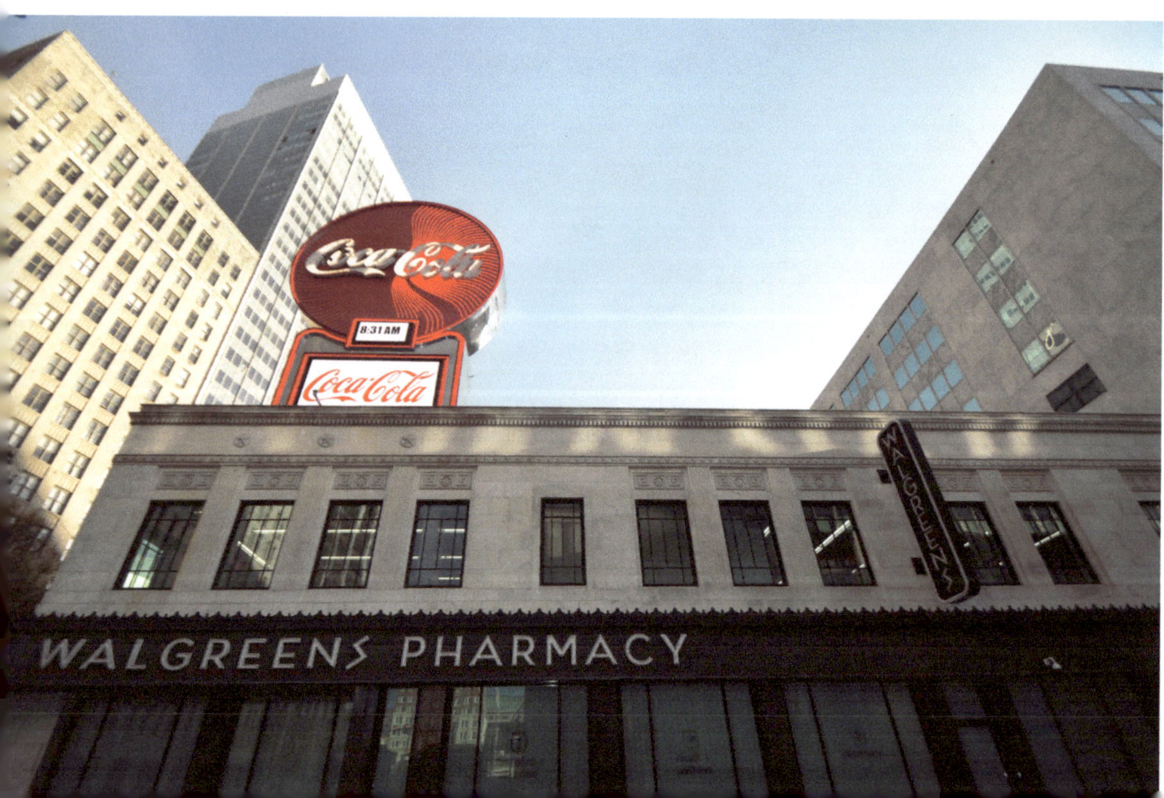

Olympia Building

The Olympia building is one of many landmarks in 5 Points where the Walgreens and Coca-Cola signage has been for years.

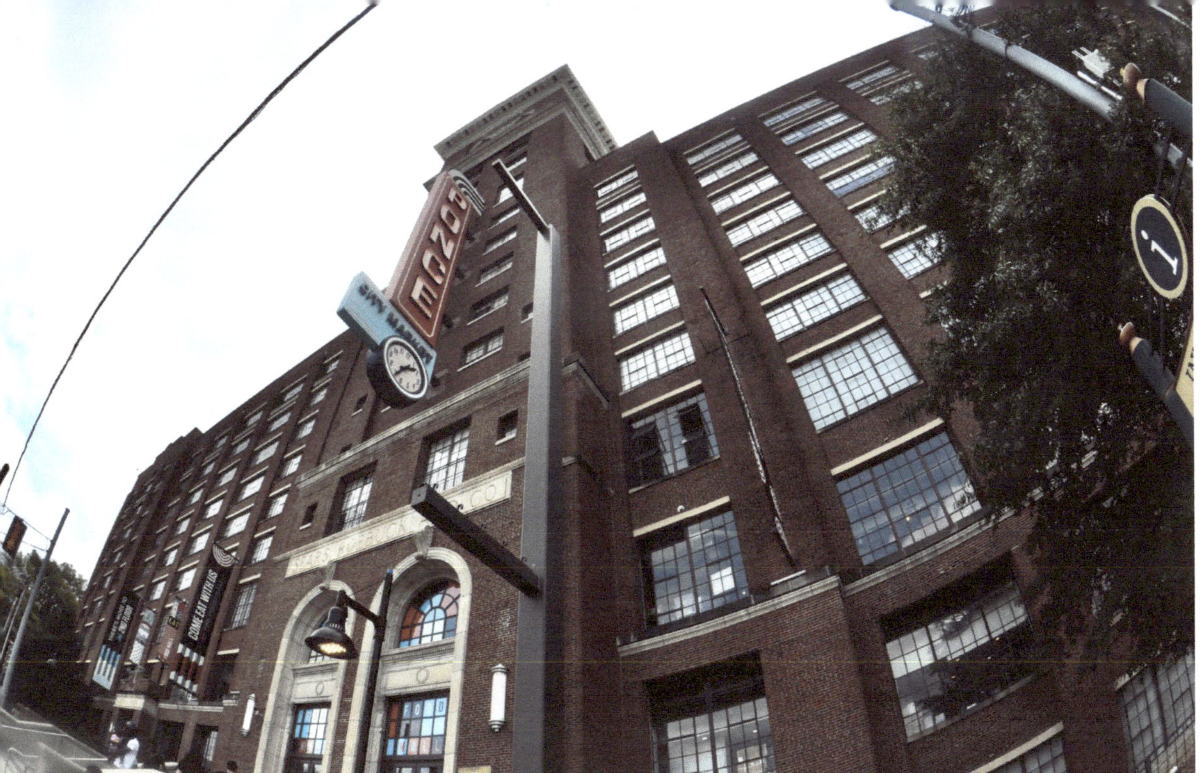

Ponce City Market
Once the site of the historic Sears building, Ponce City Market is now a vibrant multiuse market with food, shops, and living spaces.

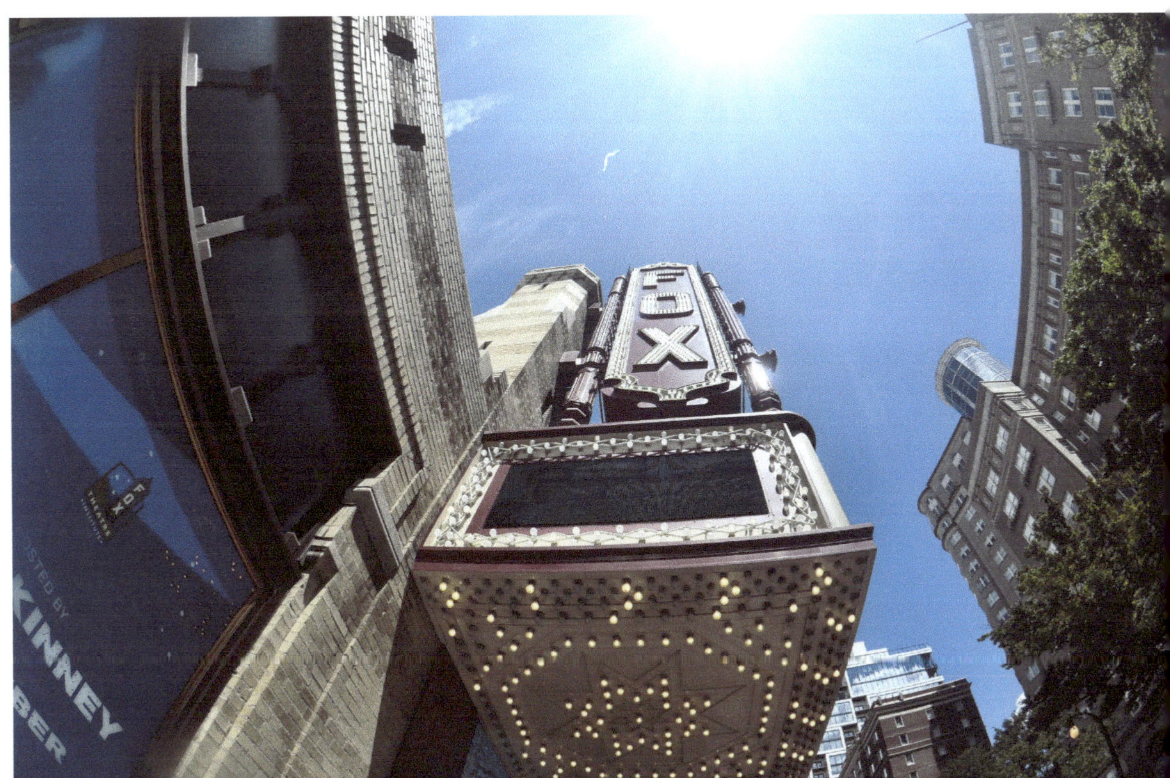

Fox Theatre
The historic and iconic "Fabulous Fox Theatre" lives up to its name as a movie palace. The size of a city block, it was one of the largest movie houses built during the height of the Golden Age.

Grady Hospital

Grady Hospital was named after the editor of the Atlanta Constitution, Henry W. Grady. Grady was concerned about the quality of care that often affected Atlanta's poor. Historic segregation led to many units being named "The Gradys" by older African American residents.

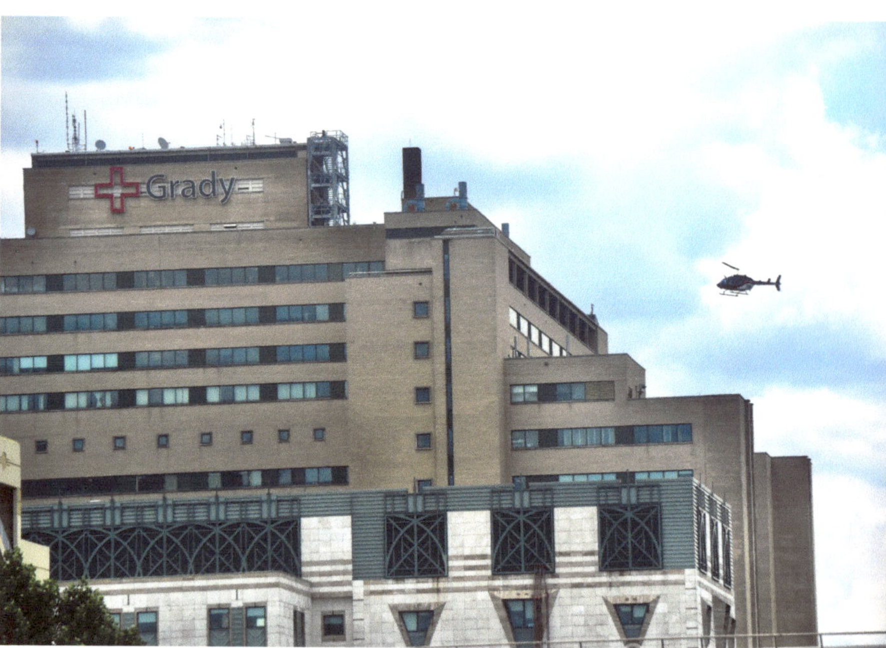

State Farm Arena and Mercedes-Benz Stadium

These stadiums serve as home to the Atlanta Falcons, the Atlanta United, and the Atlanta Hawks while also being entertainment meccas in the city.

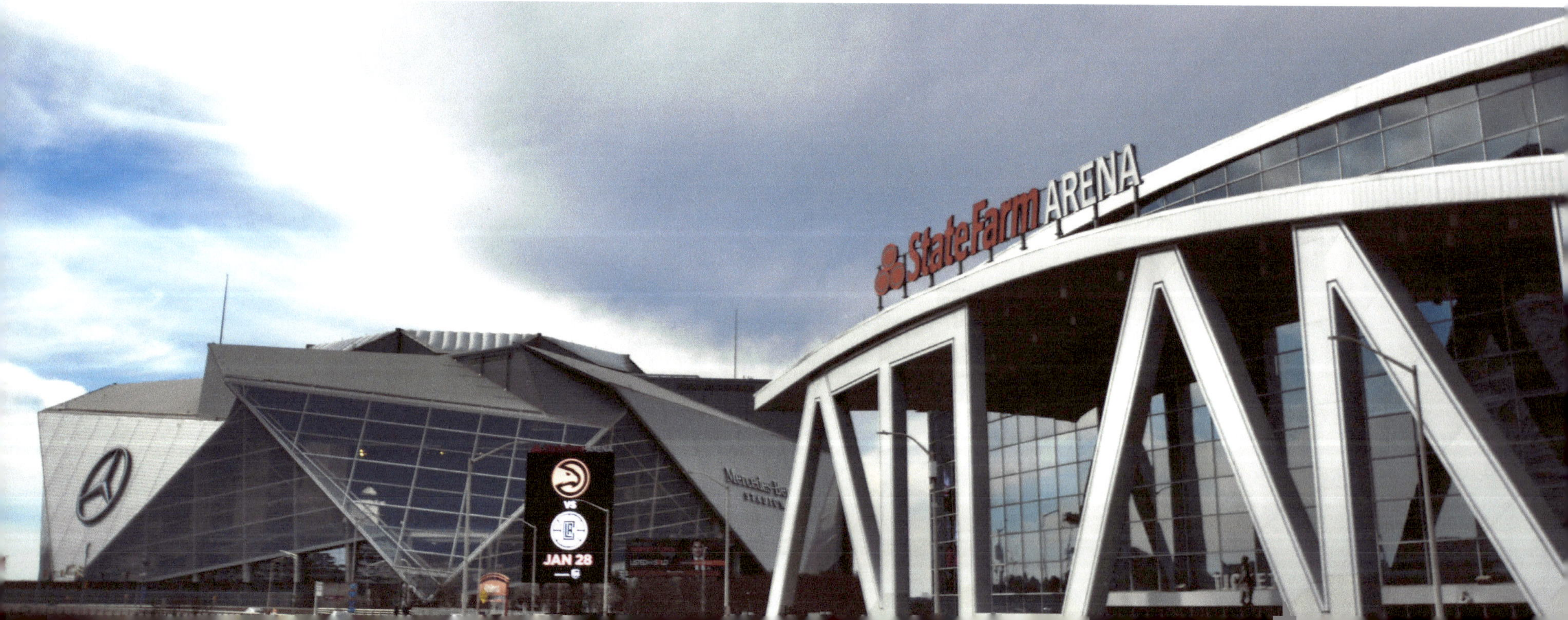

Iconic Restaurants

Soul Vegetarian

Soul Vegetarian, located in the West End District, was vegan before it was cool.

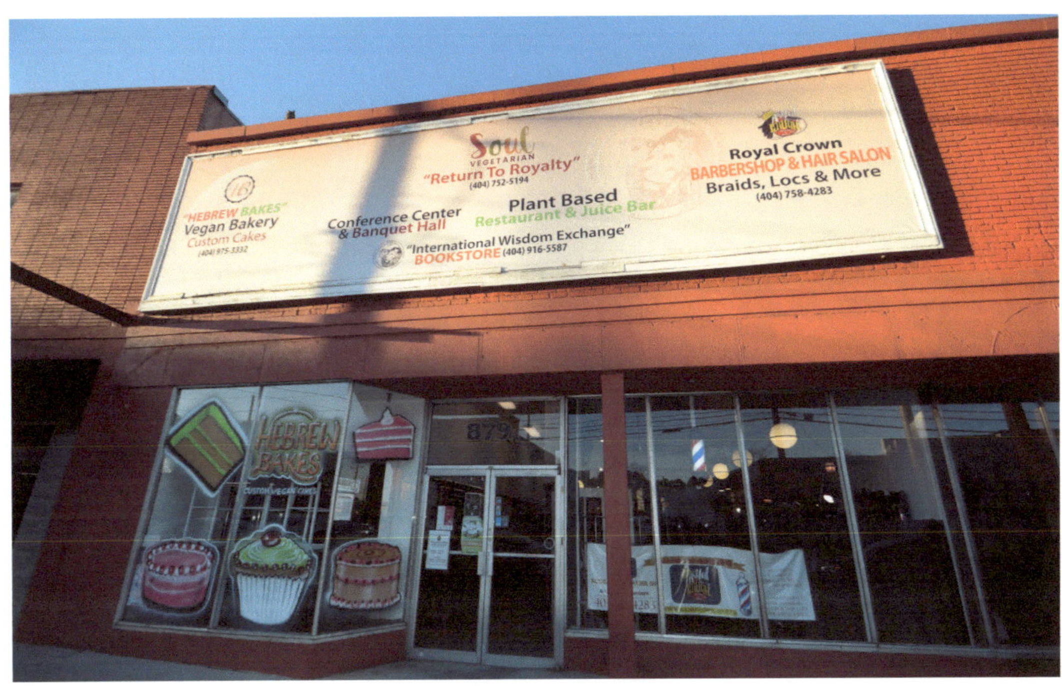

Mary Mac's Tea Room

Opening in 1945, Mary Mac's Tea Room is the last standing of sixteen tea rooms.

Fat Matt's Rib Shack

This is an electric and unpretentious spot integrating blues and some of the best barbecue around the city.

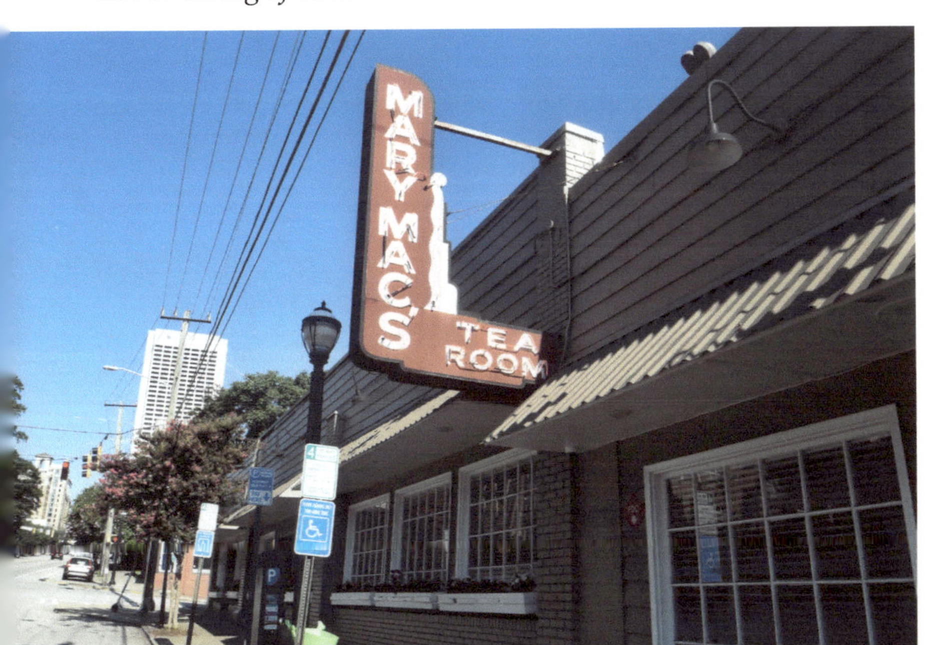

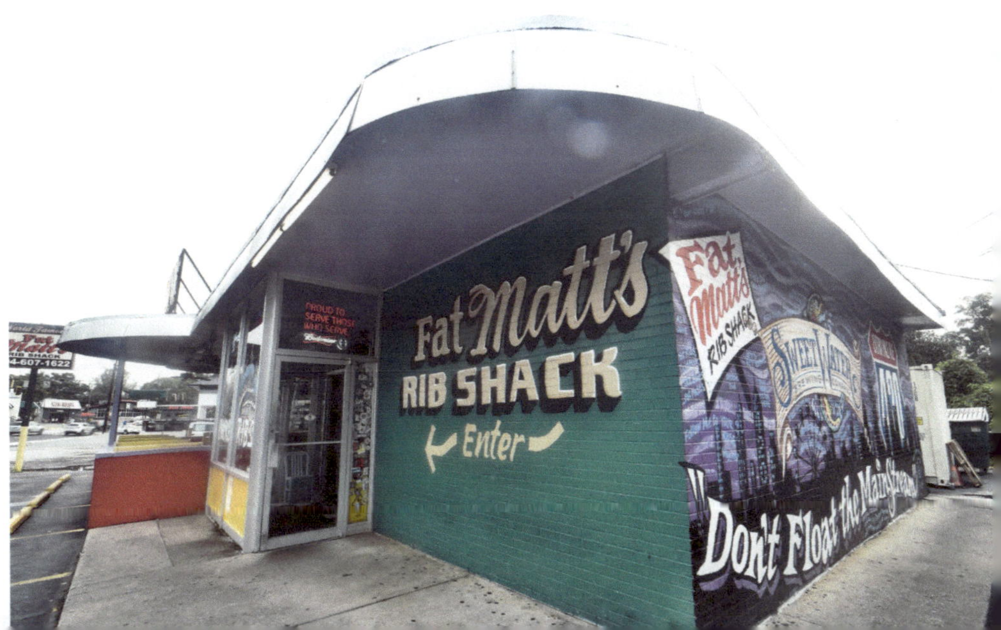

The Varsity

Founded by Frank Gordy in 1928, the original Varsity drive-in food restaurant still stands today on North Avenue. Frank was a man with a two-thousand-dollar nest egg and million-dollar taste buds.

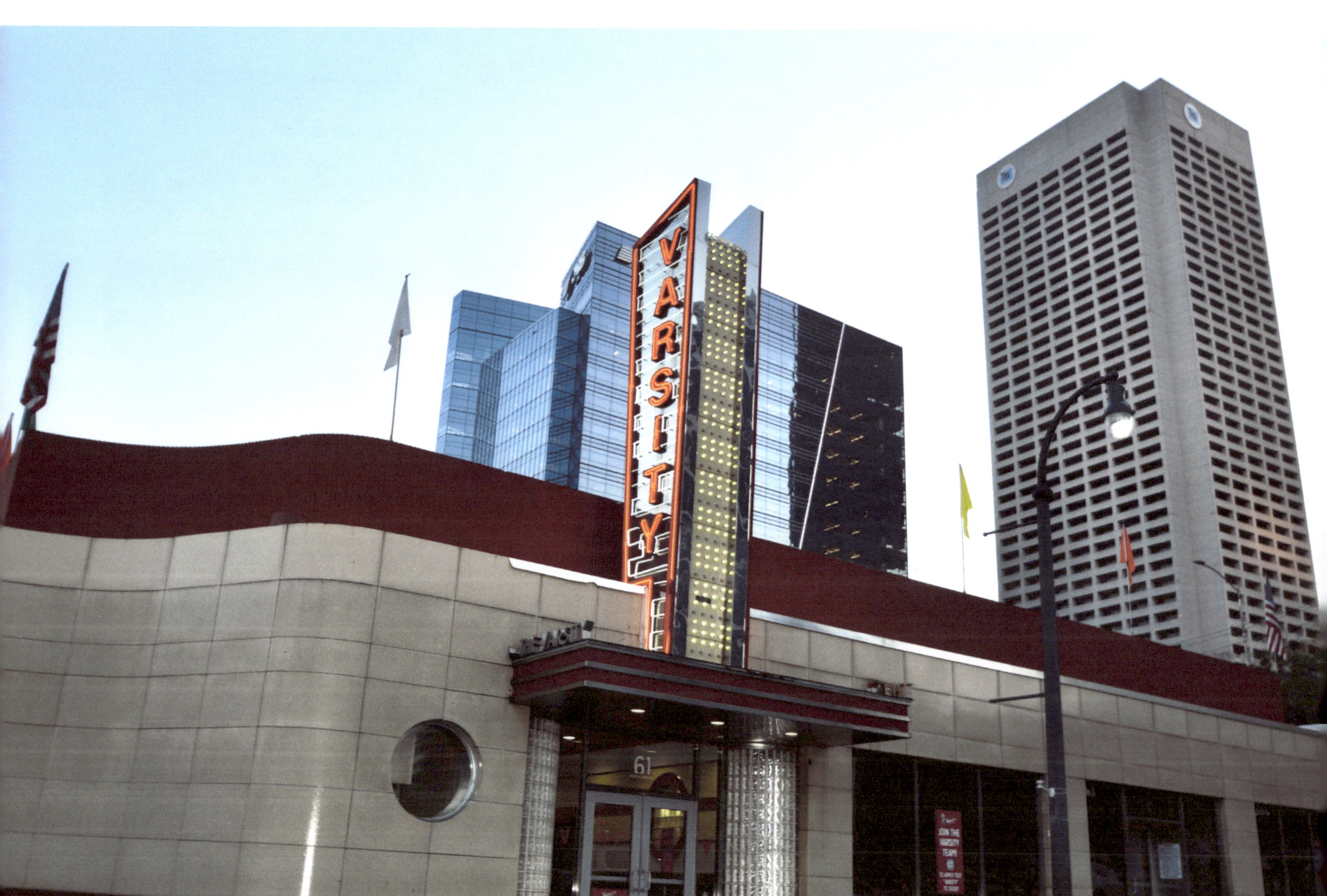

The Vortex Bar & Grill

The Vortex is an Atlanta fixture known for its burgers and selection of beer and wine with a rock and roll atmosphere.

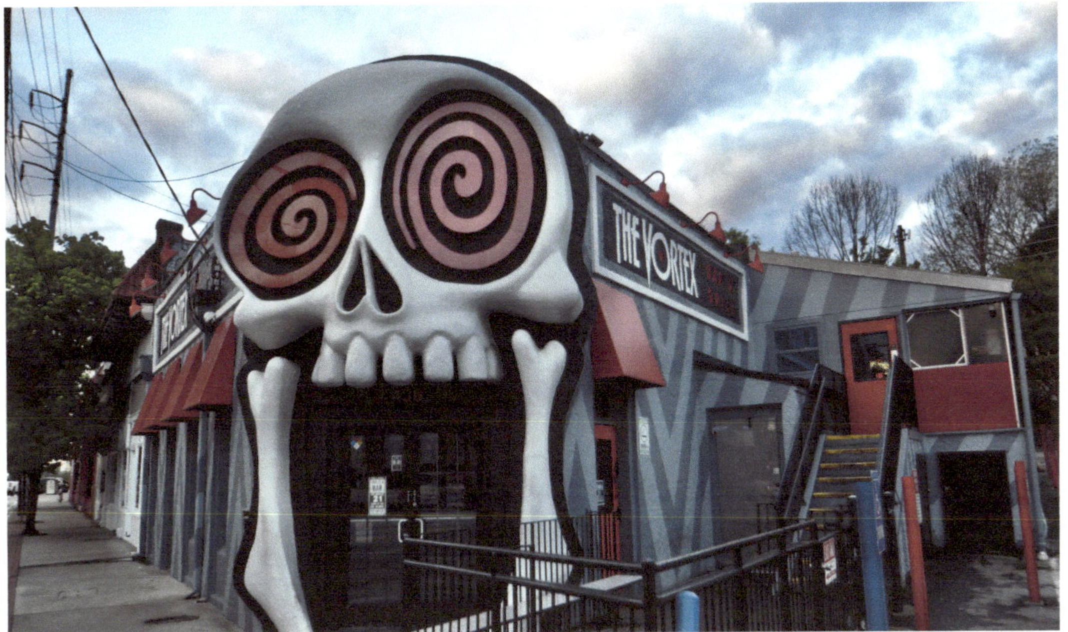

The Beautiful Restaurant

Since 1979, this restaurant is known for its healthy soulful homestyle tastes of the South.

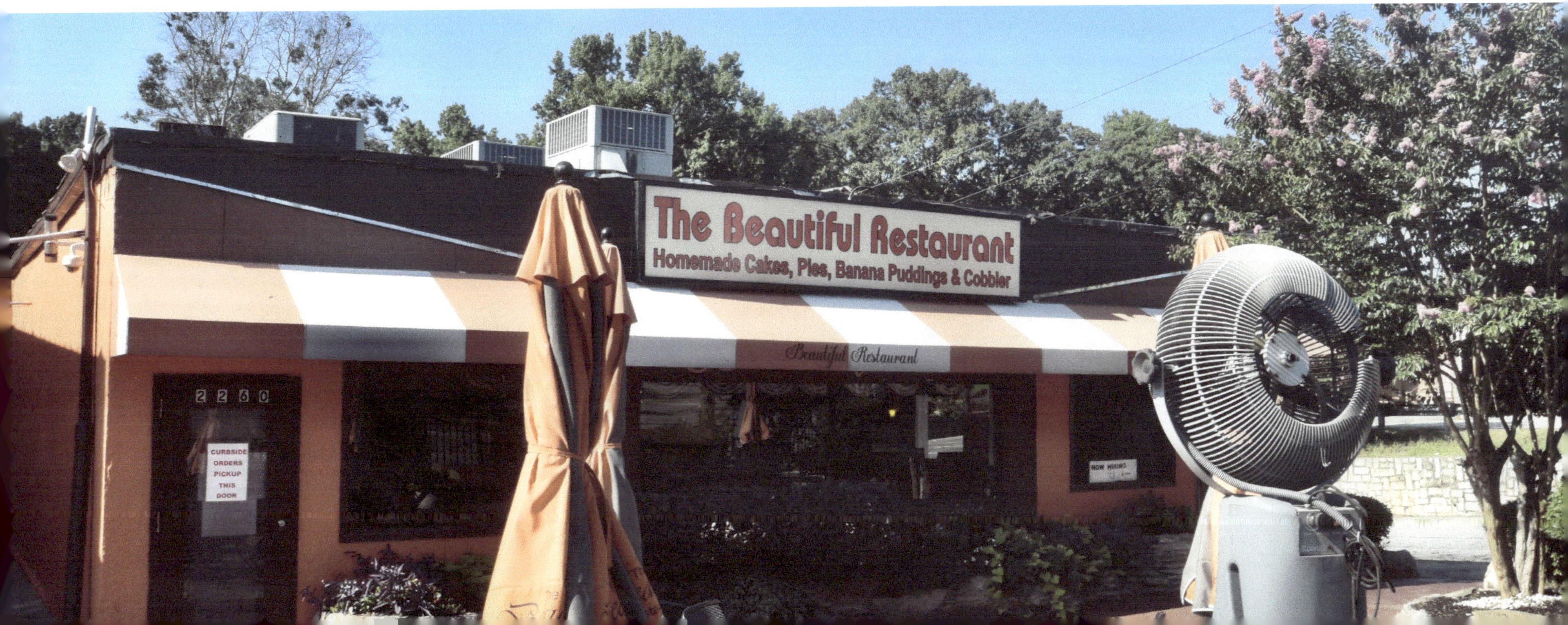

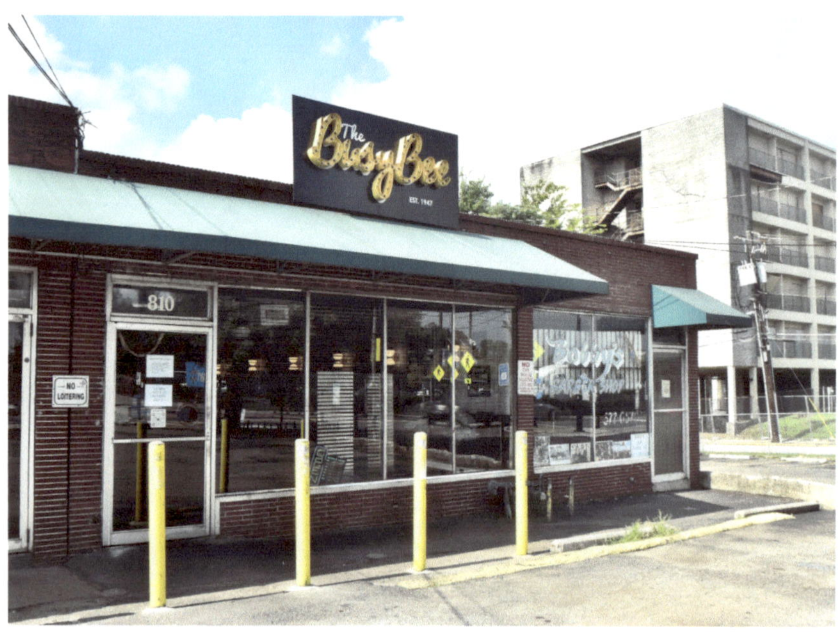

The Busy Bee

Founded in 1947, this restaurant is known for its traditional soul food.

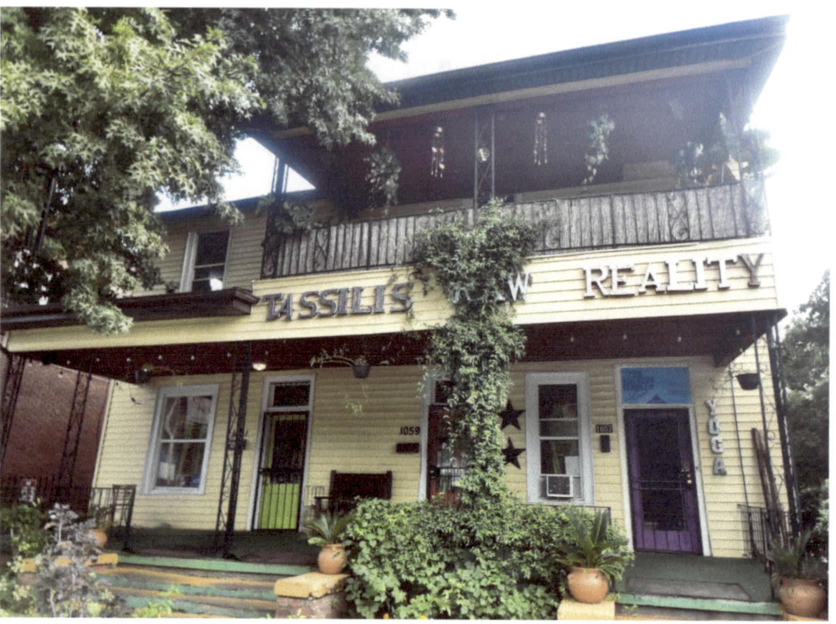

Tassili's Raw Reality

Located in the West End of Atlanta, this African American-owned restaurant prepares raw vegan cuisine right in front of the customer.

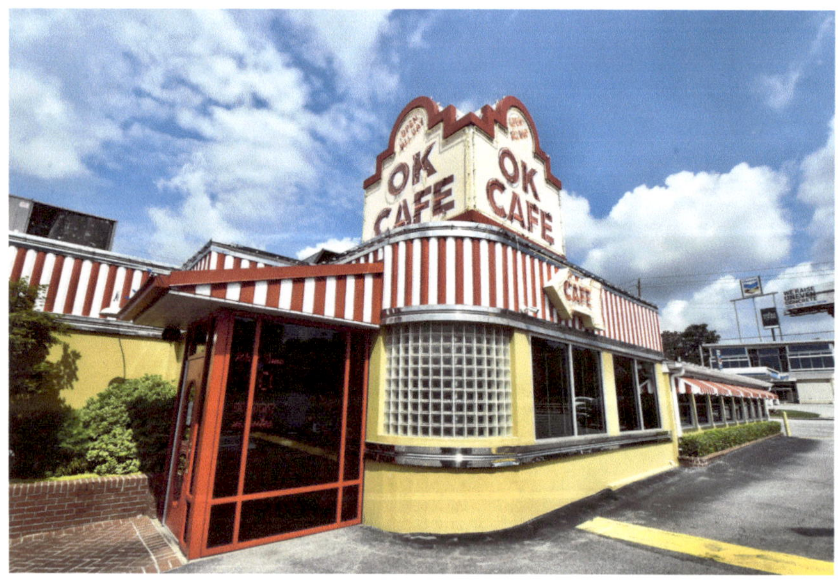

OK Cafe

This Atlanta staple is an old-fashioned-style diner, originally opened in 1987, and offers breakfast, lunch, and dinner with southern hospitality.

Paschal's

Paschal's was originally founded as a sandwich shop in 1947 by brothers Robert and James Paschal. It became a restaurant known for its soul food, as well as the unofficial headquarters for the Civil Rights Movement in the 1960s. Paschal's was originally located on West Hunter Street, later renamed Martin Luther King Jr. Drive. Notable patrons such as Dr. Martin Luther King Jr., John Lewis, Reverend Jessie L. Jackson, Julian Bond, Ted Kennedy, Hubert Humphrey, and many other Civil Rights leaders convened at Paschal's for strategy sessions, planning protest marches and voter registration drives. The Paschal brothers defied the law and served and seated White and Black patrons at the same tables. The new location is on Northside Drive.

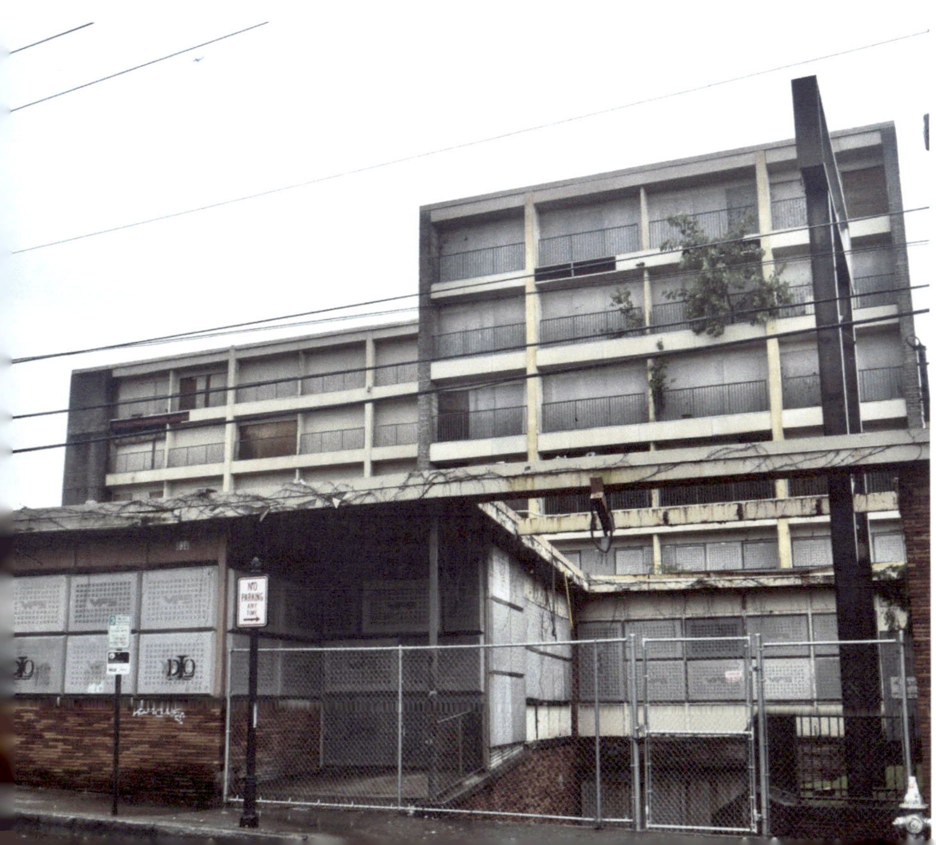

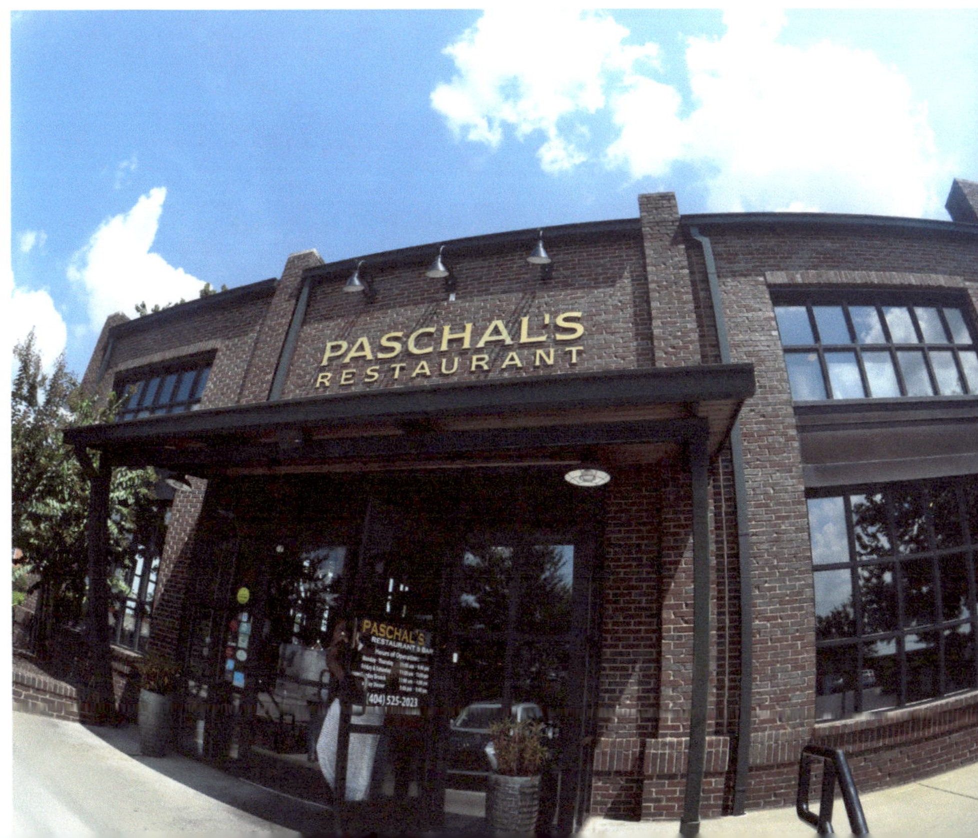

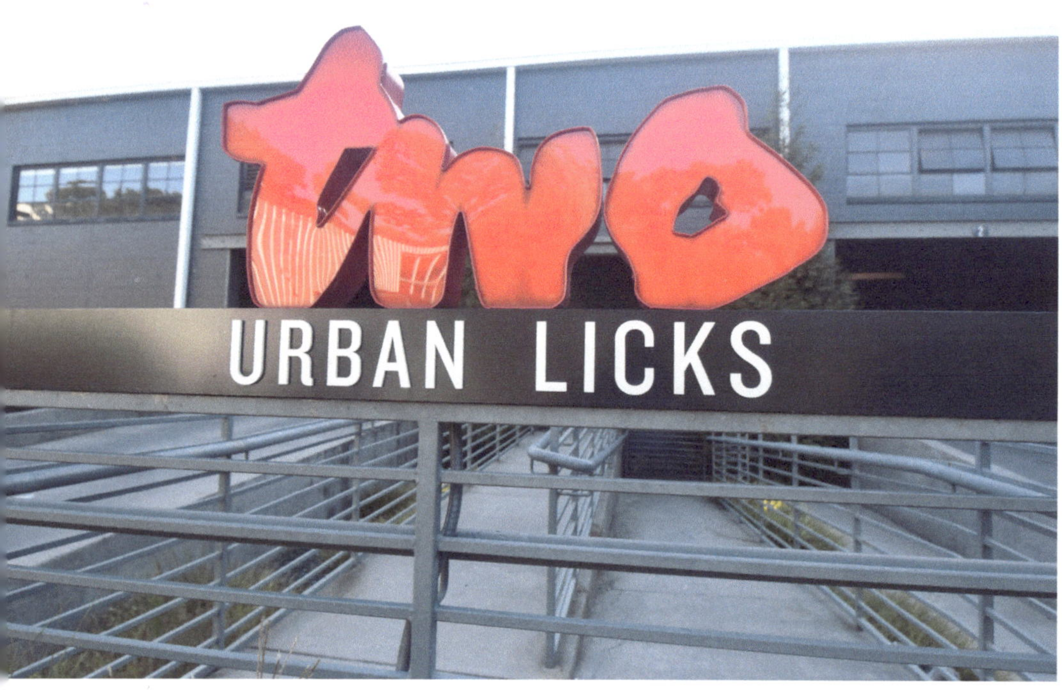

Two Urban Licks

An American rotisserie fare that offers live blues in a warehouse with easy access to the Atlanta Beltline and a view of the city.

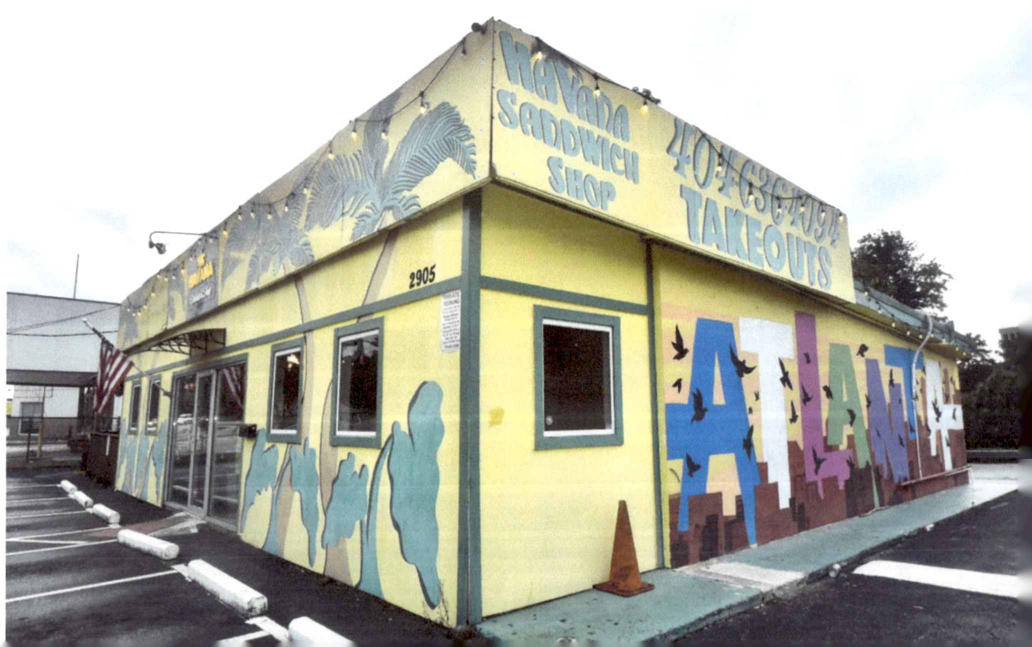

Havana Sandwich Shop

Since 1976, Havana Sandwich Shop has served authentic Cuban sandwiches.

Historic Buildings

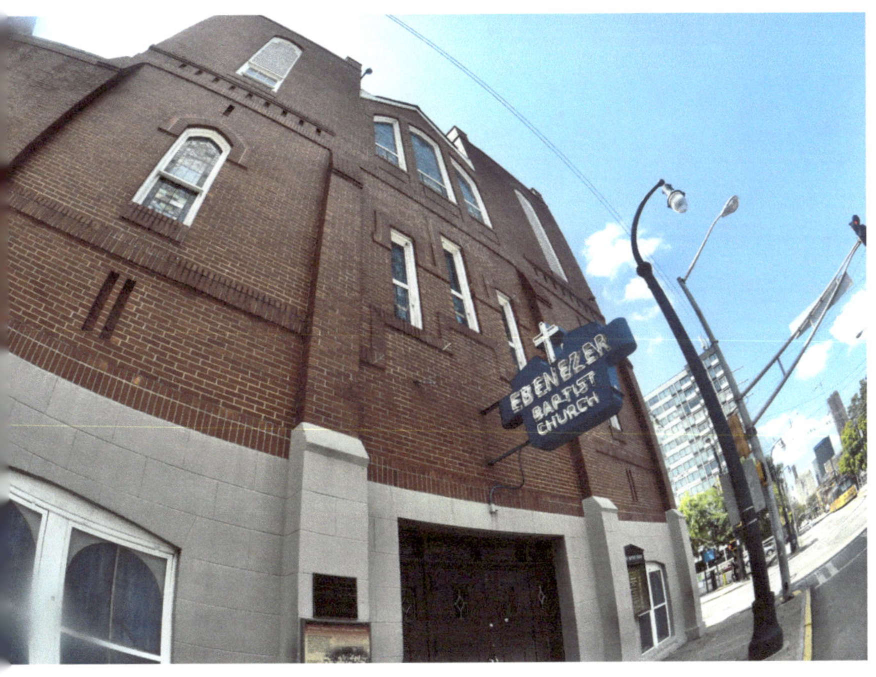

Ebenezer Baptist Church

Ebenezer Baptist Church was founded in 1886 by Pastor John A. Parker along with eight people. The church's name derives from the Books of Samuel, where Samuel names a place Ebenezer, meaning a stone of help. Notably, this was a baptismal place and the place where the funeral of Reverend Dr. Martin Luther King Jr. was held. Dr. Martin Luther King Jr. served as copastor along with his father, Dr. Martin Luther King Sr. Since 2005, the honorable reverend, doctor, and senator Raphael Warnock has served as the pastor (now at the new location, directly across the street). He is only the fifth person to serve as Ebenezer's senior pastor since its founding 137 years ago. The original church still stands.

Ebenezer Baptist Church Organ

The Ebenezer Baptist Church organ was once played by Alberta King, mother of slain Civil Rights leader, Dr. Martin Luther King Jr., until her untimely assassination six years after her son's assassination. On June 30, 1974, after playing a hymn, mayhem erupted in the sanctuary. Marcus Wayne Chenault leaped from the pew and fired a handgun, fatally wounding Mrs. King and Deacon Edward Boykin. An unidentified woman was also shot, yet she survived.

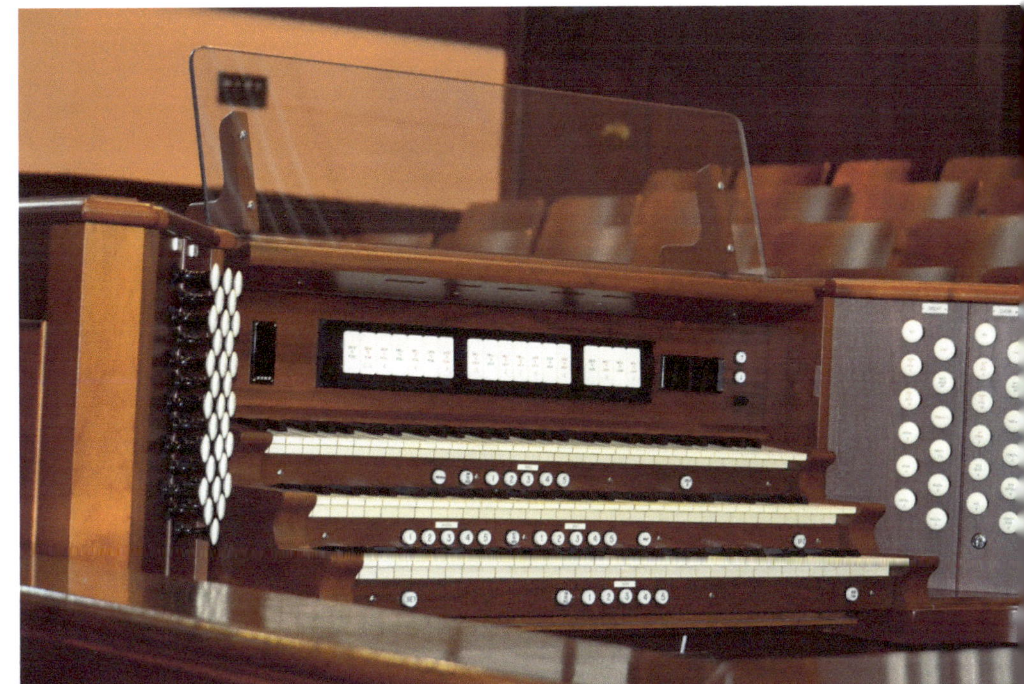

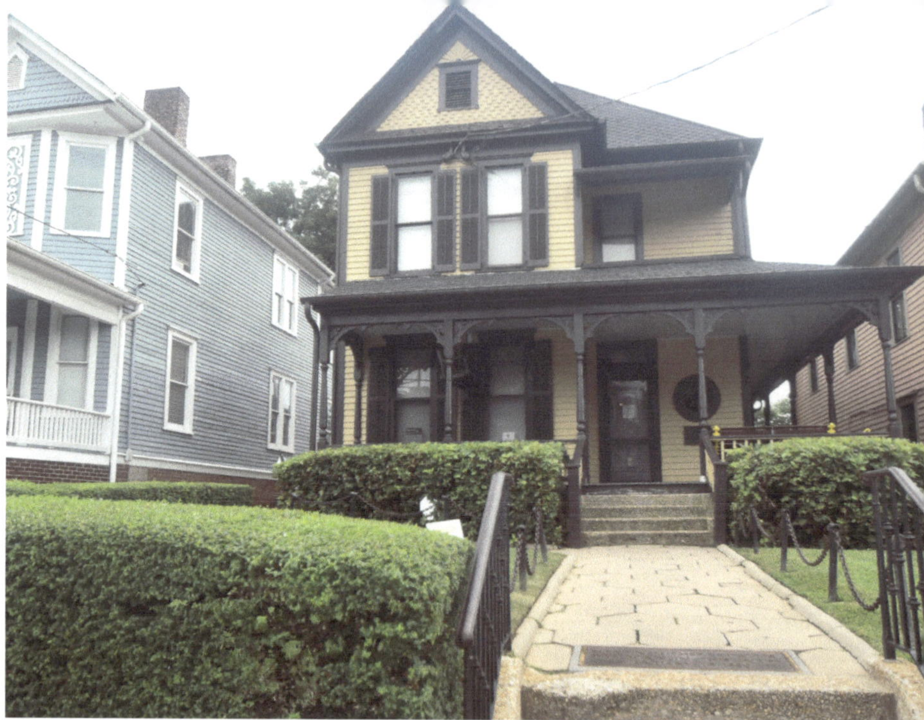

Reverend Dr. Martin Luther King Jr.'s Homes
The home where Dr. Martin Luther King Jr. was born (above) and the last home he resided in before he was assassinated (below).

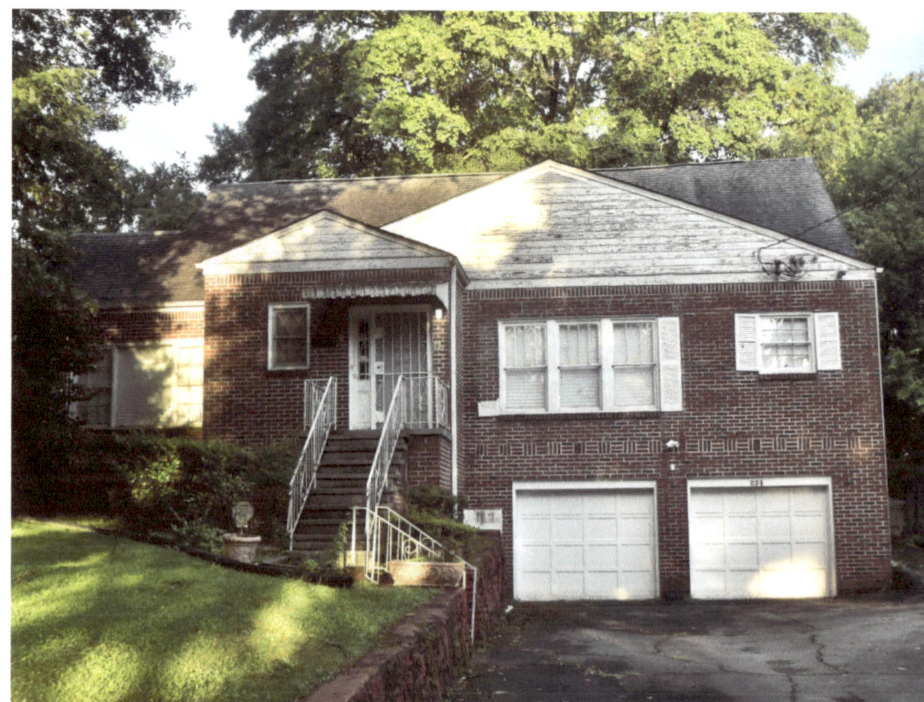

Resting Place of Reverend Dr. Martin Luther King Jr. and Coretta Scott King

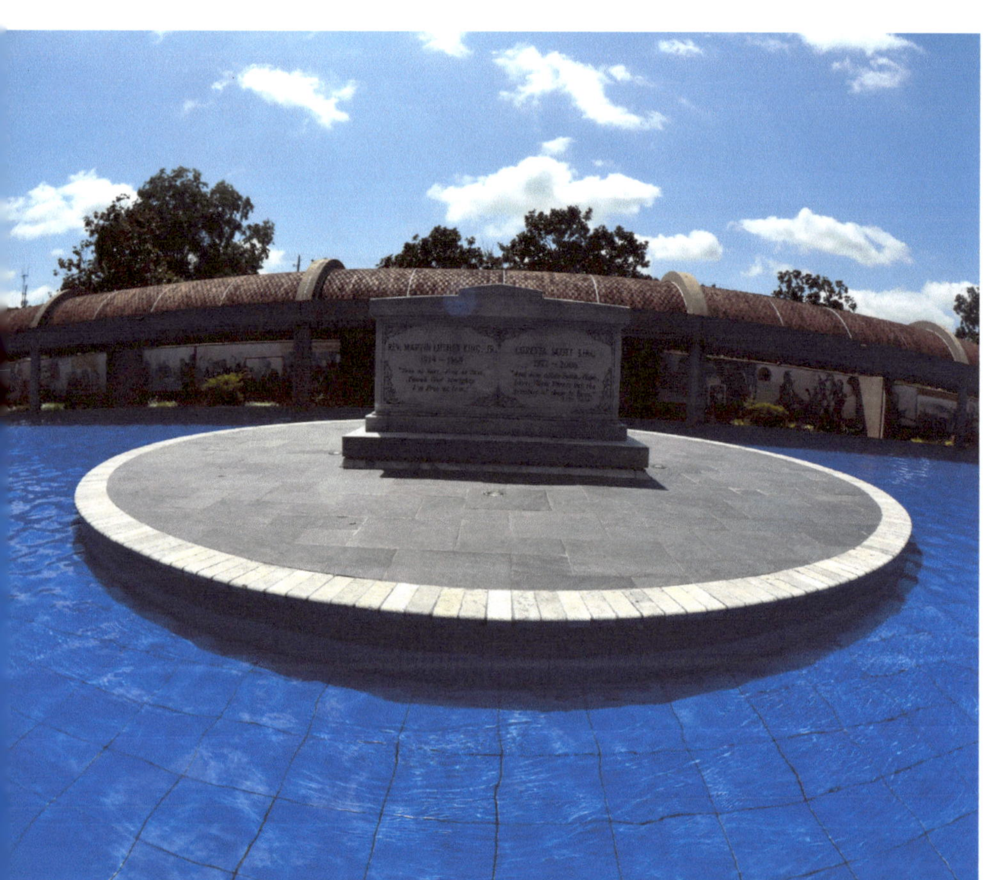

Shrine of the Immaculate Conception

The shrine is the city's oldest parish, first built in 1848. After suffering damage during the Civil War, a new structure was built in 1869.

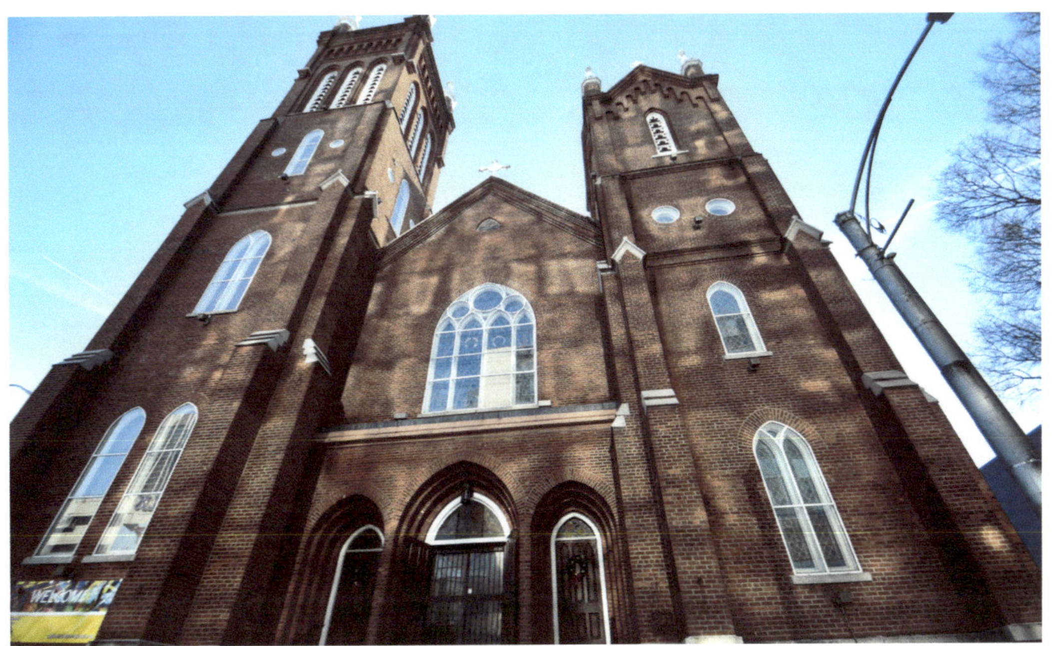

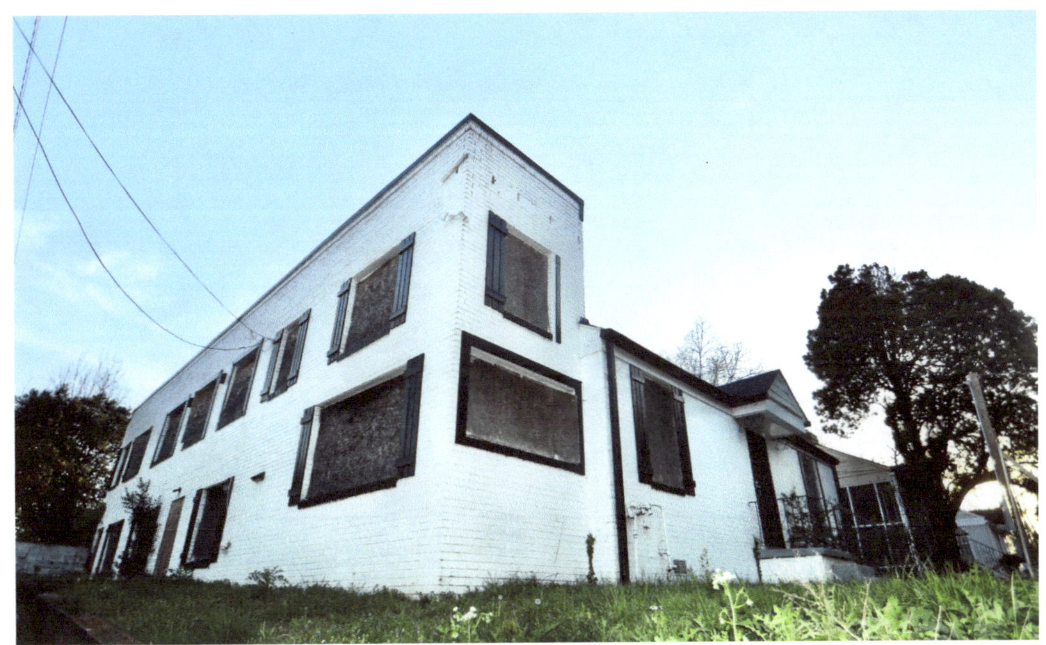

The McLendon Hospital

The McLendon Hospital, founded by Dr. Frederick Earl McLendon, opened in 1945 to serve and meet the needs of African Americans who were denied healthcare throughout Atlanta. Originally, the hospital had three buildings along Sharon Street in the Hunter Hills/Mozley Park neighborhood. Today, only one structure remains.

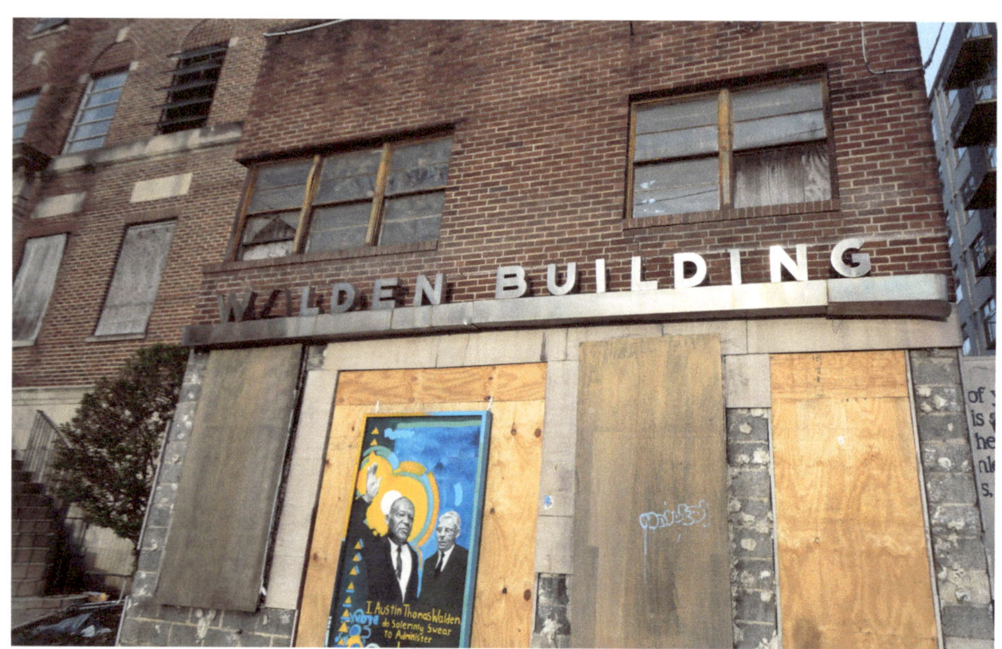

The Walden Building

Built in 1948, its namesake is of prominent Black Atlanta attorney, Austin Thomas Walden. Walden established the Gate City Bar Association, the first bar association in the state of Georgia, and the Atlanta Negro Voters League. He also fought to obtain equal pay for Black teachers and desegregate lunch counters, buses, and public schools.

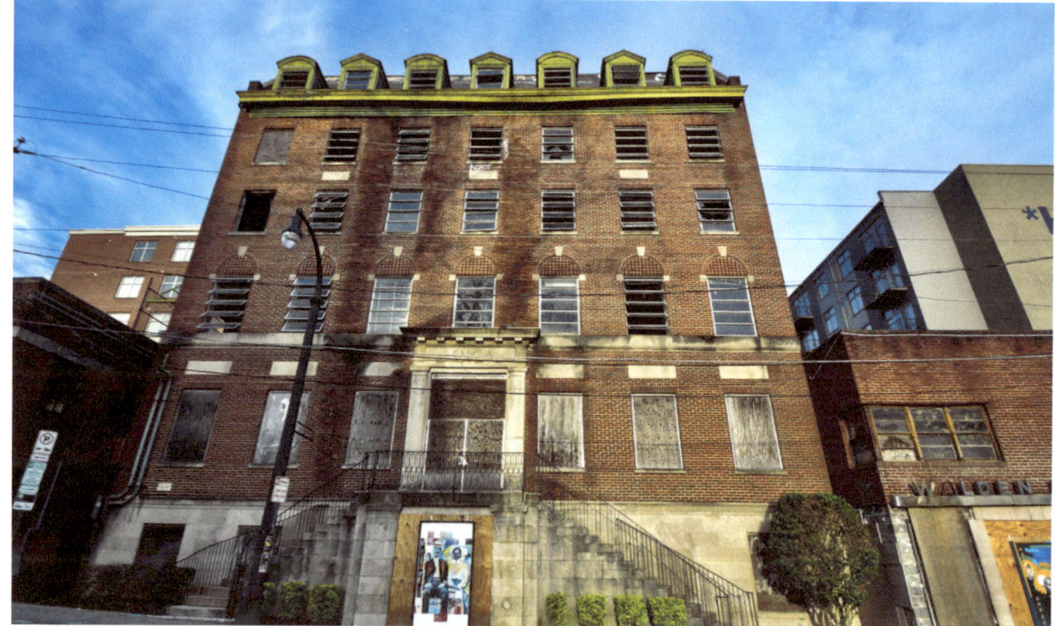

The Butler Street YMCA

Known as the "Black City Hall," this was a communal cornerstone in the Black community. It provided the African American community with a place to gather and enjoy the luxuries of swimming pools, restaurants, game rooms, a gymnasium and more. Notable members were Dr. Martin Luther King Jr., Vernon Jordan, Maynard Jackson, and Jesse Hill Jr.

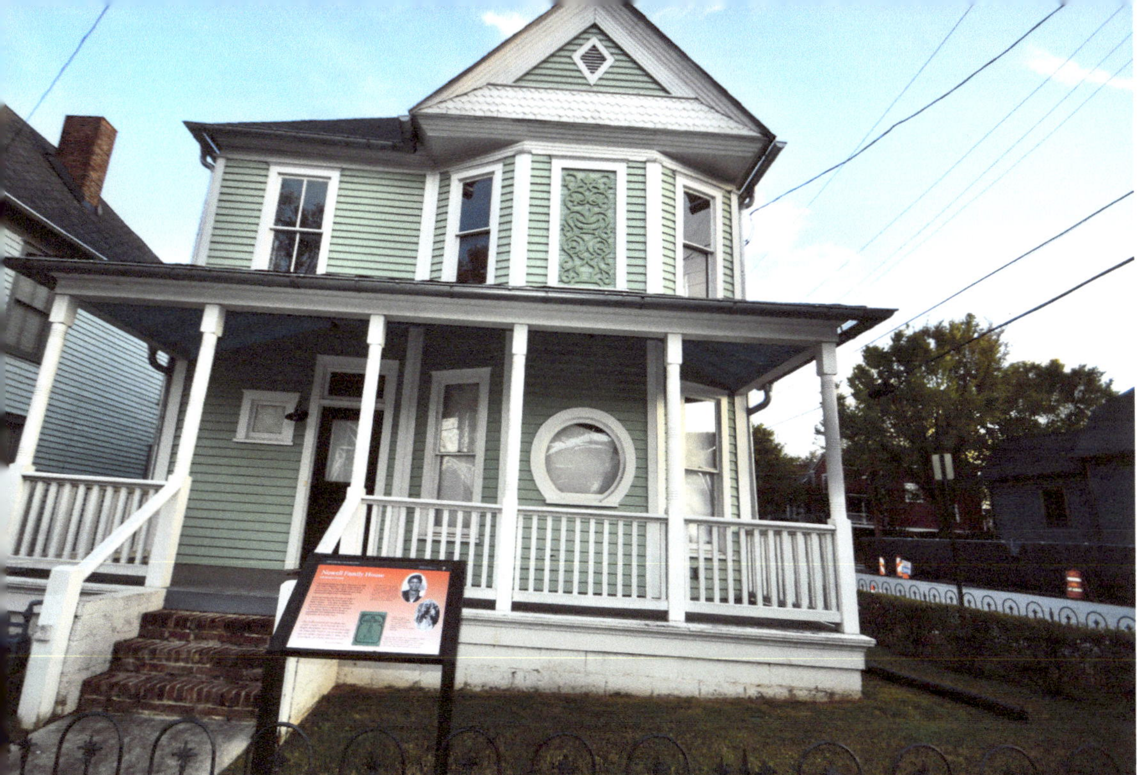

Nowell Family Home

Annie Nowell-Johnson's home was the only option provided to Black boarders and renters who traveled and needed a place to live when Black people were denied lodging for over seventy years.

WERD

Home to the first Black-owned and operated radio station in the United States. I had the pleasure years ago to meet the first radio DJ on this station, Jack Gibson, also known as Jack the Rapper.

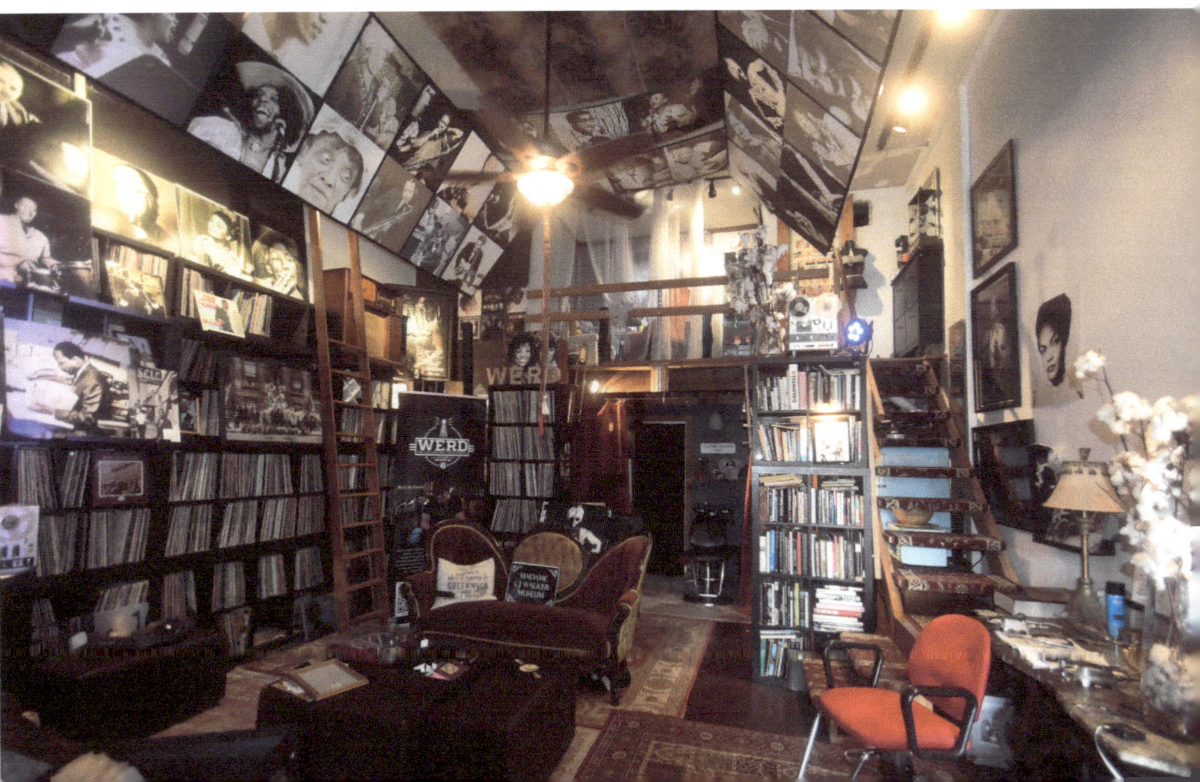

Atlanta Daily World

The historic home of the world's oldest Black newspaper. On August 5, 1928, William Alexander Scott II founded the first successful African American daily newspaper in the United States.

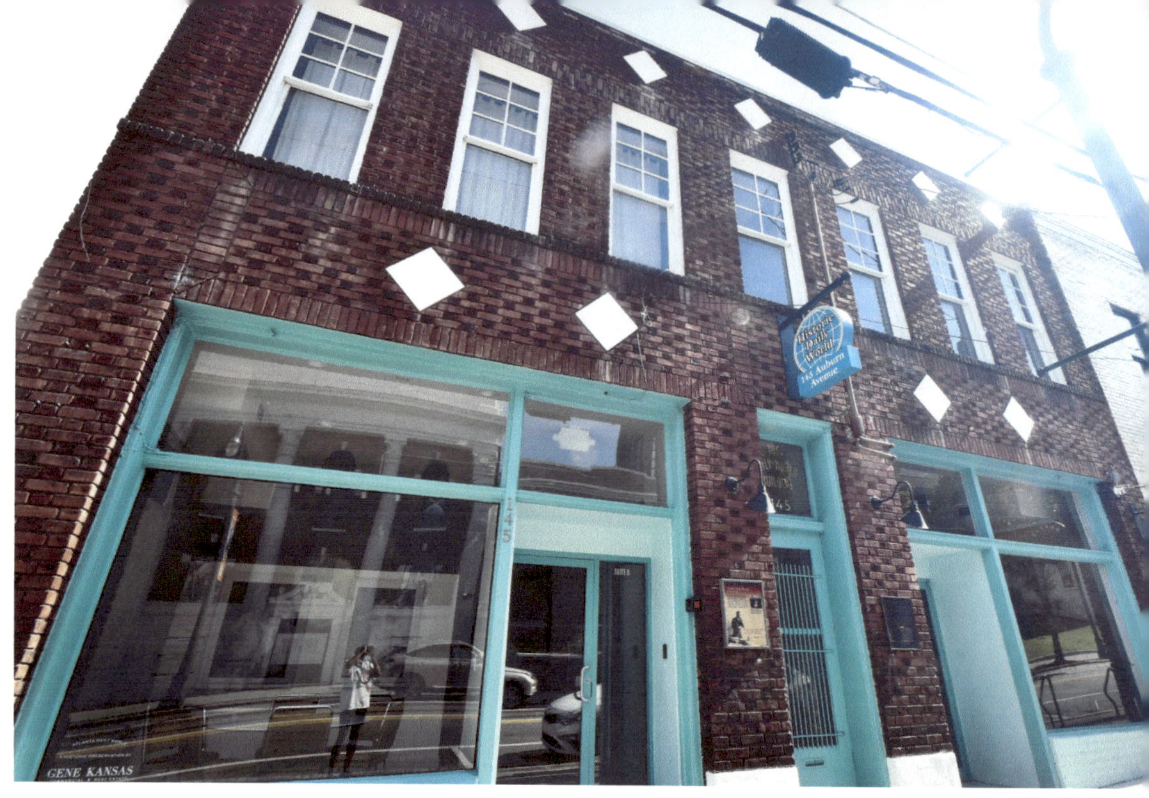

Atlanta Life Insurance

In 1905, Alonzo Herndon founded Atlanta Life Insurance Company which became one of the leading African American insurance companies in the nation. Born into slavery, he became one of the first African American millionaires in the United States.

The Herndon Mansion
Home to Alonzo Herndon.

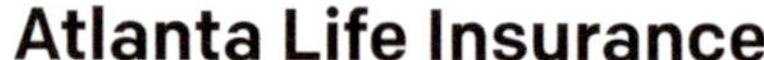

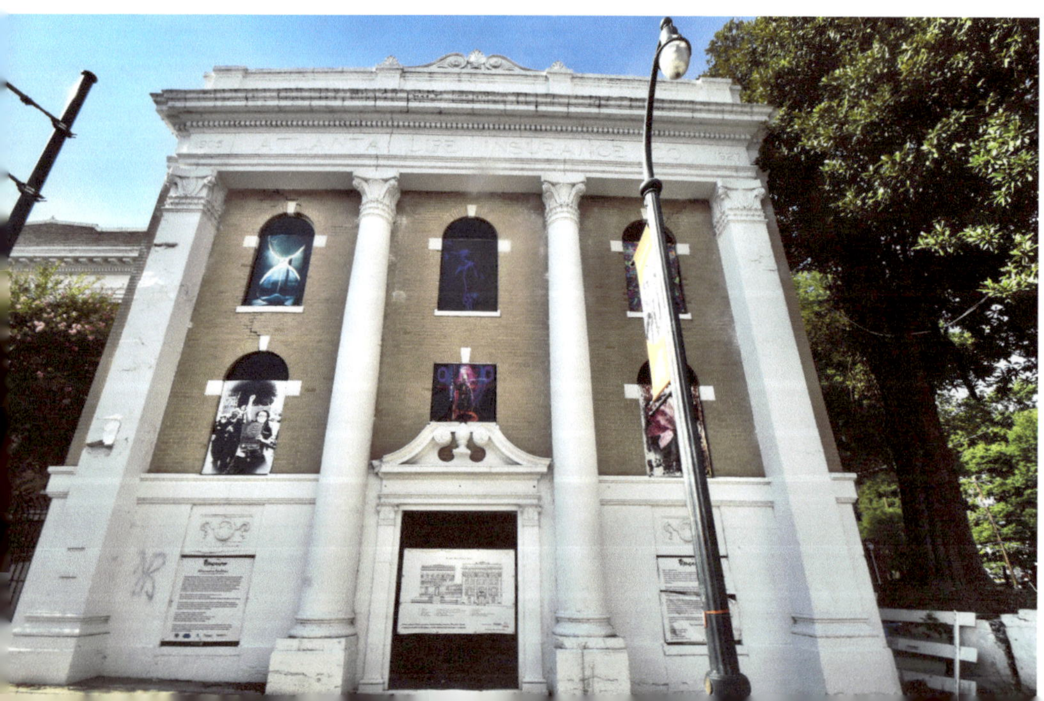

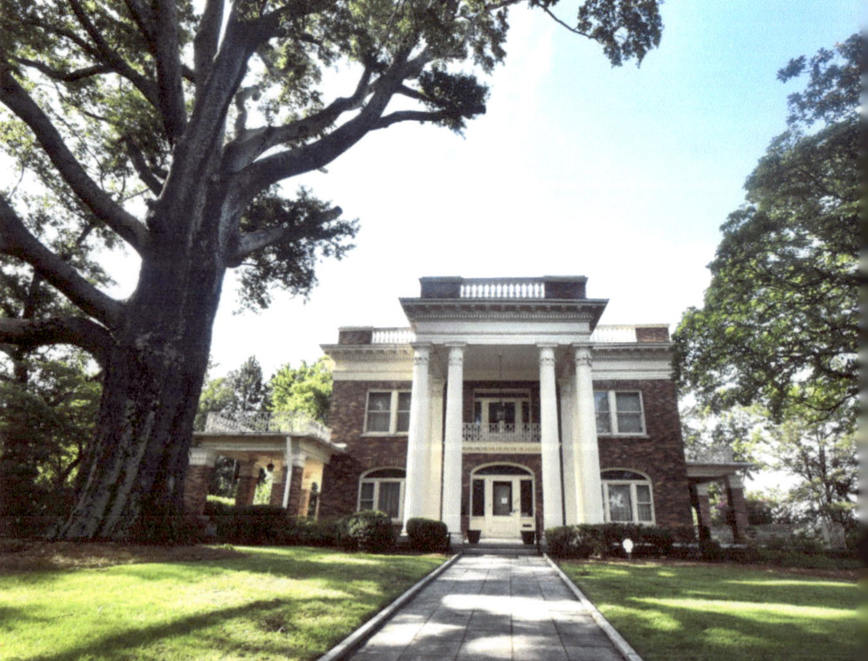

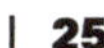

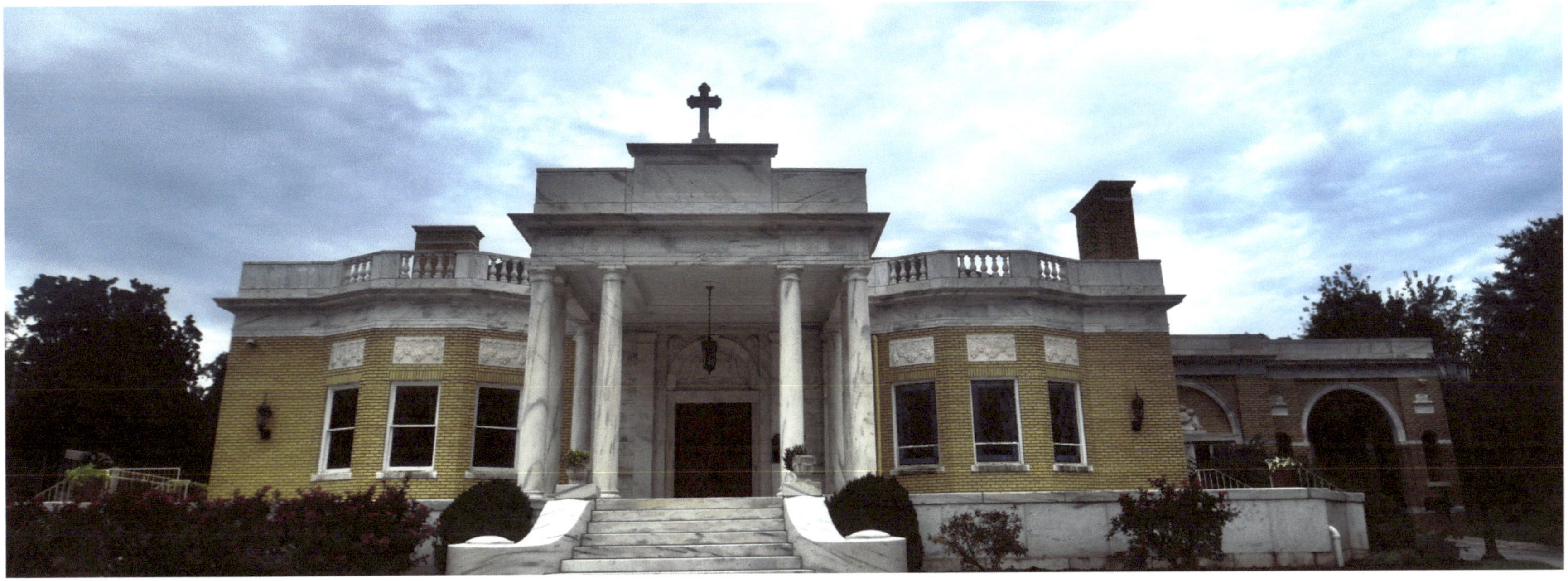

Former Homes of Asa Griggs Candler, Founder of The Coca-Cola Company

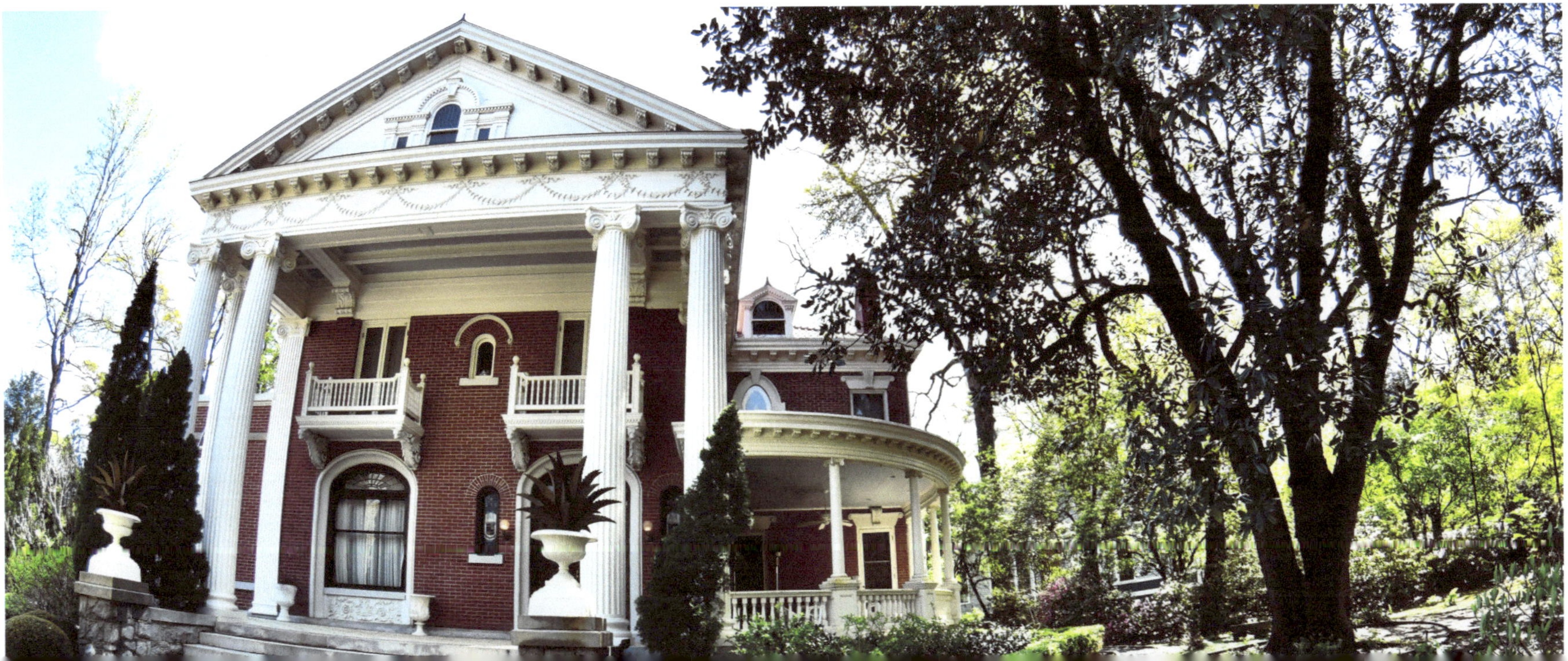

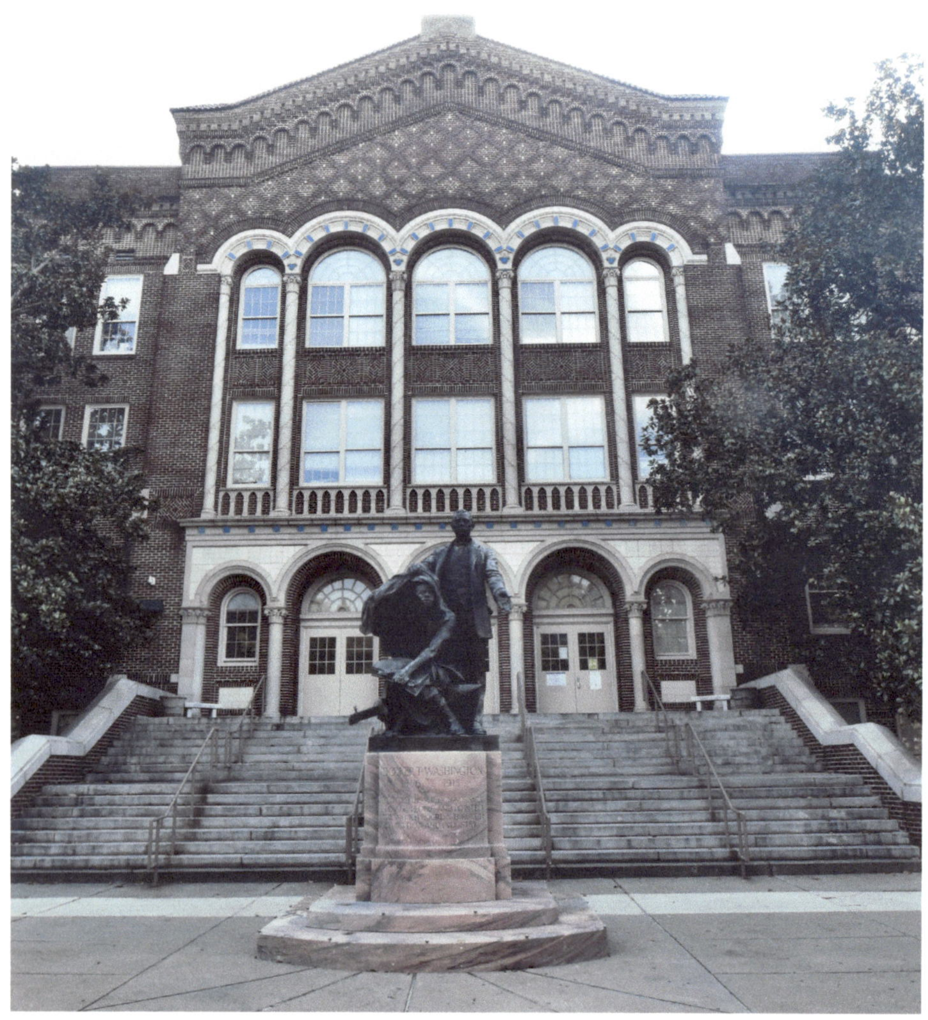

Booker T. Washington High School

In 1924, named for the influential educator, Booker T. Washington opened its doors. It was the first African American public school in Atlanta. Many notables who graduated there included Lena Horne and Dr. Martin Luther King Jr.

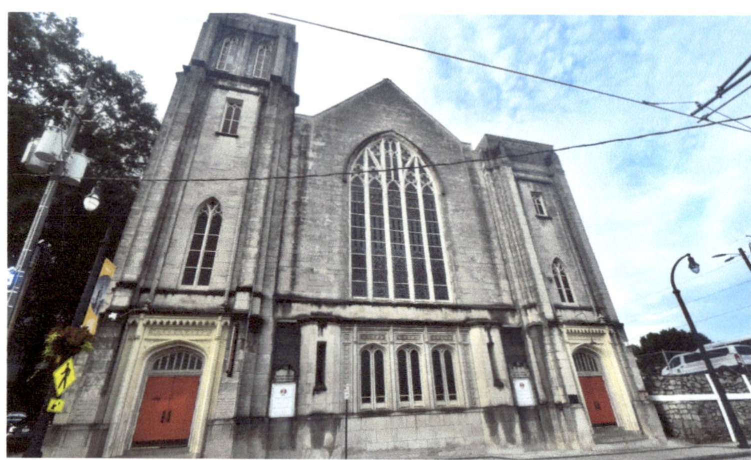

Wheat Street Baptist Church

Founded in 1869, Wheat Street Baptist Church was organized during Reconstruction to serve African American communities. Wheat Street created one of the first federal credit unions in the South.

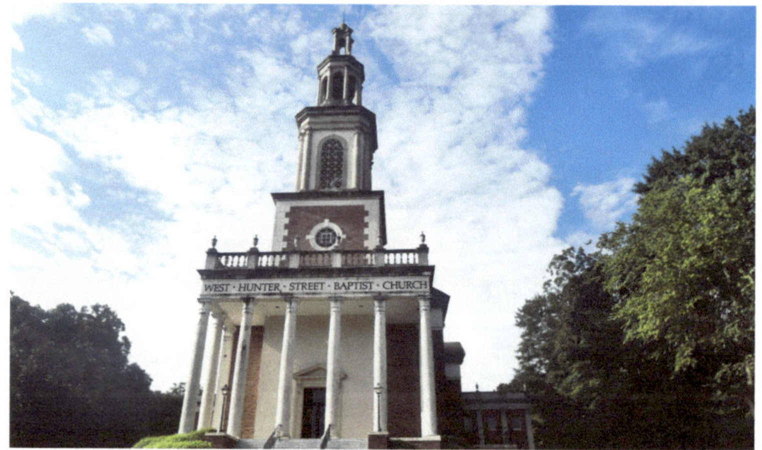

West Hunter Street Baptist Church

Organized in 1881 by a small group of dedicated believers, West Hunter Street Baptist Church has stood tall for the past 135 years. The distinguished Civil Rights leader and activist, Ralph David Abernathy, served as pastor from 1961–1990.

Atlanta Communities

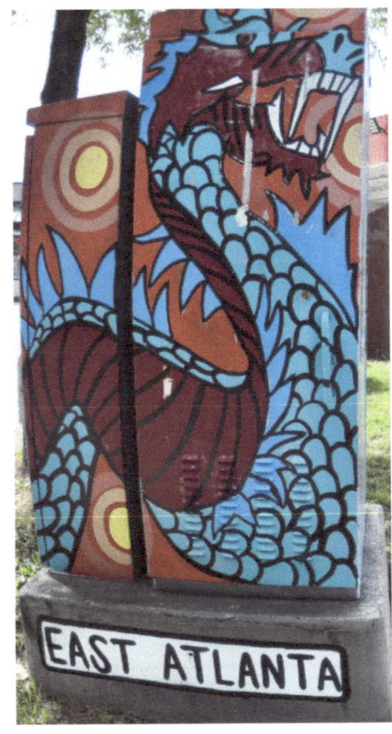

East Atlanta Village

East Atlanta Village is located near Little Five Points. The community . . . hip, and not showy, is known for its' amazing bars and nightlife. Earth day is one of many outdoor events featuring yoga, live music, and vendors showcasing the arts and homemade crafts.

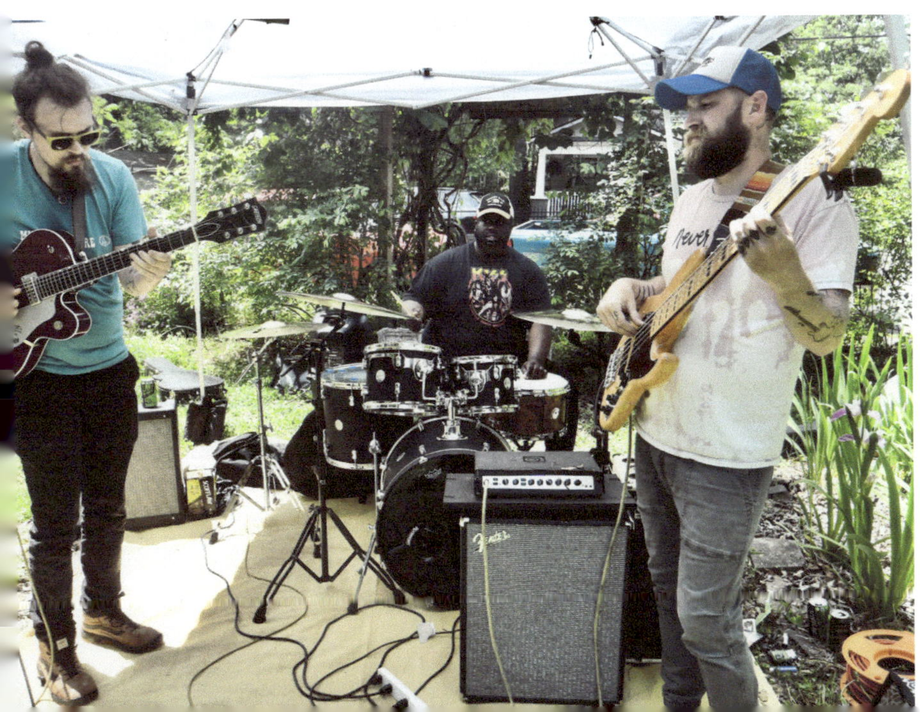

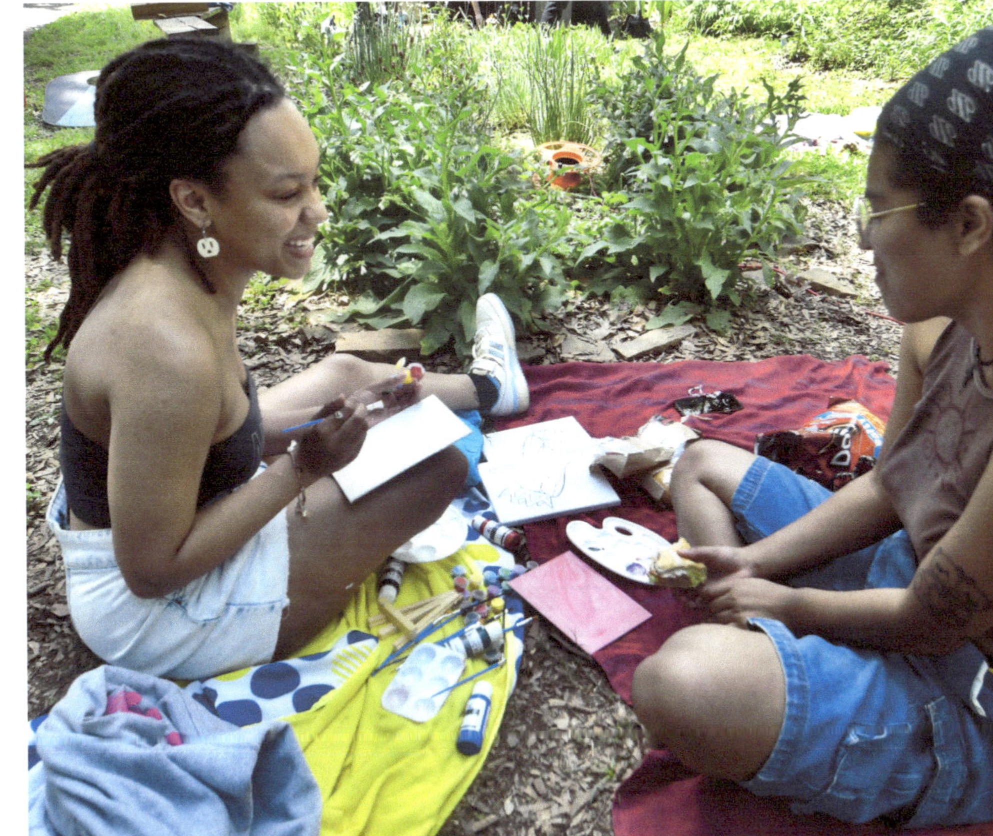

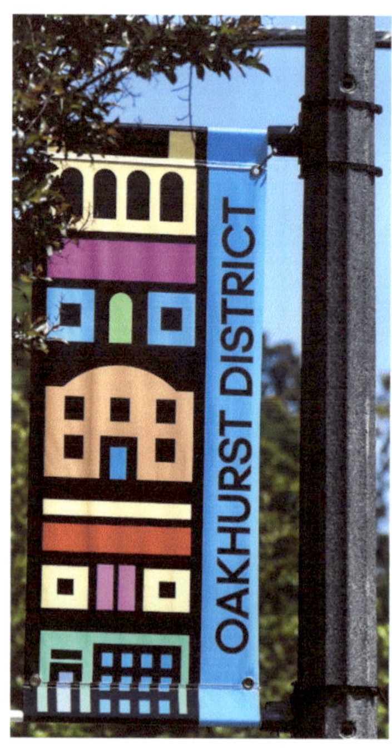

Oakhurst Village

The Oakhurst neighborhood is an eclectic community located in Decatur, a suburb of Atlanta. Here, you will find The Old Scottish Rite Hospital, quaint eateries, coffee shops . . . and phenomenal outdoor Jazz concerts.

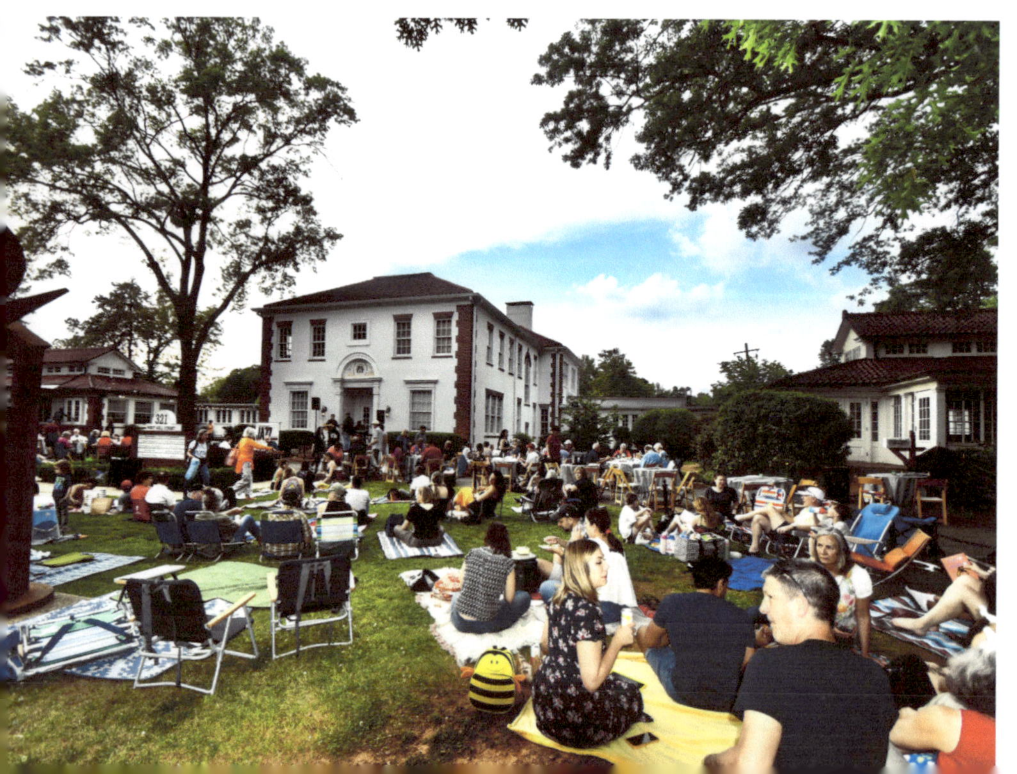

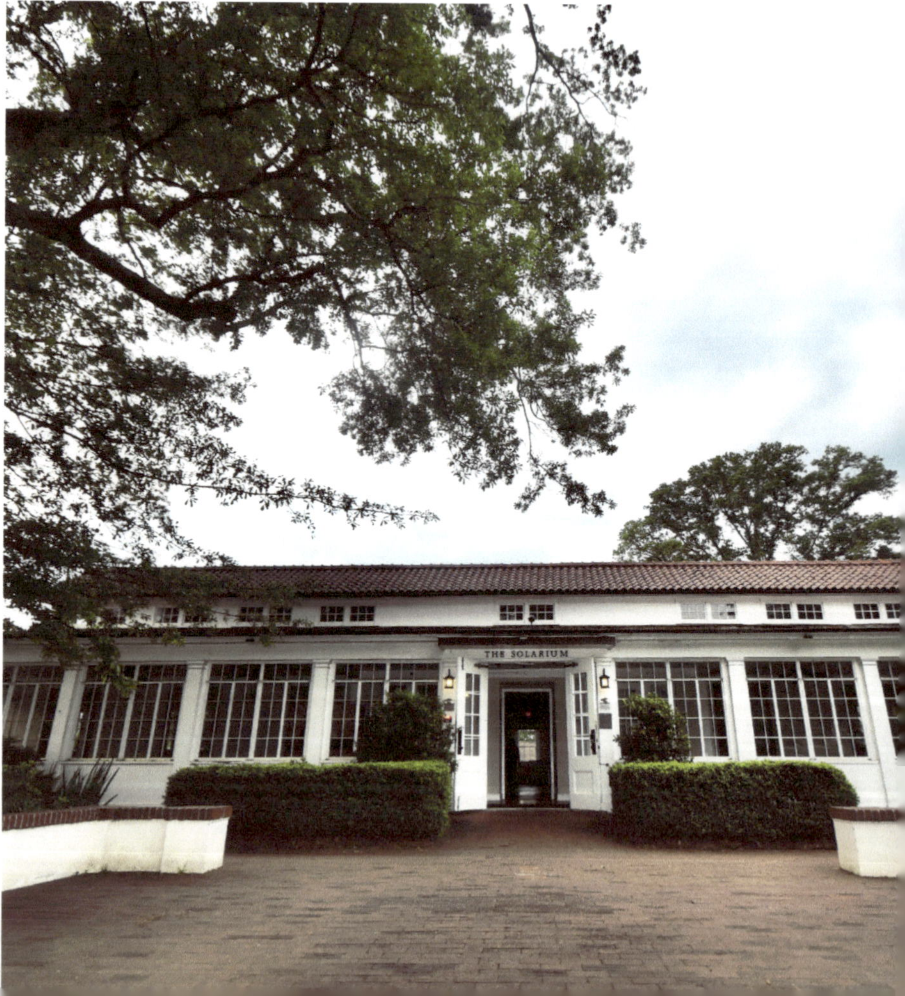

Little Five Points

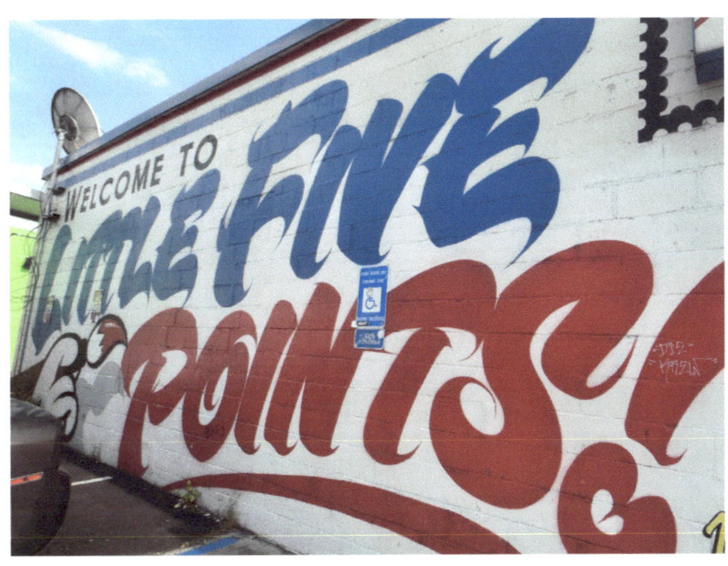

Variety Playhouse

It was originally the Euclid Theatre, a sister to the Fabulous Fox, the entertainment palace in Midtown.

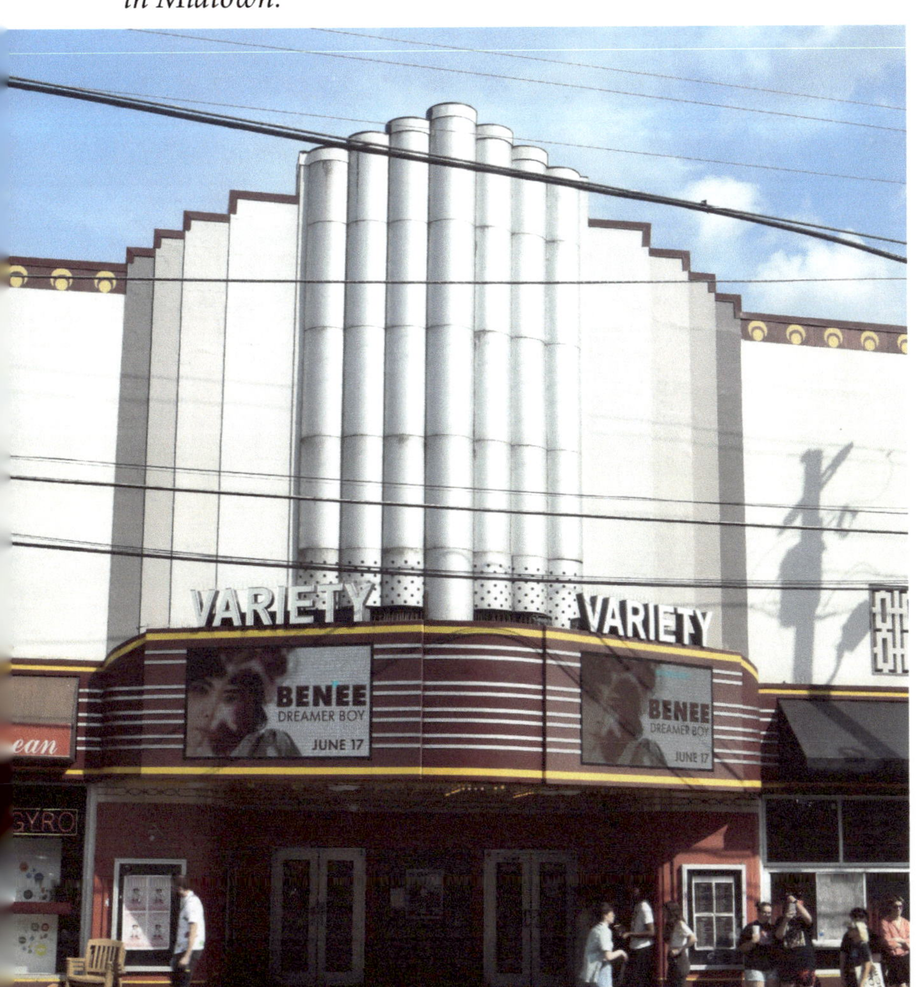

Sevananda

Sevananda is Atlanta's original natural food store and has served the community since 1974.

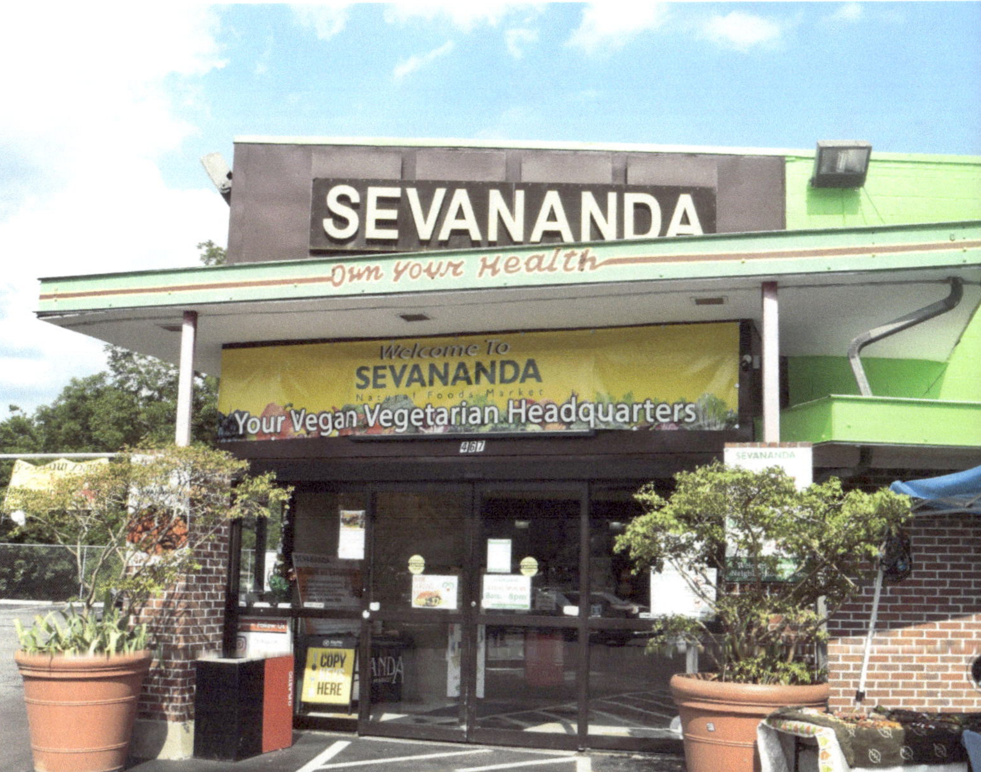

Virginia Highland

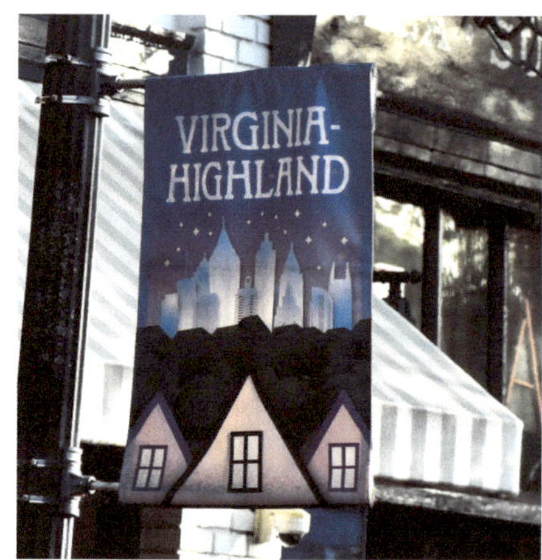

Virginia Highland Church

*This progressive community of faith has been part of
the Virginia Highland community for over a century.*

Blind Willie's

*Located in the heart of historic Virginia Highlands,
serving up blues, brews, and amazing Southern cuisine,
Blind Willie's is the perfect spot for anyone, especially
if you're craving a fun, cozy and warm ambience.*

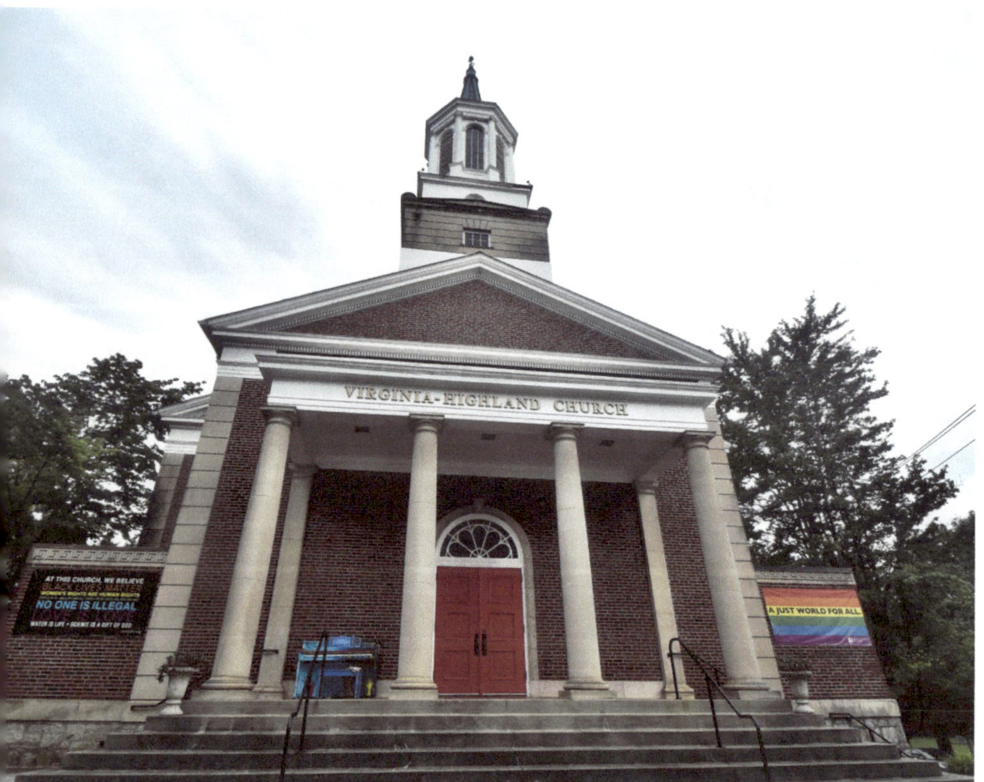

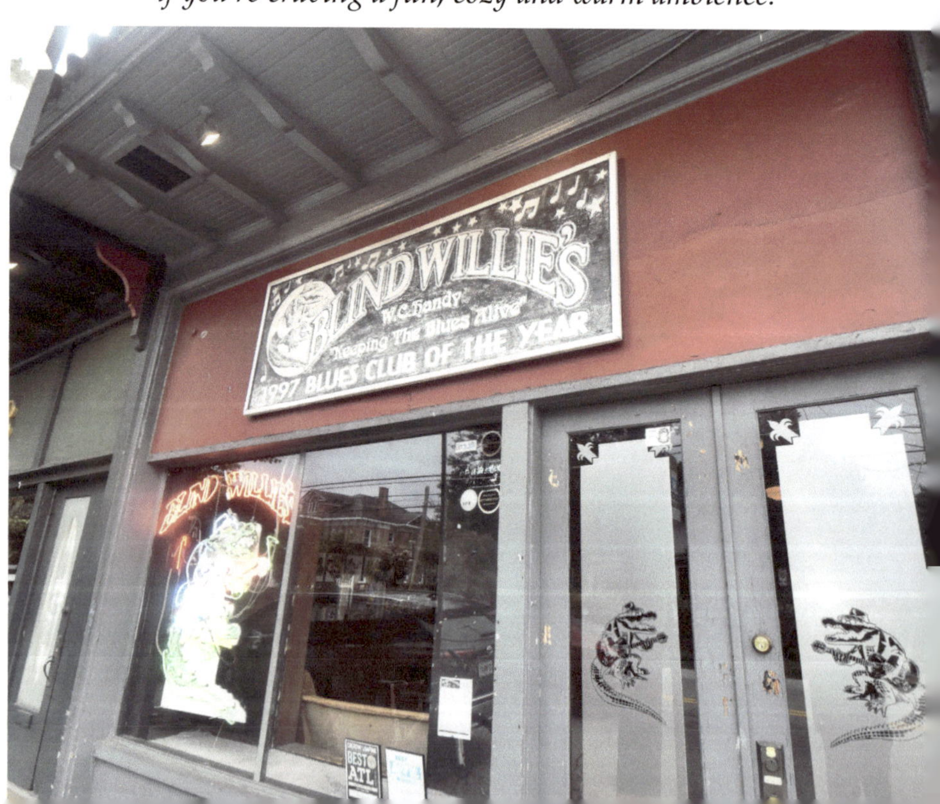

Atlanta Colleges

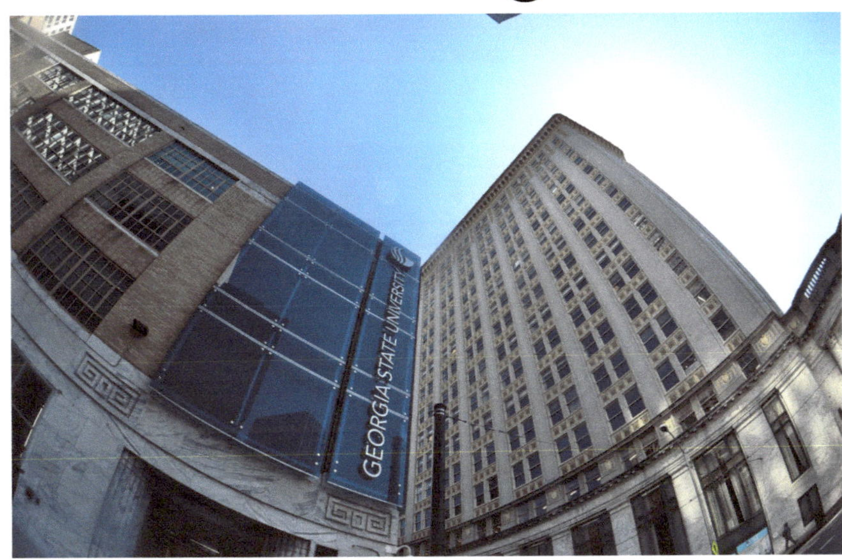

Georgia State University

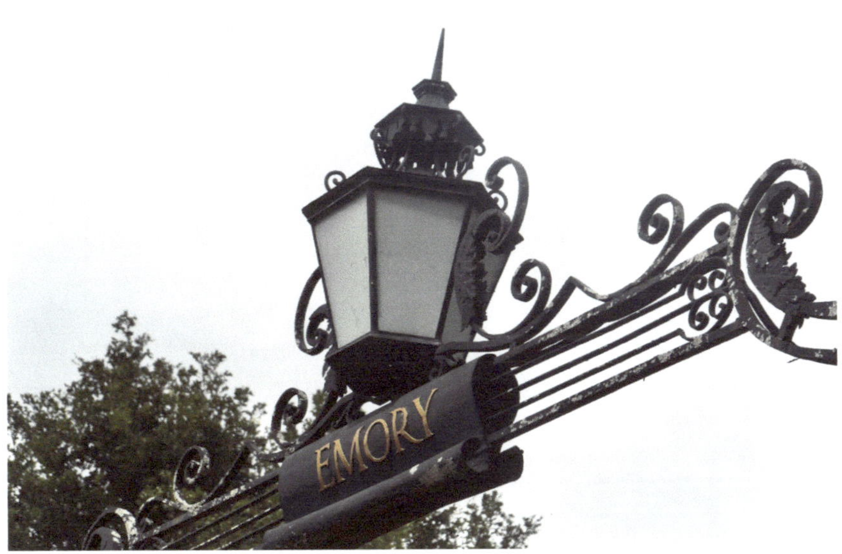

Emory University

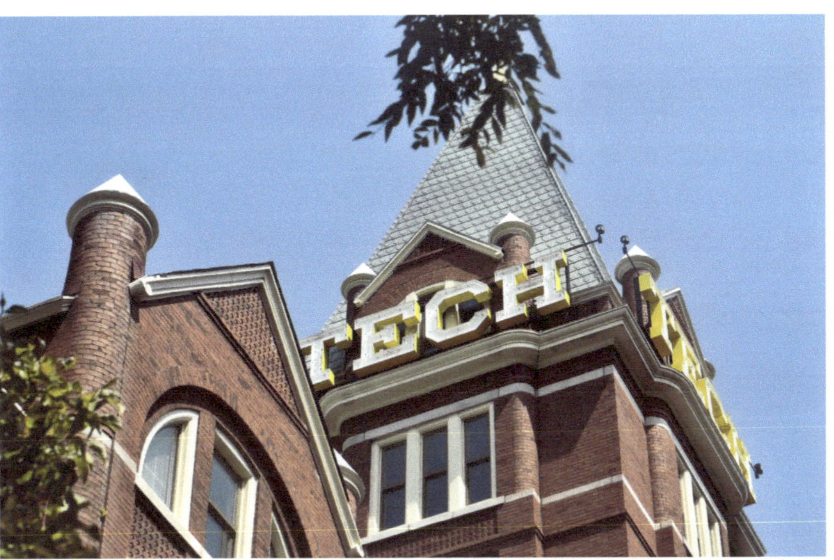

Georgia Institute of Technology (Georgia Tech)

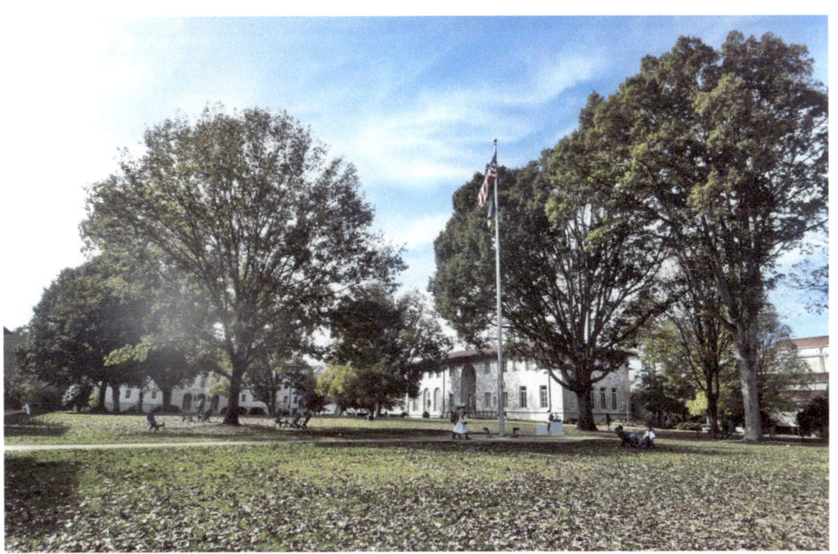

Emory University, The Quad

The formation of Emory's quadrangle occurred over a period of eighty years, beginning in 1915. This eclectic structure is a gathering place for students to study and unwind.

Oglethorpe University

Oglethorpe University was chartered in 1835, named in honor of General James Edward Oglethorpe, founder of the Colony of Georgia.

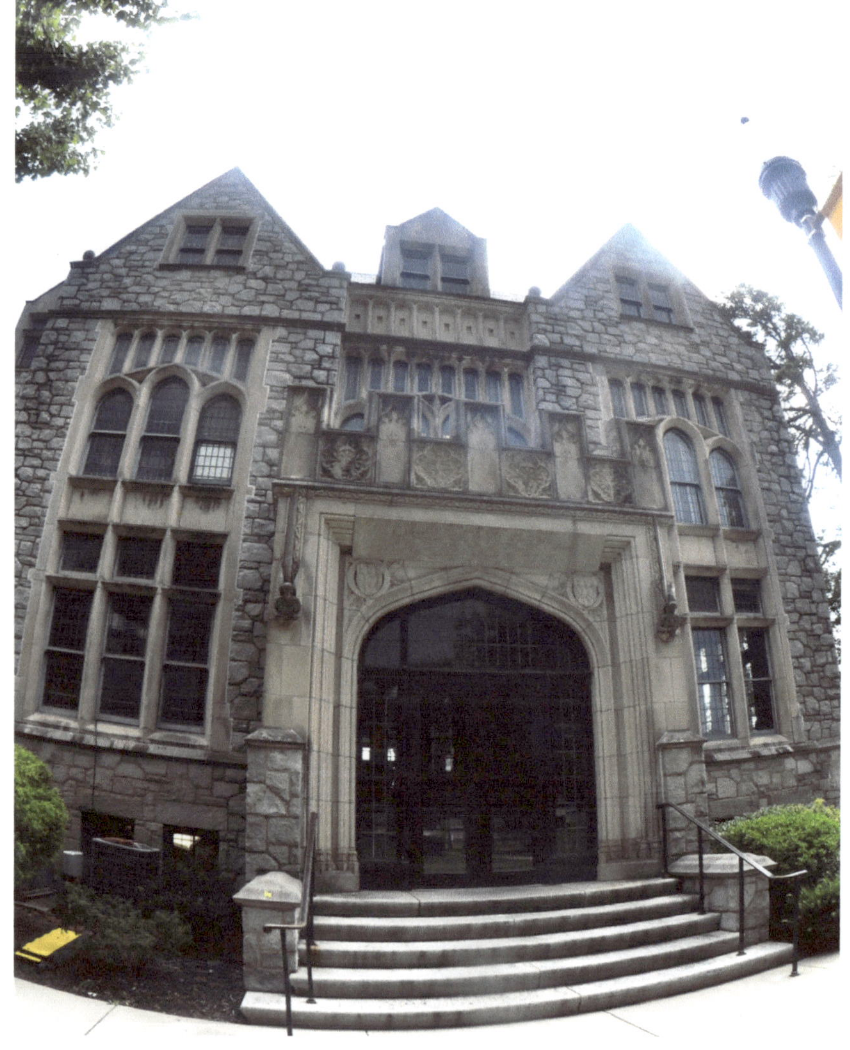

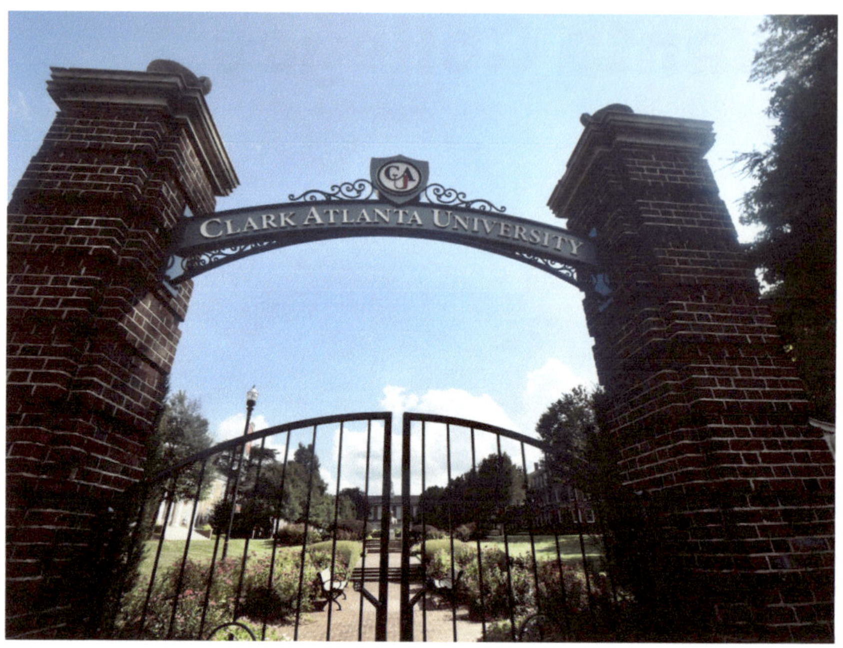

Clark Atlanta University Student Center

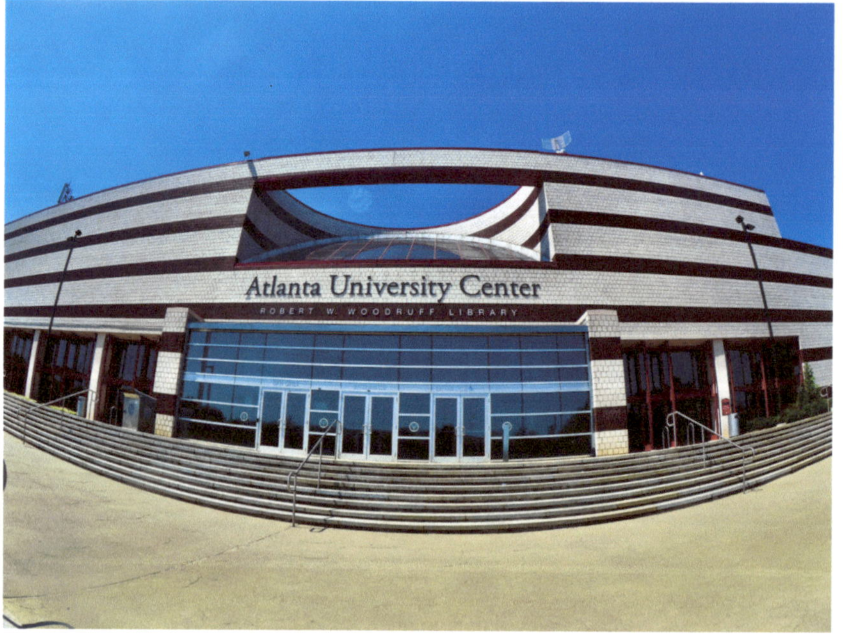

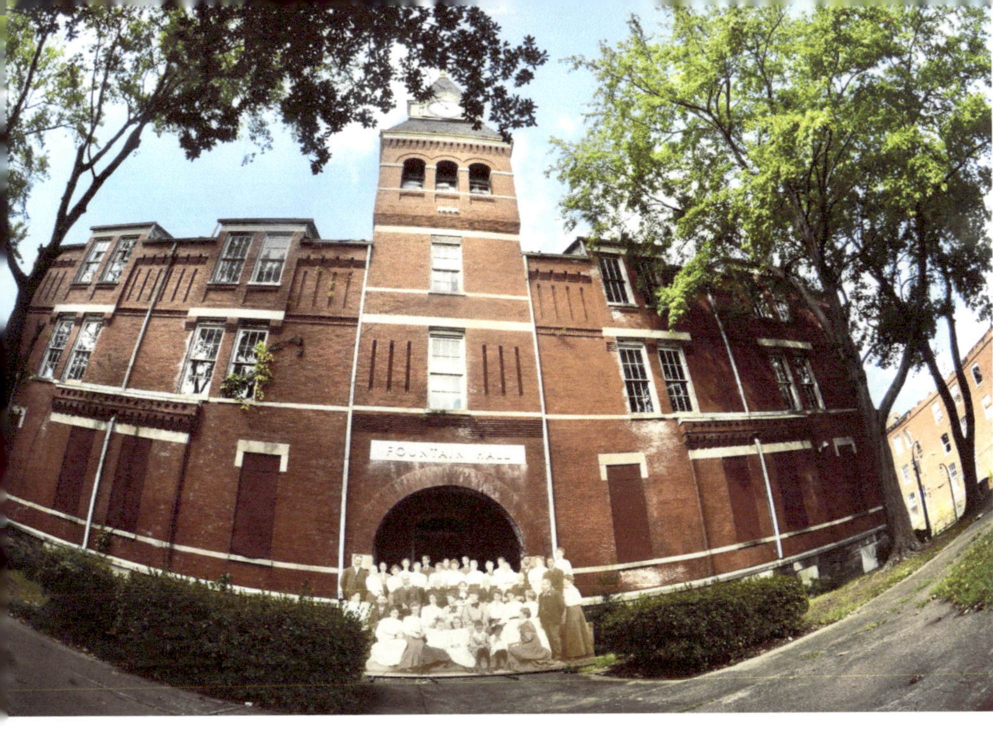

Morris Brown College

Morris Brown is home to the classroom and office of W. E. B. Du Bois, the first African American to earn a PhD from Harvard. Fountain Hall, one of the oldest buildings that was once affiliated with Atlanta University, is a historic landmark on the Morris Brown College campus.

The Unity Statue stands tall on the Morris Brown College campus

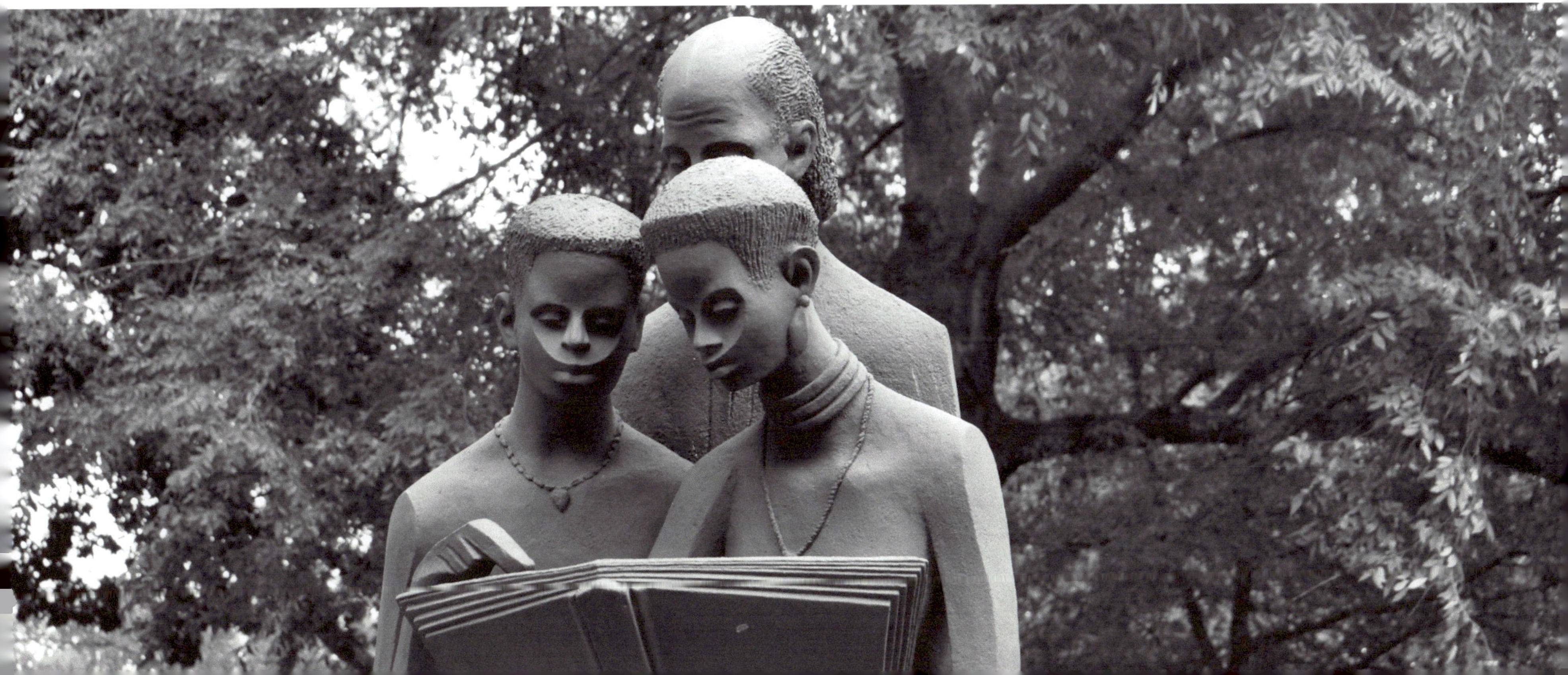

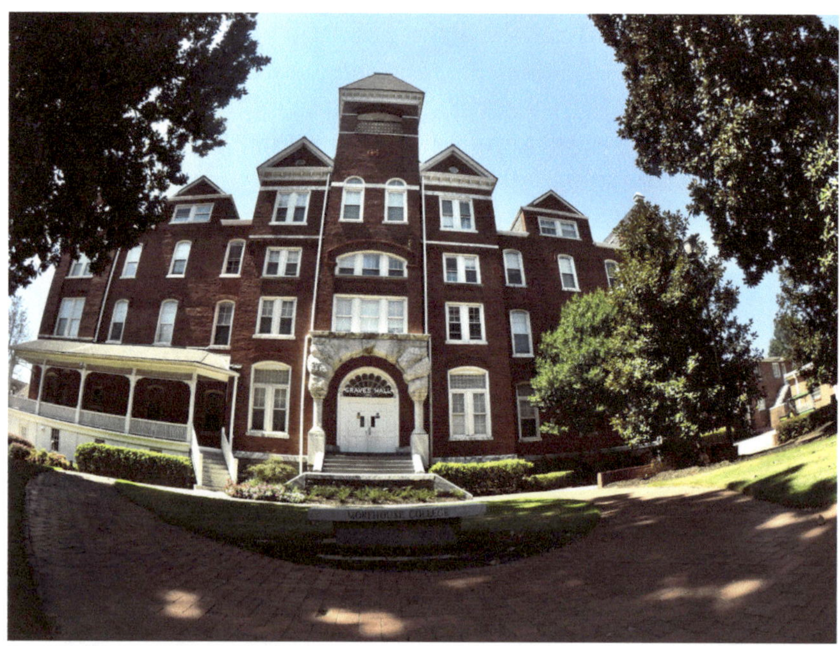

Graves Hall—Morehouse College

Built in 1889, it is the oldest building on the campus. Notable people who either lived in or studied at Graves Hall include Dr. Martin Luther King Jr., movie director Spike Lee, Olympic gold medalist Edwin Moses, former Atlanta mayor Maynard Jackson, and former Health and Human Services Director Dr. Louis Sullivan.

Letitia Pate Evans Dining Hall, Agnes Scott College

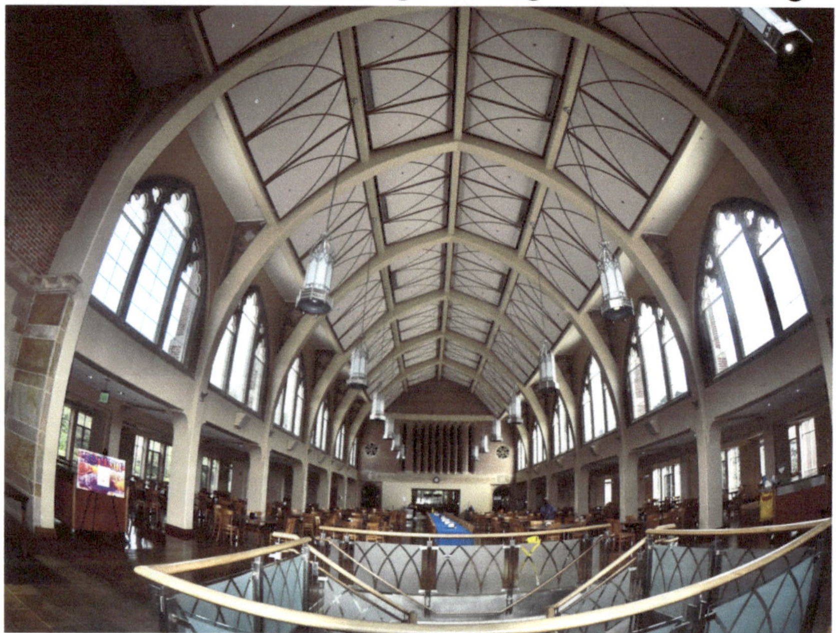

Agnes Scott College

Agnes Scott College is a private women's liberal arts college and is considered one of the Seven Sisters of the South.

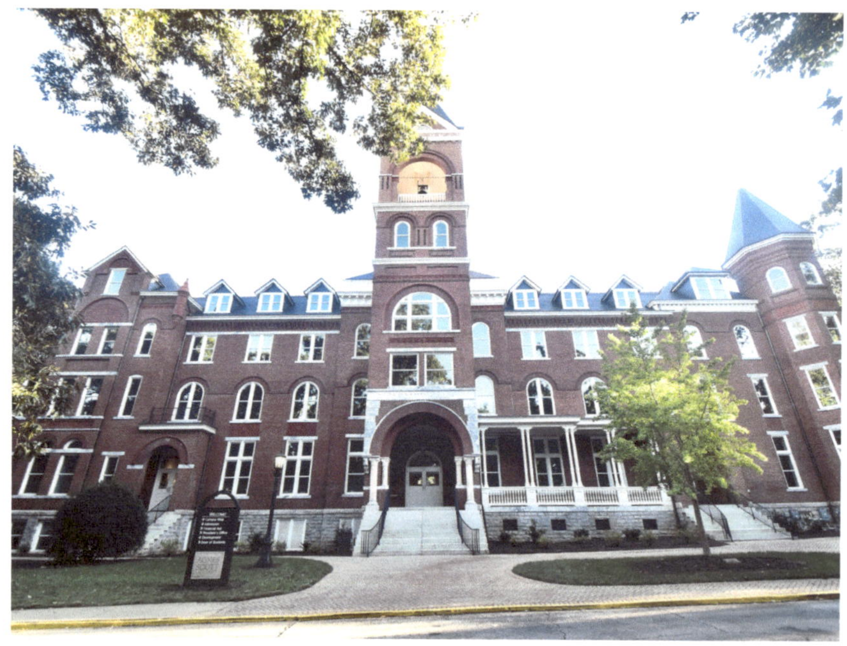

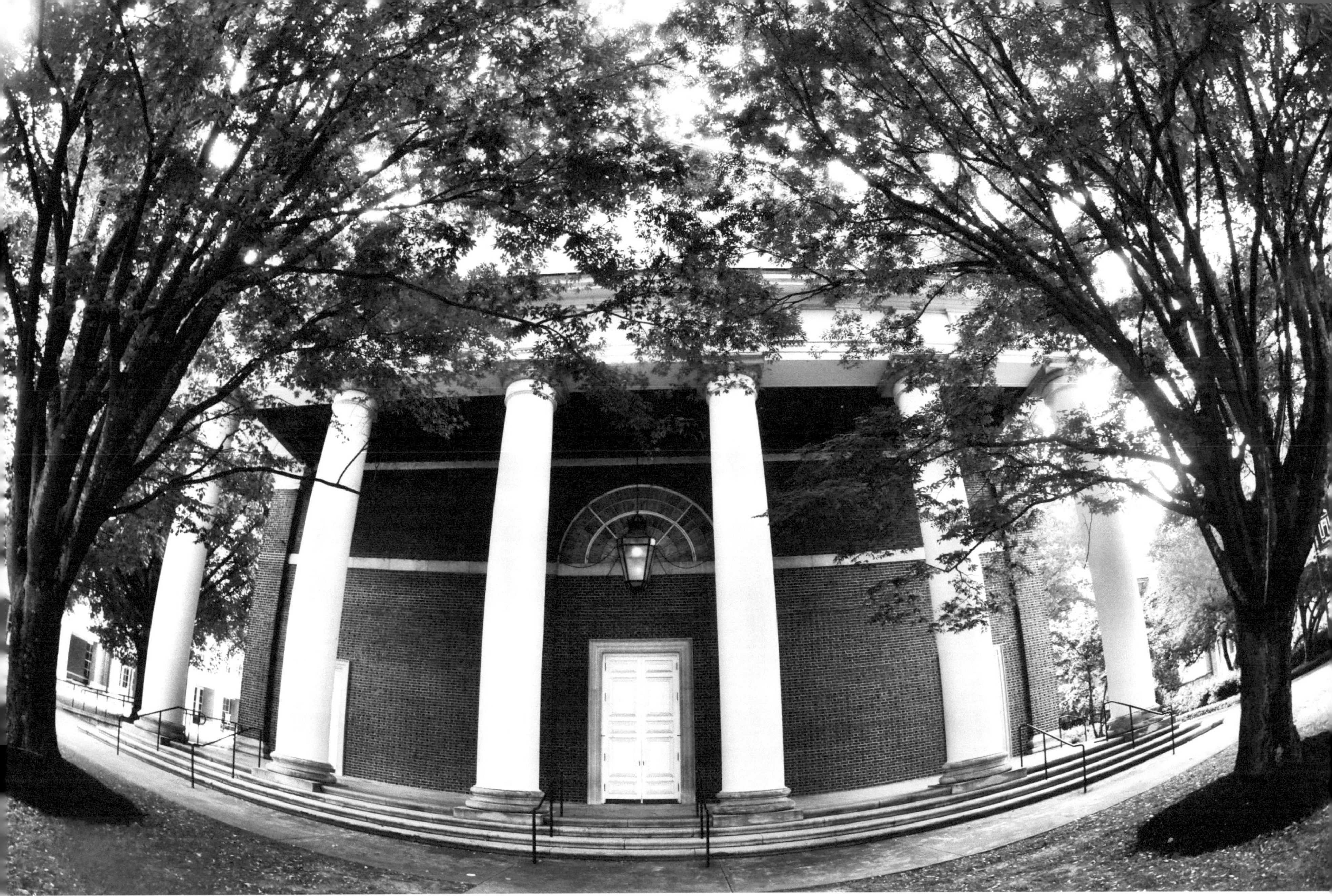

Sisters Chapel, Spelman College

Sisters Chapel is the religious and spiritual center of Spelman College. In 1968, the public viewing of the body of Martin Luther King Jr. was displayed for forty-eight hours and then later transported to Ebenezer Baptist Church.

Atlanta Sports

Midtown Celebration
The Atlanta Braves celebrate after winning the World Series in 2021.

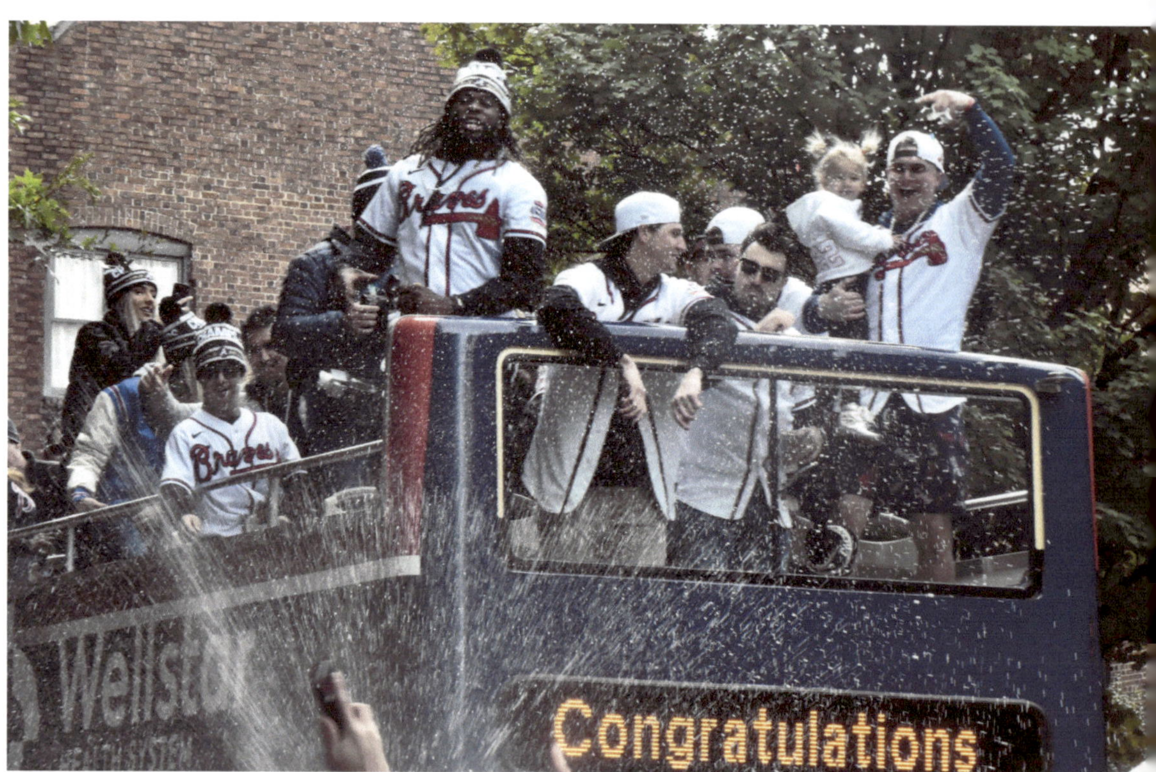

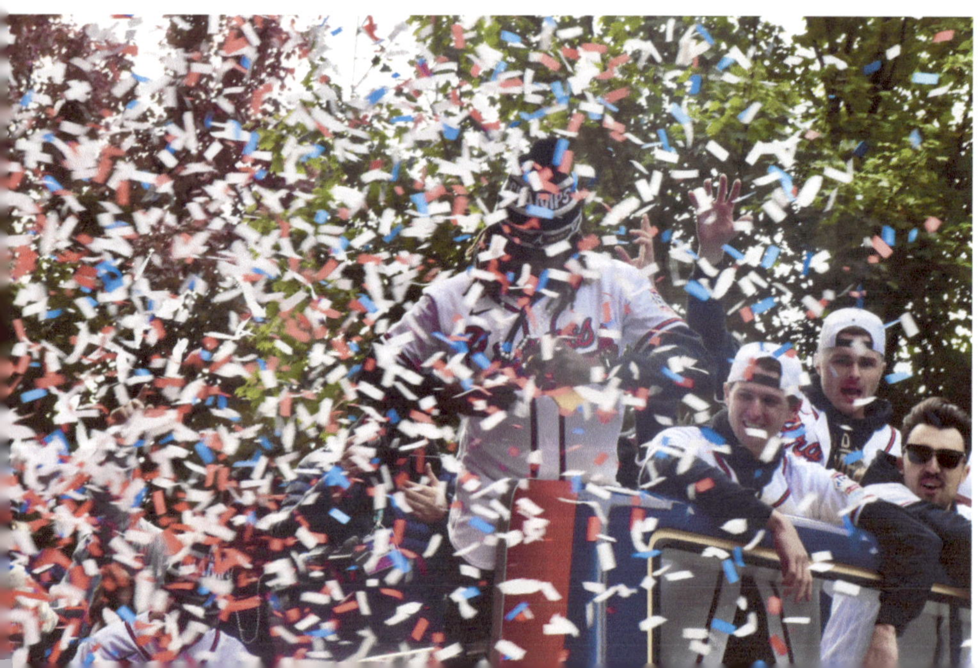

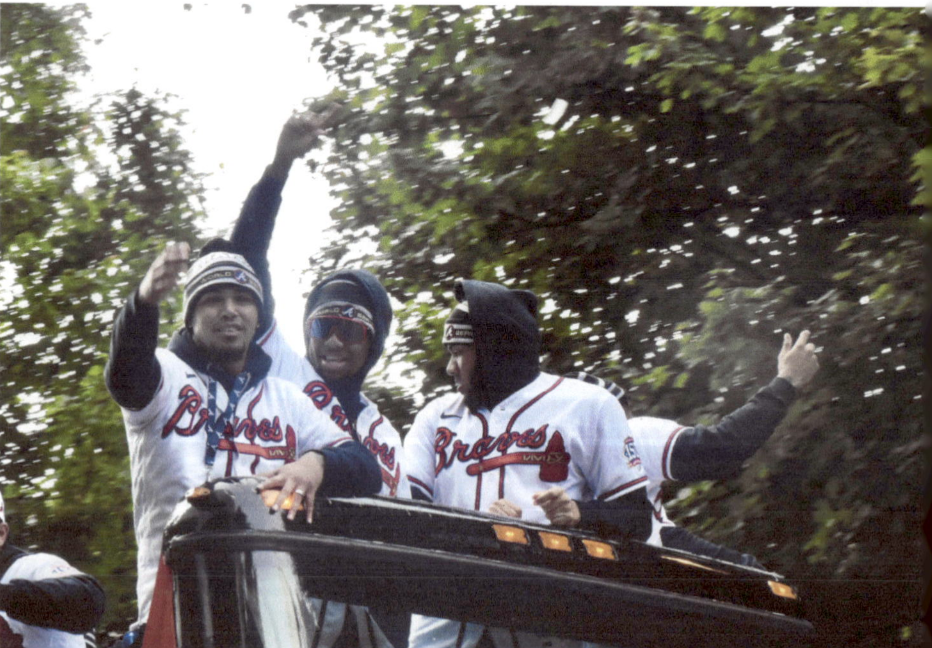

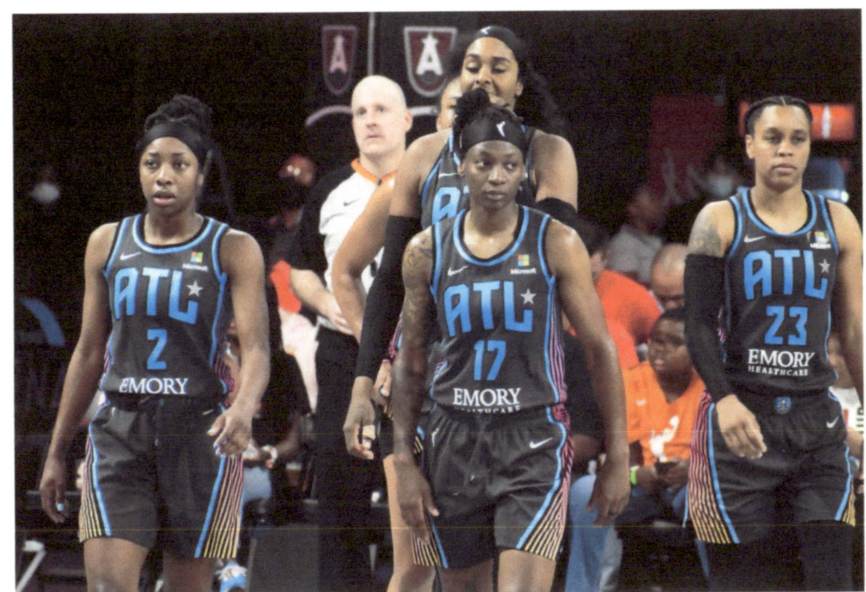

Atlanta Dream

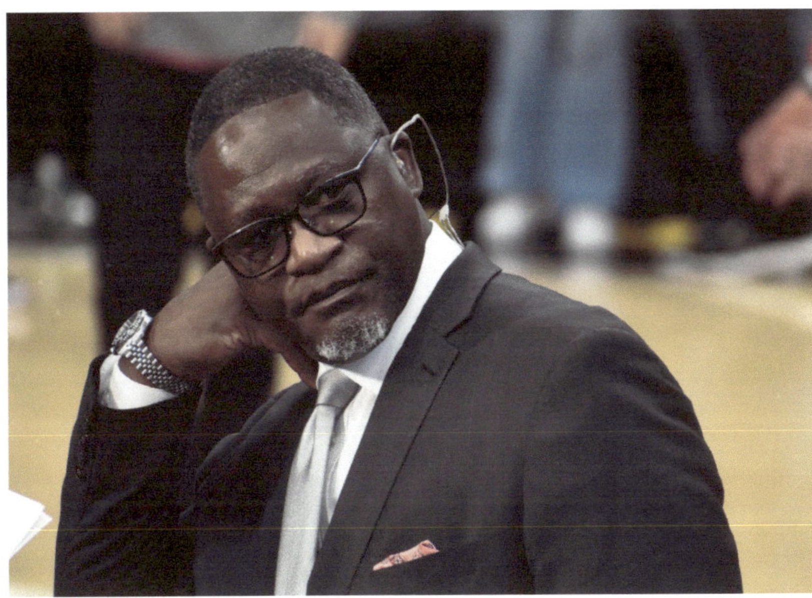

Atlanta Hawks Former Forward, Dominique Wilkins

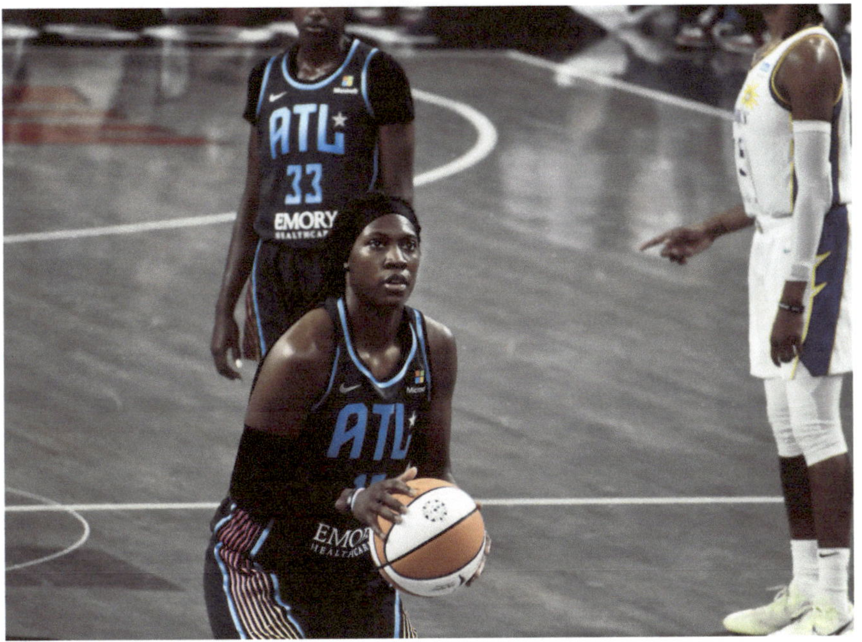

Atlanta Dream Guard, Rhyne Howard

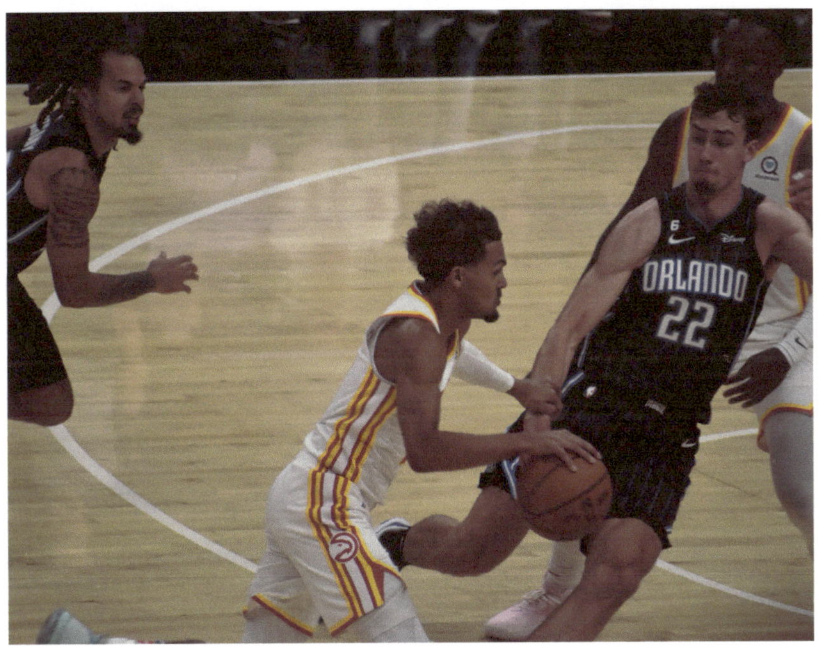

Atlanta Hawks Point Guard, Trae Young

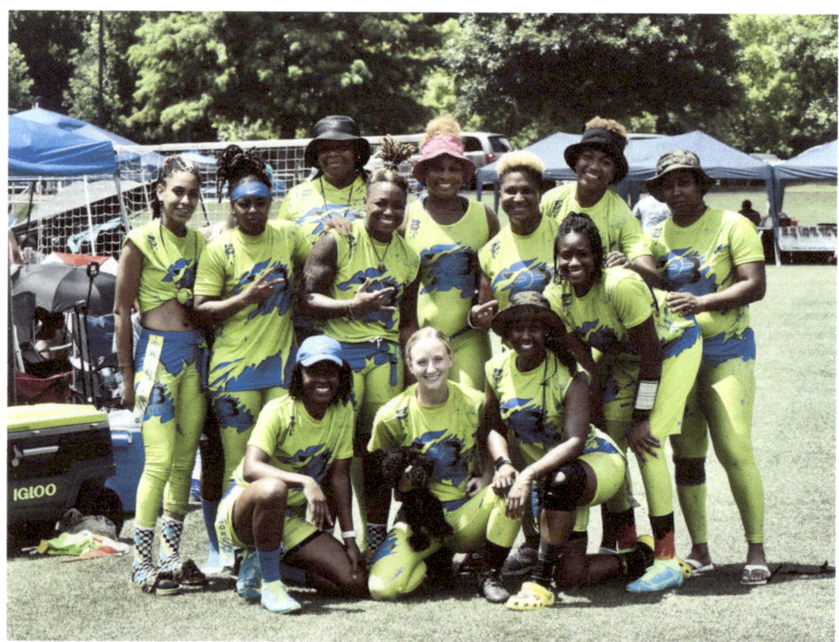

Atlanta's Women's Flag Football, the Rebels

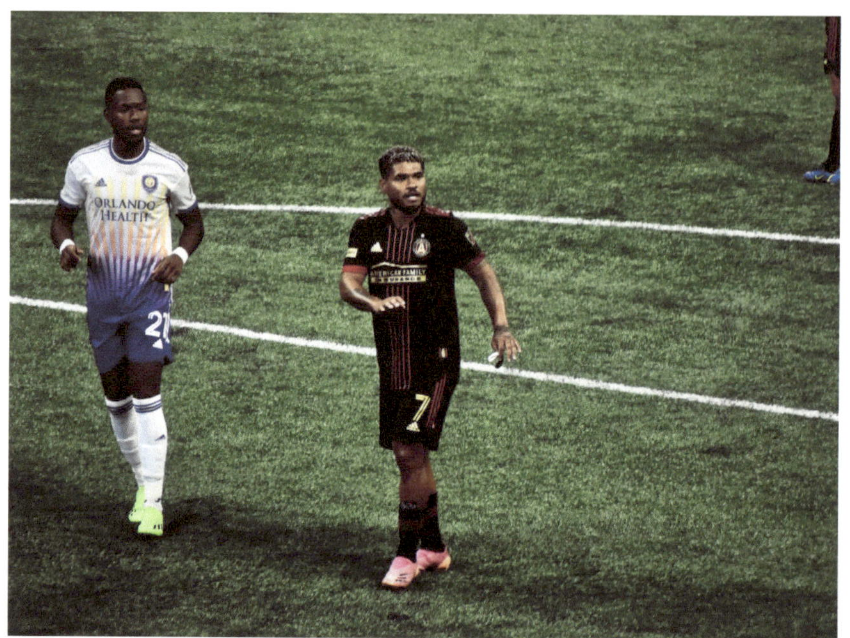

Atlanta United Soccer standout, Josef Martinez

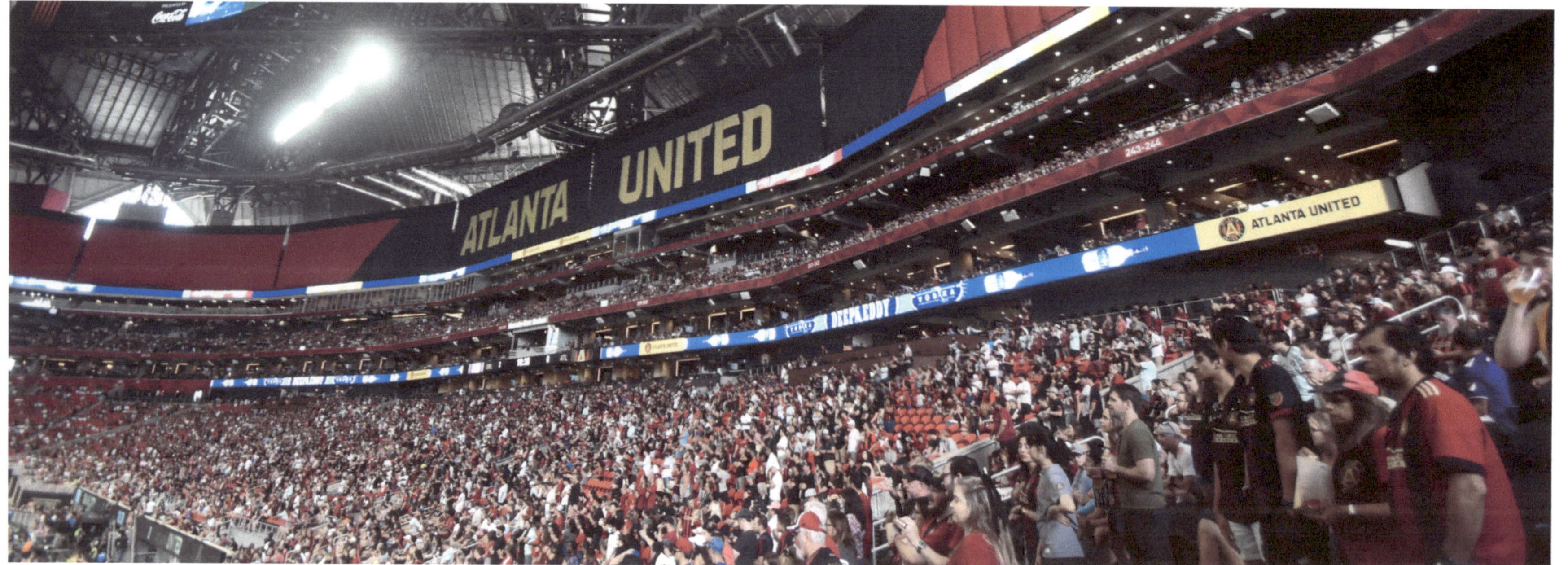

Atlanta Falcons' Former Quarterback, Matt Ryan

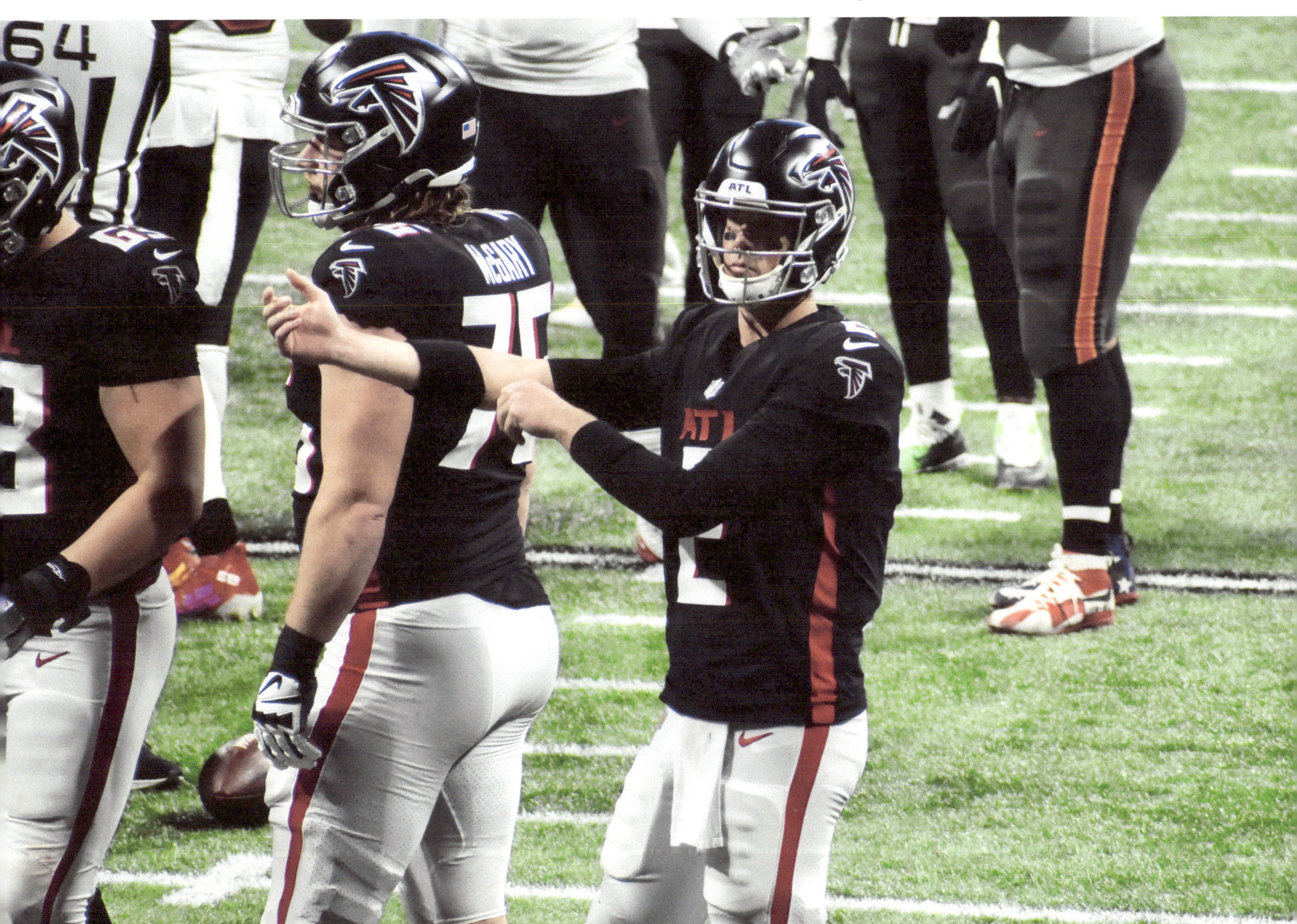

Things to See Around Atlanta

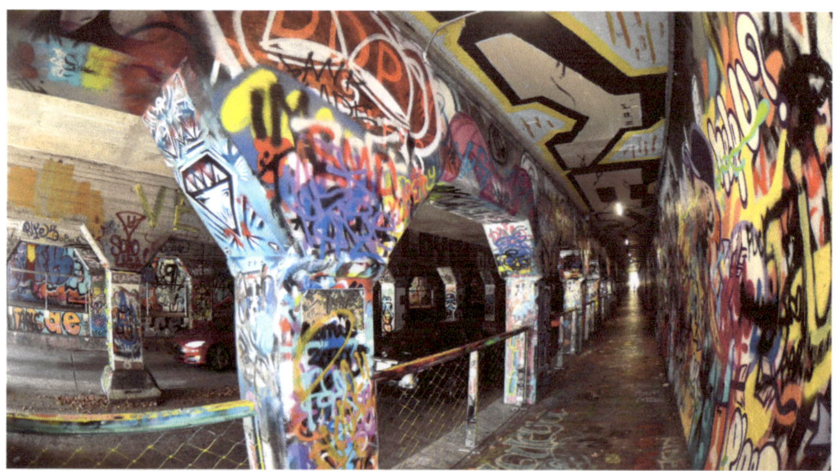

Krog Street Tunnel

Covered from top to bottom in paint by street artists from all over Atlanta, this two-lane tunnel is constantly filled with the smell of fresh spray paint.

CNN Center Sign,
Once an Atlanta Fixture, Is Now History

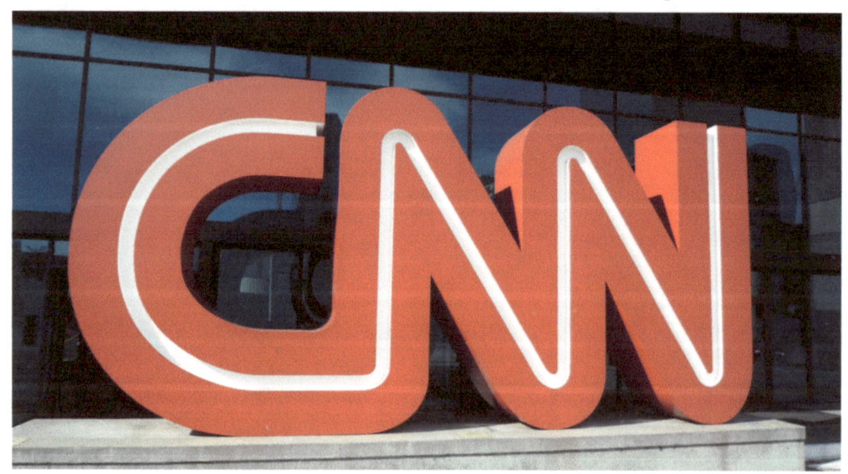

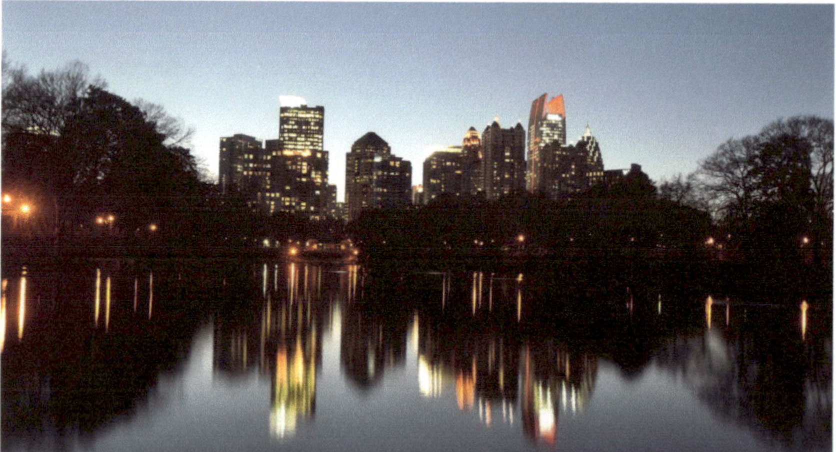

Lake Clara Meer, Piedmont Park

Tyler Perry Studios

Tyler Perry Studios is a major motion picture studio located on a 330-acre lot in the heart of Atlanta. This site was once the home of Fort McPherson US Army base.

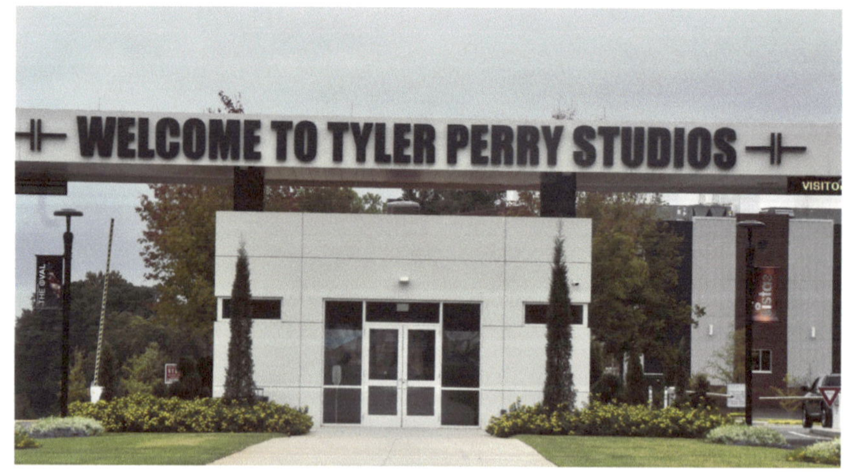

Centennial Olympic Park

The home of the 1996 Olympic games.

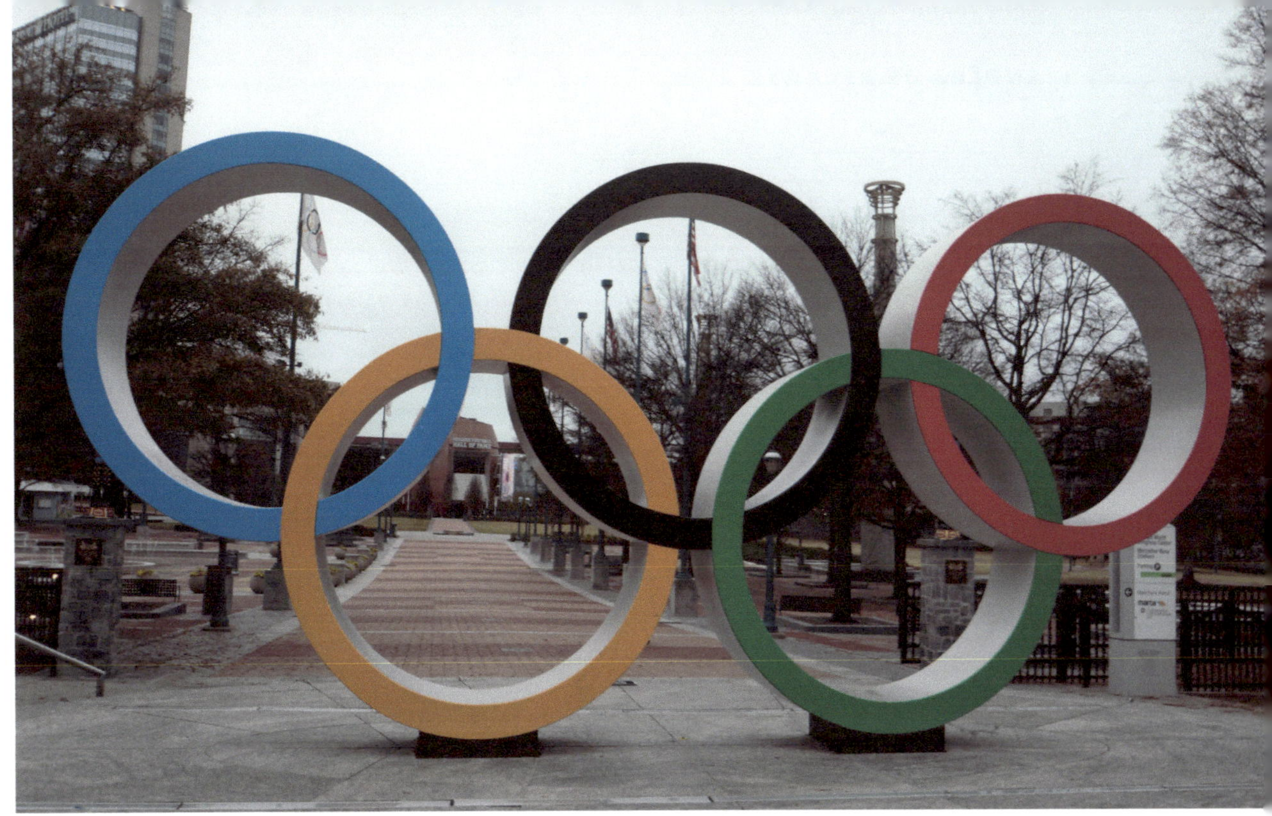

Skyview Atlanta

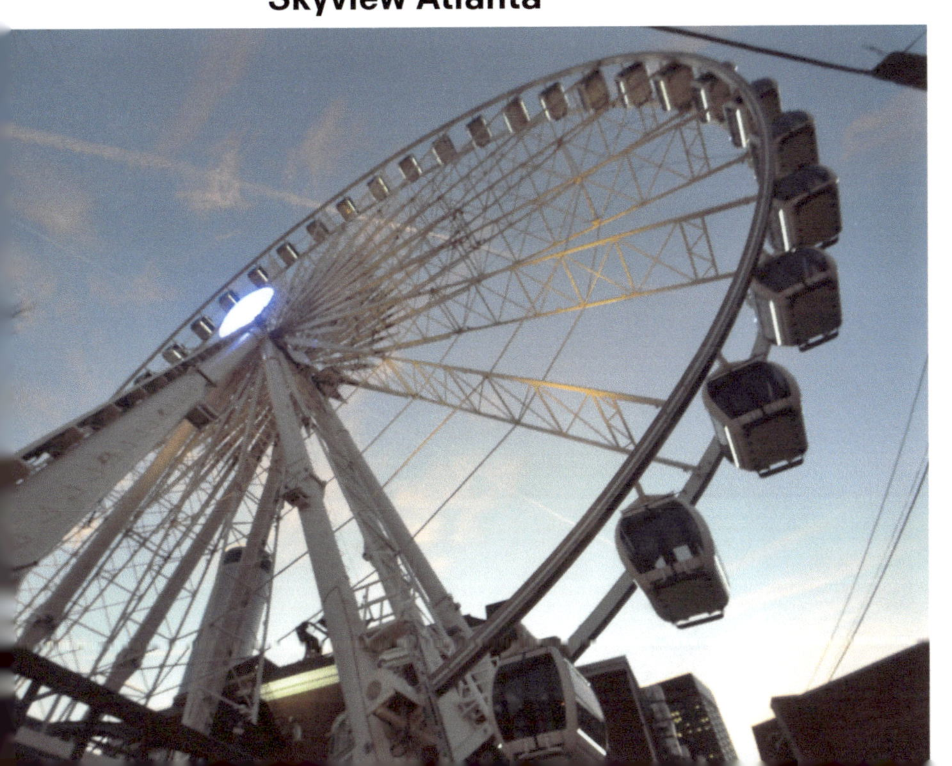

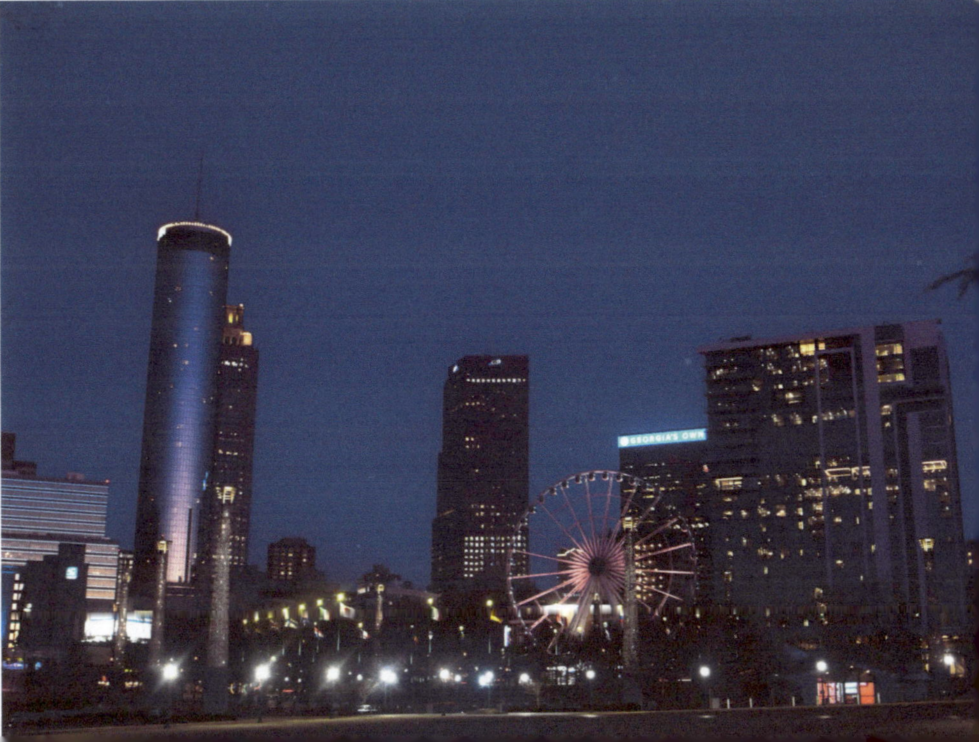

Atlanta Botanical Garden

The Atlanta Botanical Garden is a thirty-acre oasis in the heart of Midtown. Earth Goddess is a twenty-five-foot sculpture that flows with locks and outward hands spilling with water. It is a permanent display and is meticulously maintained daily.

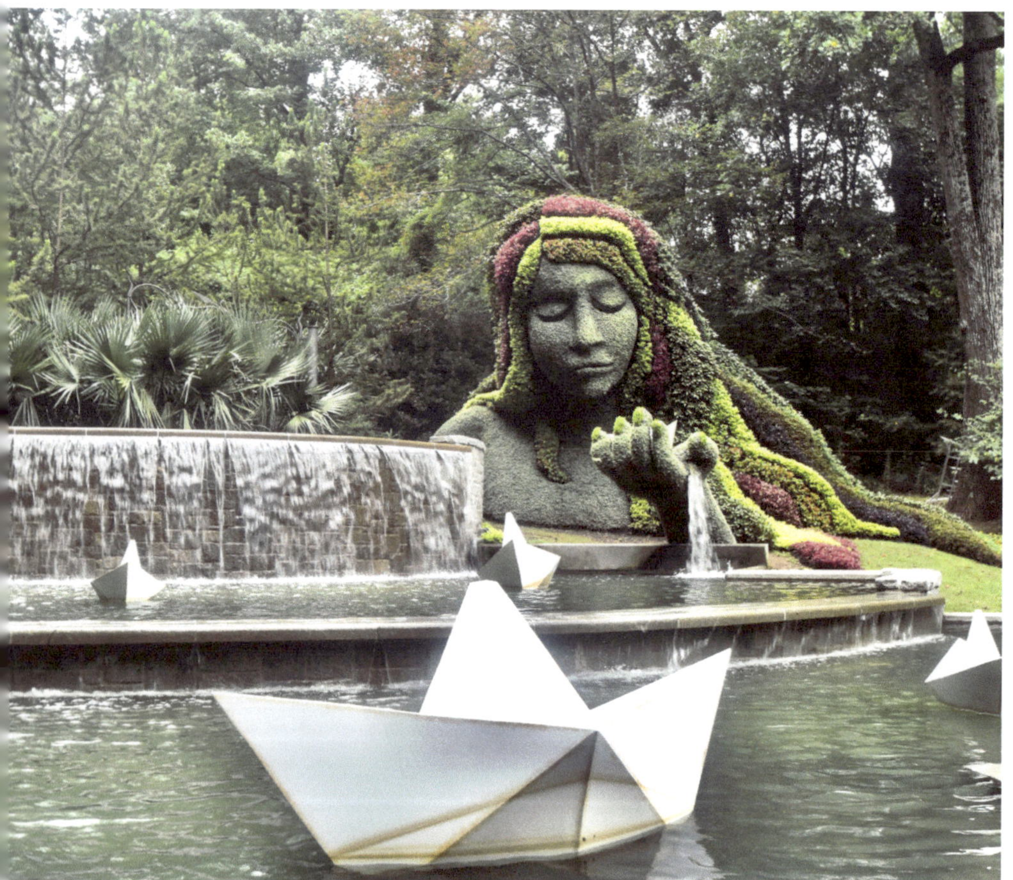

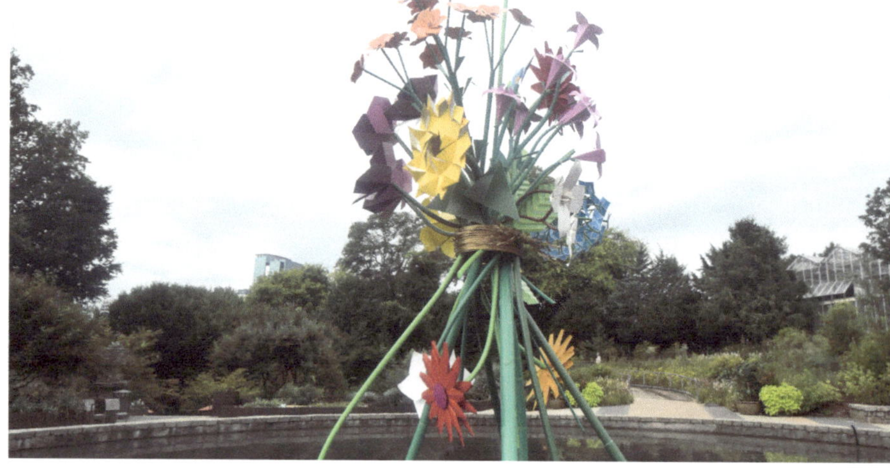

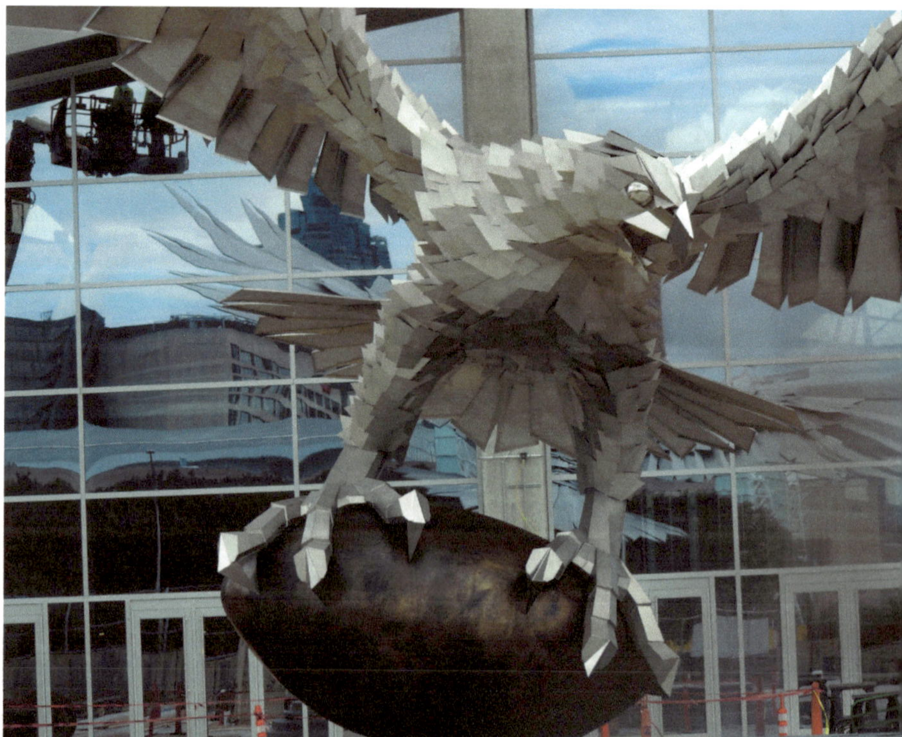

Falcons Statue at Mercedes-Benz Stadium

Weighing at 73,000 pounds, this steel artwork was created by Gabor Miklos Szoke, a Hungarian artist, for the home of the Atlanta Falcons. It is also known to be the largest bird sculpture in the world.

Stone Mountain

Stone Mountain, engraved with the sculptures of Jefferson Davis, president of the Confederate States, and generals Robert E. Lee and Stonewall Jackson, is the largest Confederate monument in the world. The effort to create this monument began in the 1910s, yet it was not completed until 1972. There was controversy following the Charleston, South Carolina, church shooting in 2015 and a political debate to remove the symbols representing the Confederacy. As of today, the monument remains in place.

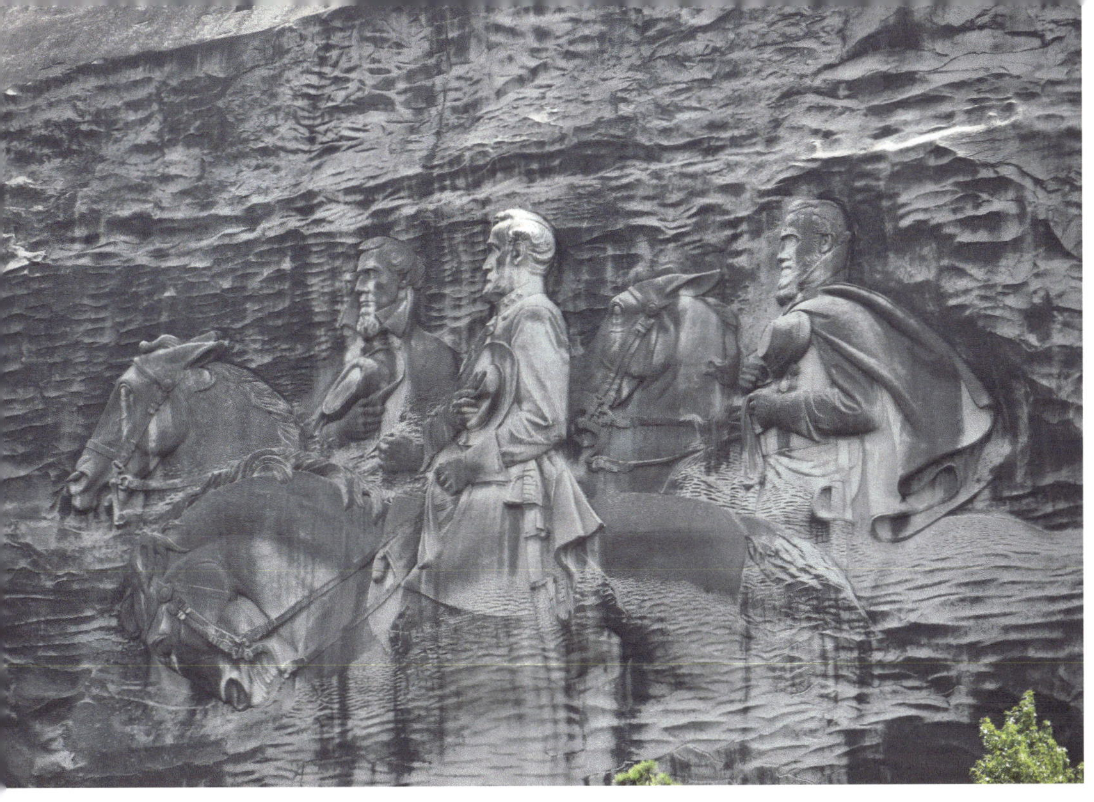

Underground Atlanta

Underground Atlanta is known as "The City Beneath the Streets."

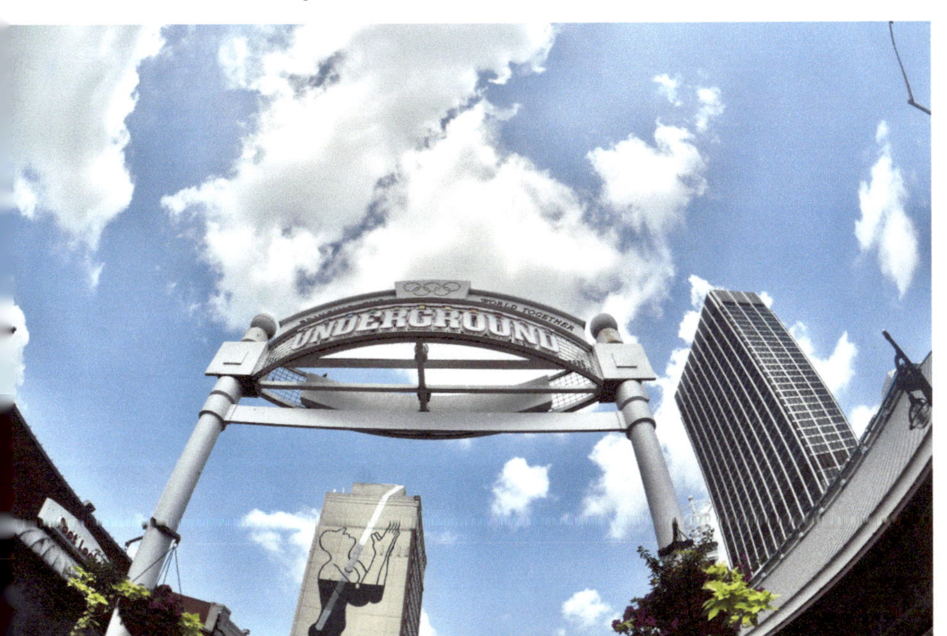

The High Museum of Art

The High Museum of Art is the largest museum of visual art in the southeastern United States.

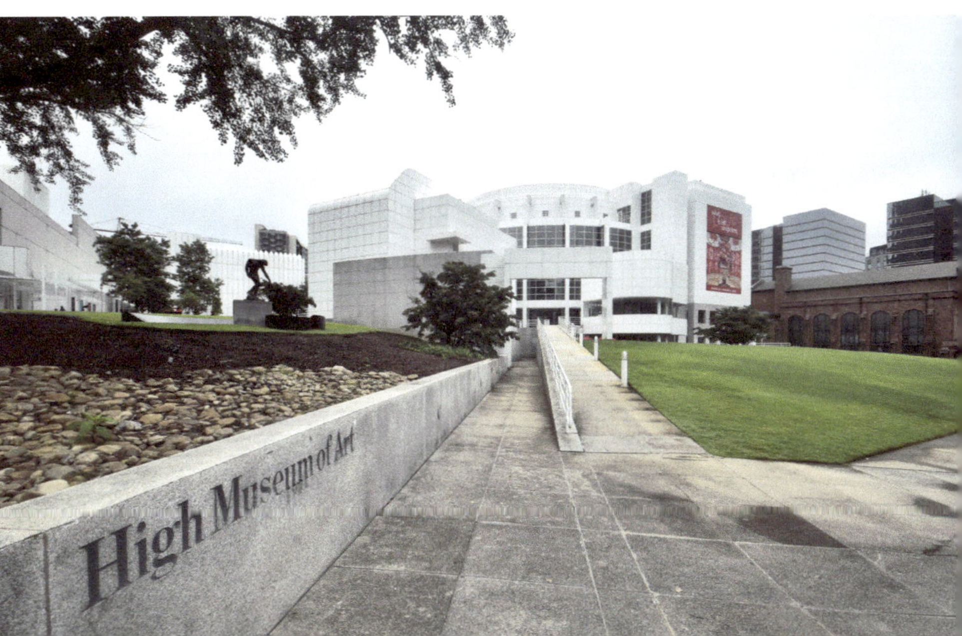

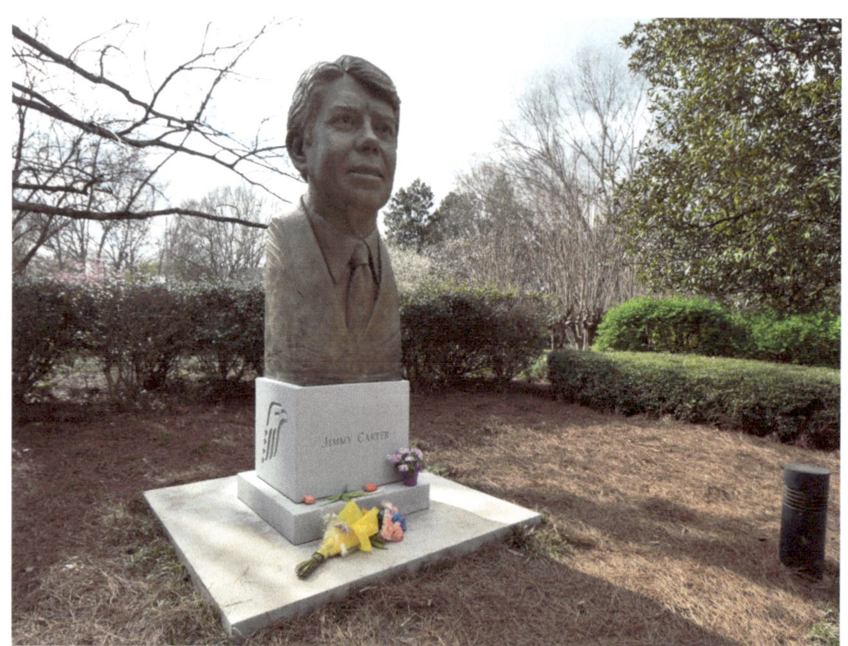

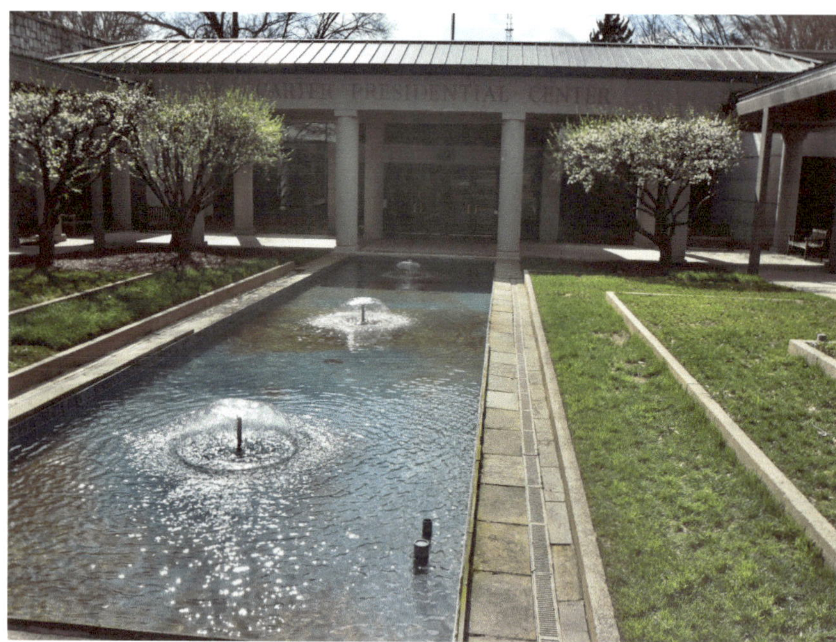

The Carter Center

The home of former President Jimmy Carter's Foundation.

The Royal Peacock

The Royal Peacock was originally known as the Top Hat Club. Its doors opened in the late 1930s as a nightclub that showcased legendary artists from Sam Cooke to Cab Calloway and Louis Armstrong, to Ray Charles, Little Richard, and Marvin Gaye. In 1998, the rap group Outkast prominently featured the Royal Peacock in its video for the song "Rosa Parks."

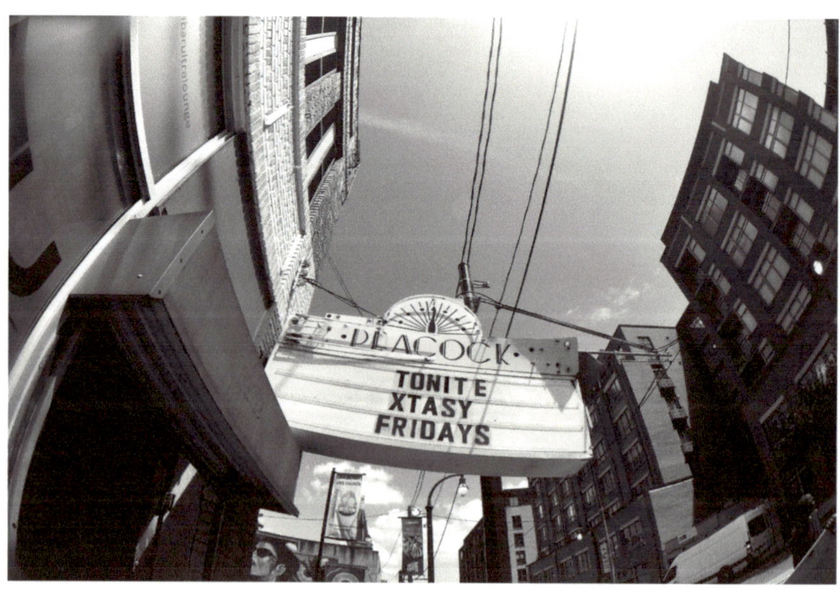

Around Town

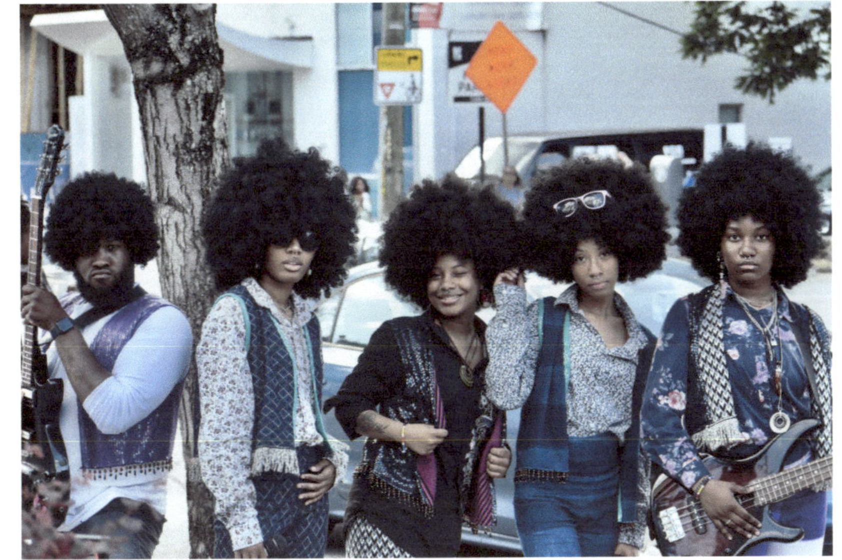

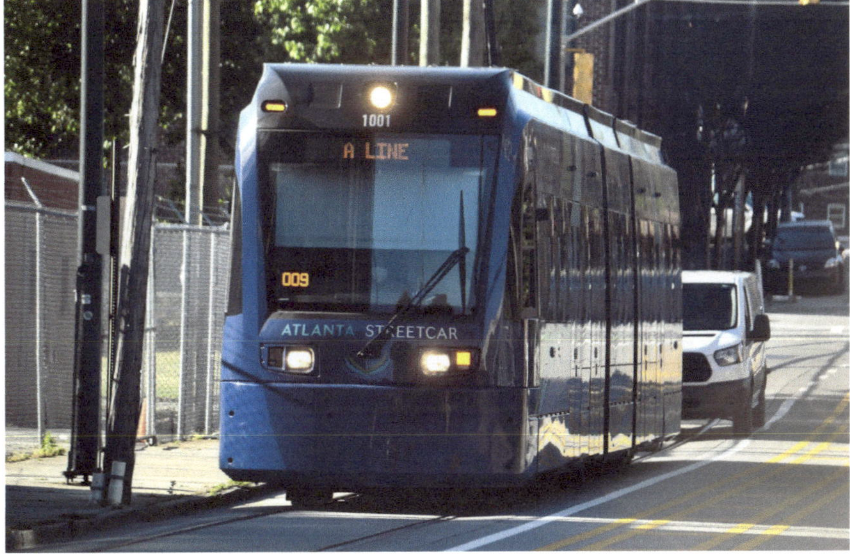

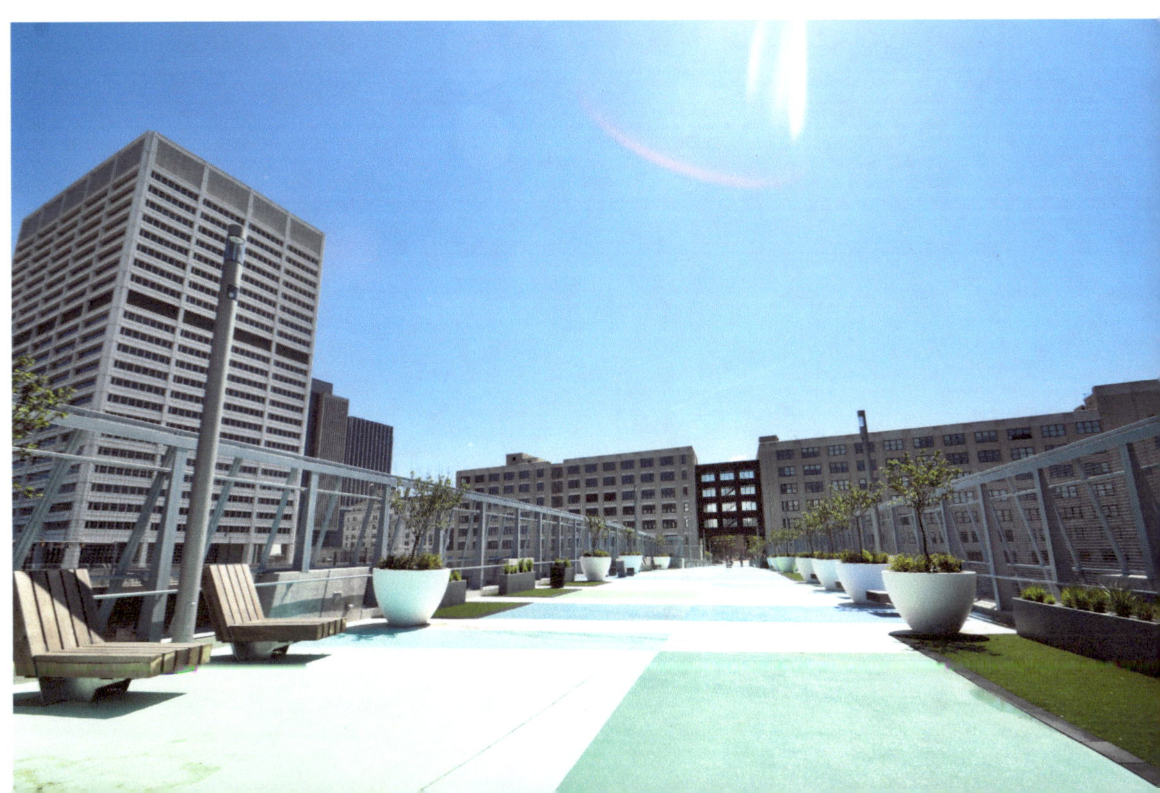

The Steele Bridge

Formerly known as the Nelson Street Bridge, this bridge was recently renamed in memory of a former enslaved Georgia resident, Carrie Steele Logan, who was responsible for founding the nation's oldest Black orphanage.

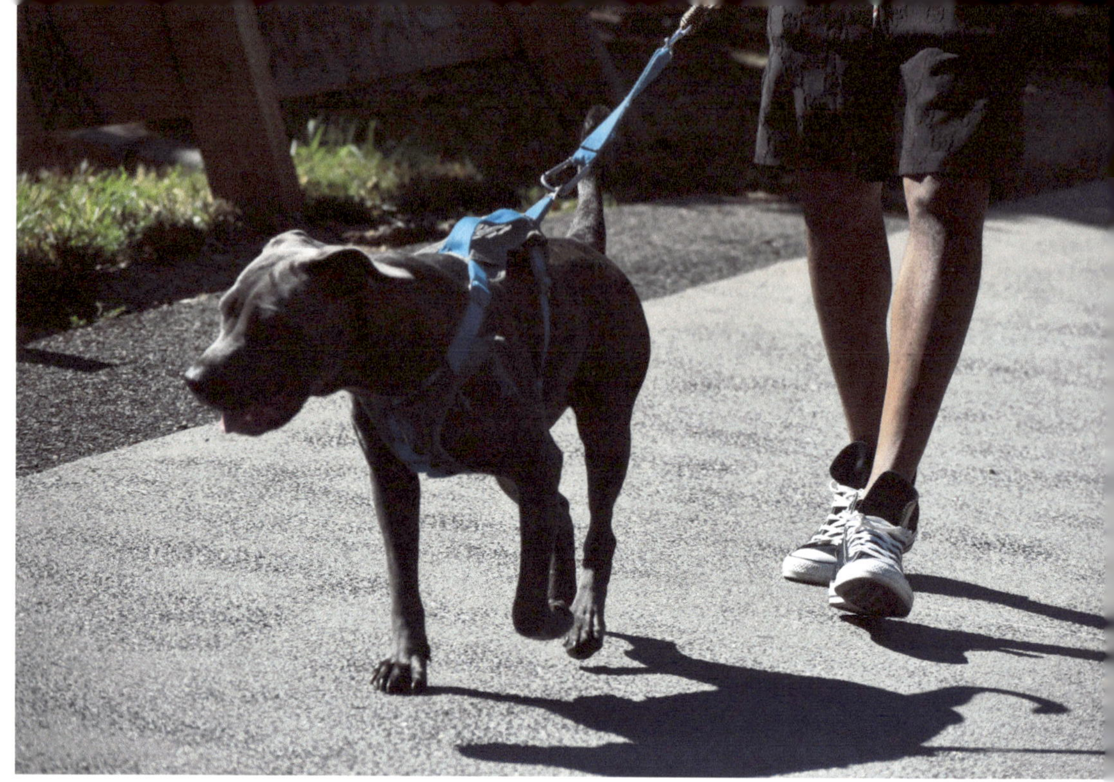

Traveling the Beltline

The Atlanta Beltline is a twenty-two-mile, multifunctional path of rail lines designated for bicyclists, runners, and is a dog-friendly environment. It exhibits the arts, culture, and flaunts the greatest atmosphere for some of the funkiest and up-to-date eateries.

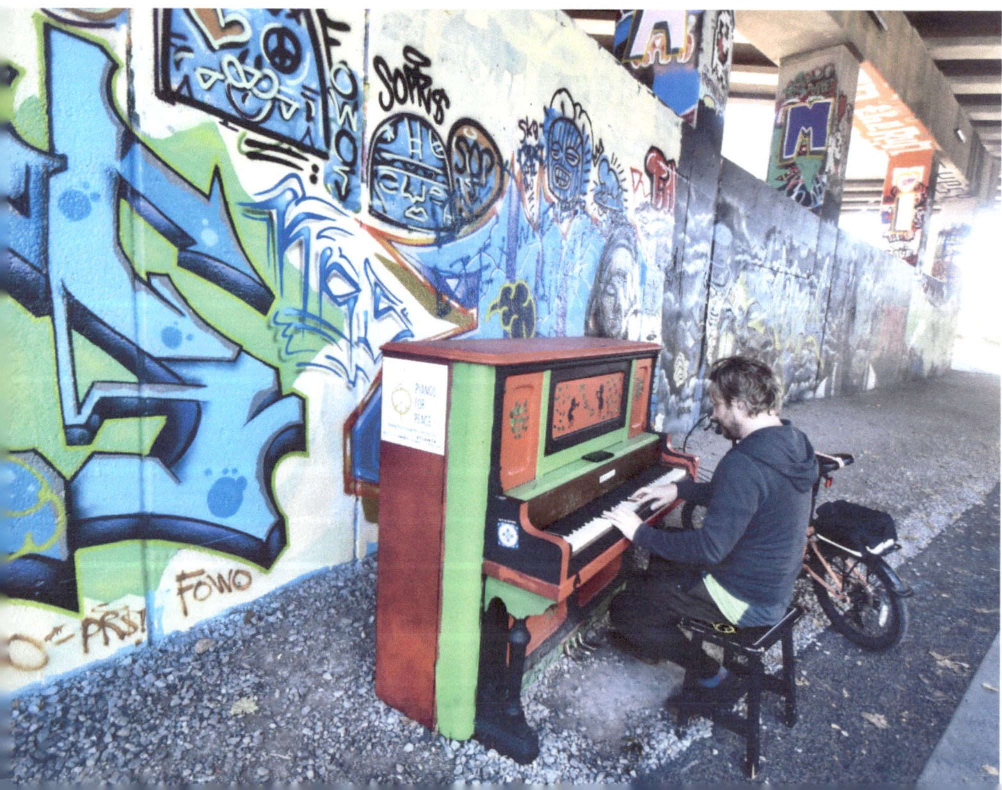

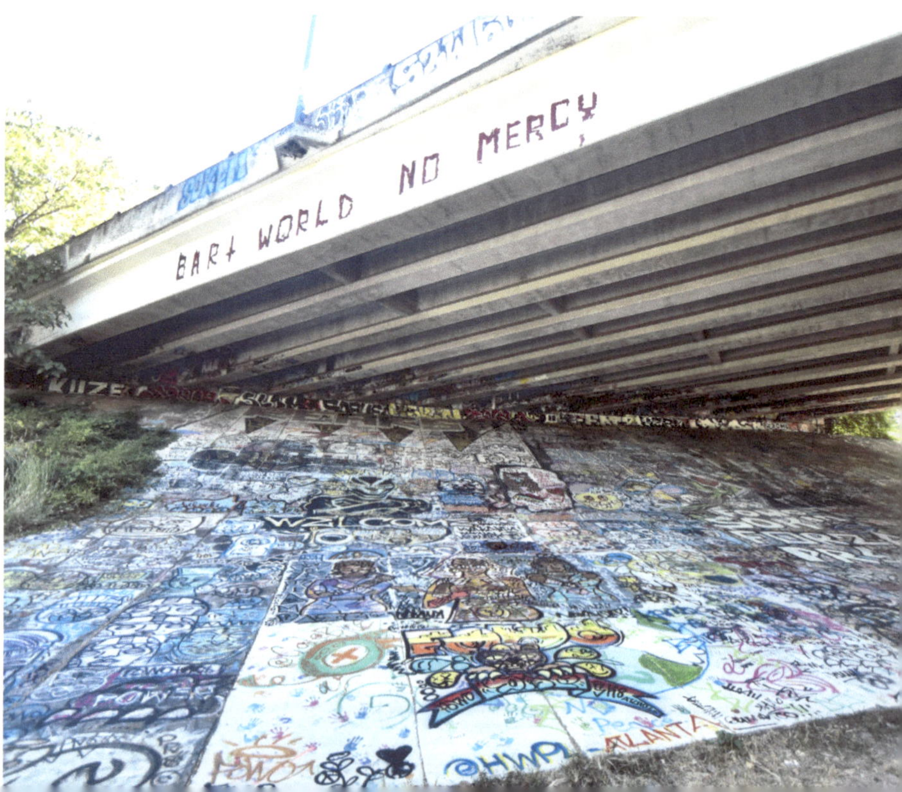

Atlanta Festivals

Tito Puente Jr. (Performing at the Reggae Festival in Atlanta's Piedmont Park 2022)

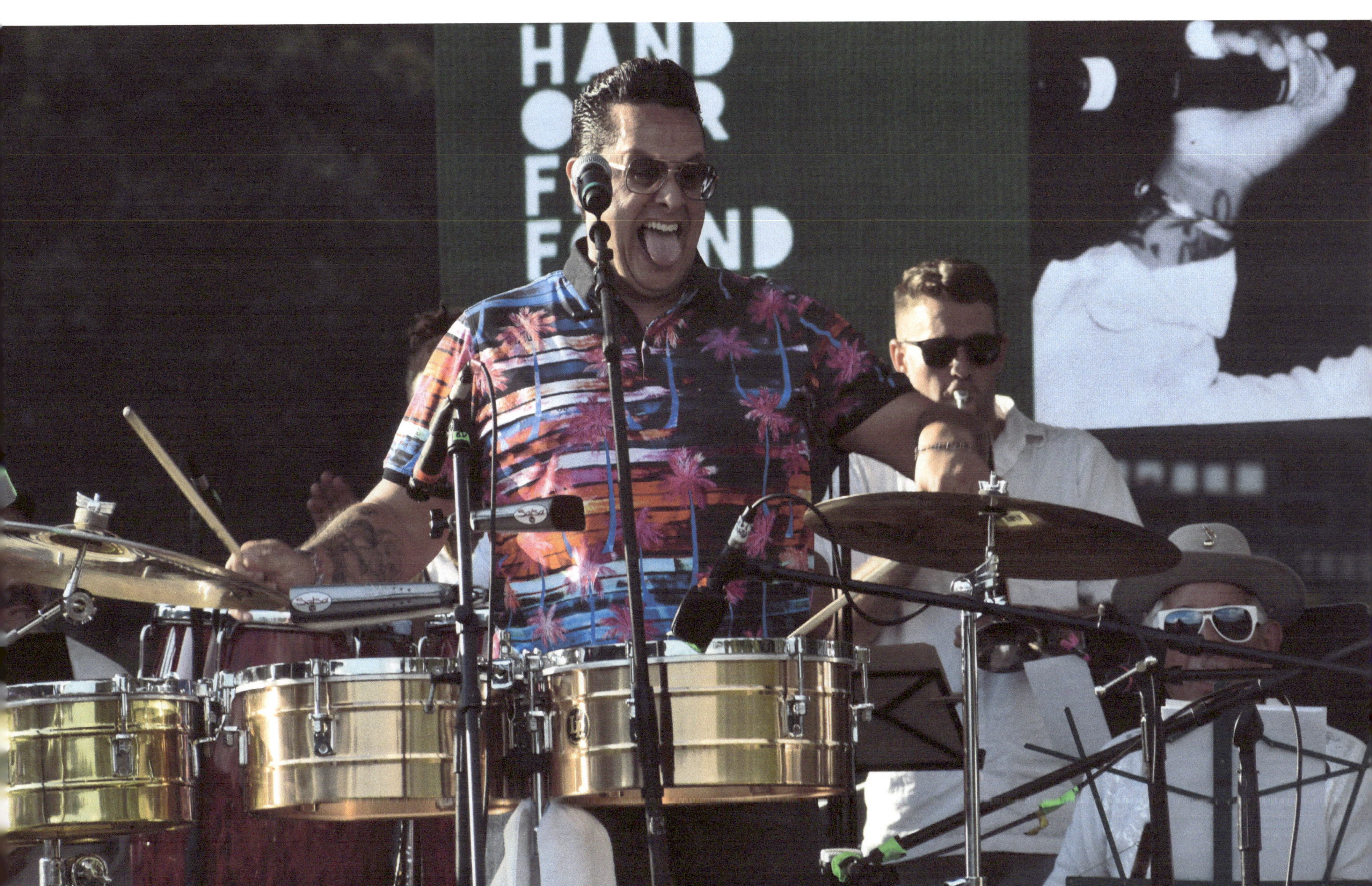

Atlanta Jazz Festival (The Largest Free Jazz Festival in the Country)

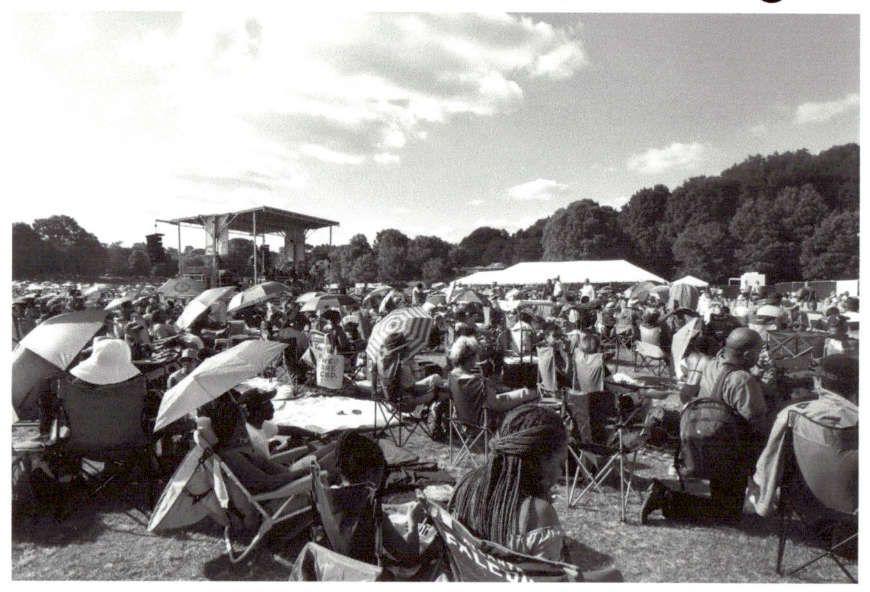

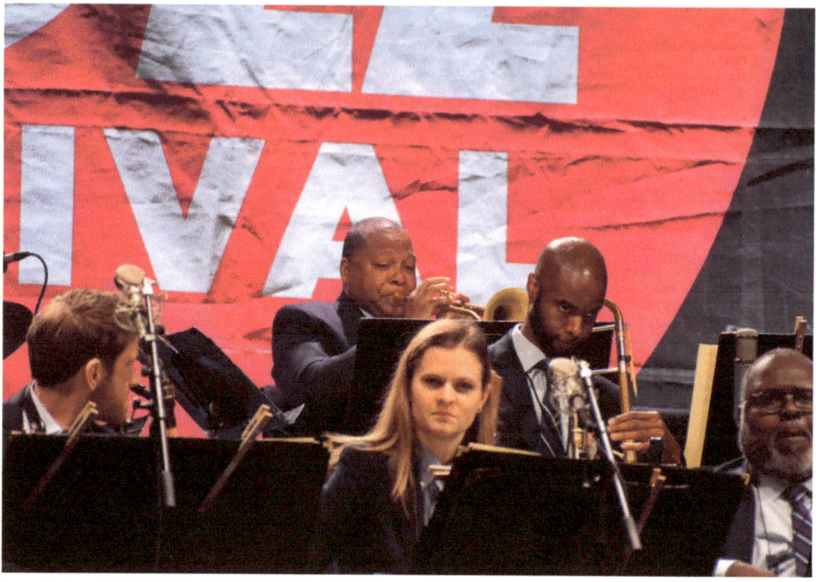

Wynton Marsalis, 2023

Jazz at the Lincoln Center Orchestra with the legendary trumpeter, saxophonist, multiple Grammy Award winner and composer, Wynton Marsalis.

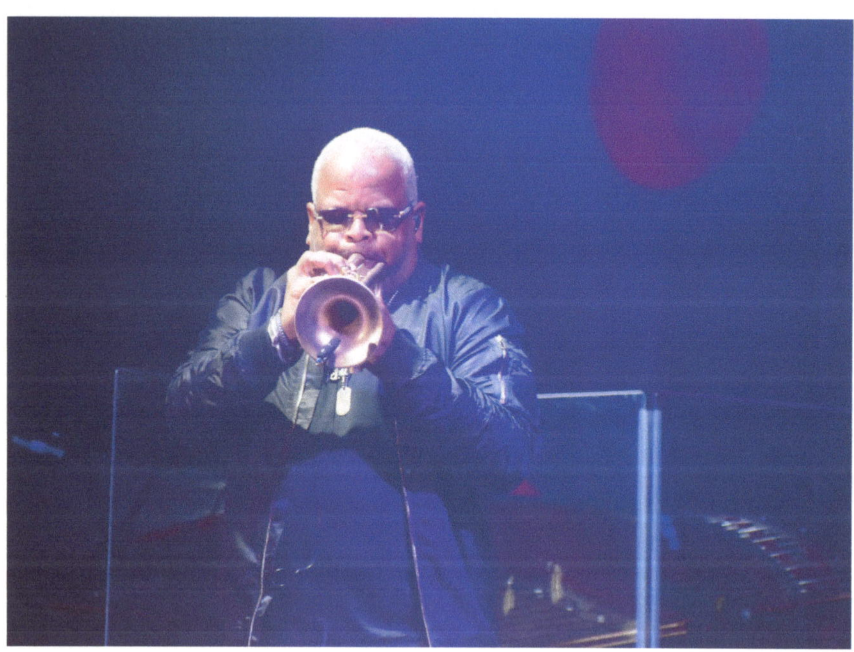

Terence Blanchard, 2022

Terence Blanchard is a Grammy Award-winning jazz musician, trumpeter, pianist, and motion-picture composer. Among many of his accomplishments, he has collaborated with Spike Lee, composing many of his film scores.

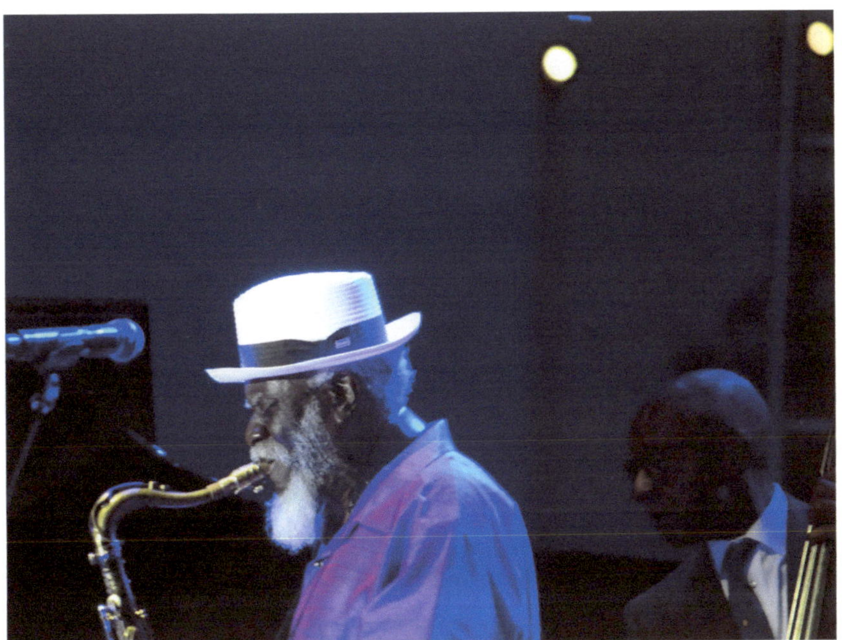

Pharoah Sanders, 2015
Pharoah Sanders is known for his contribution to what we know as free and spiritual jazz.

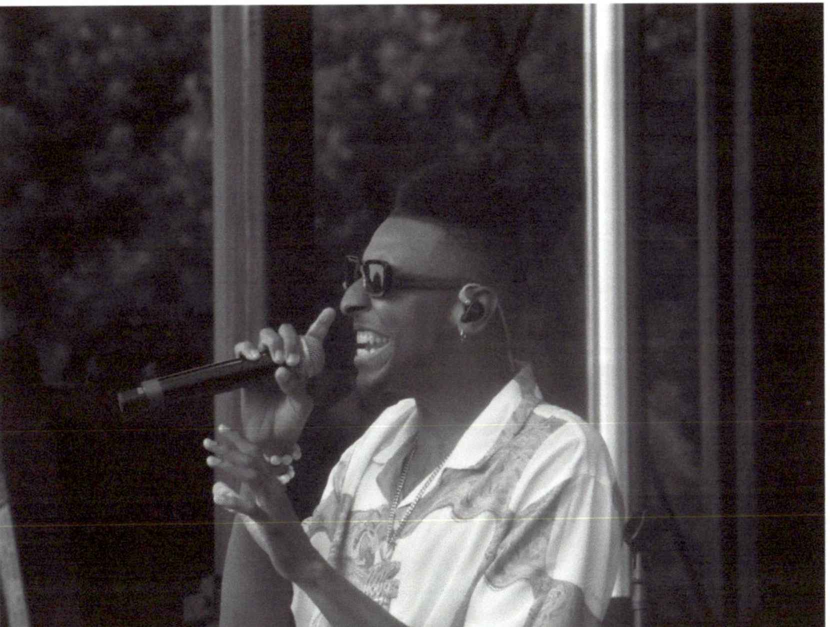

Masego, 2022
Masego's musical style is considered to be in the category of "TrapHouse Jazz."

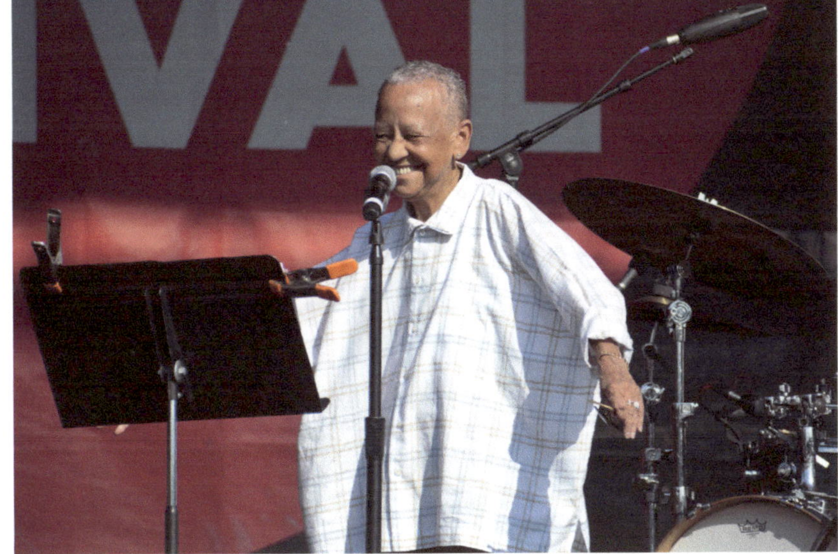

Nikki Giovanni, 2023
Nikki Giovanni was nominated for a Grammy Award for her poetry album, The Nikki Giovanni Poetry Collection, and has won multiple awards including the Langston Hughes Medal and the NAACP Image Award.

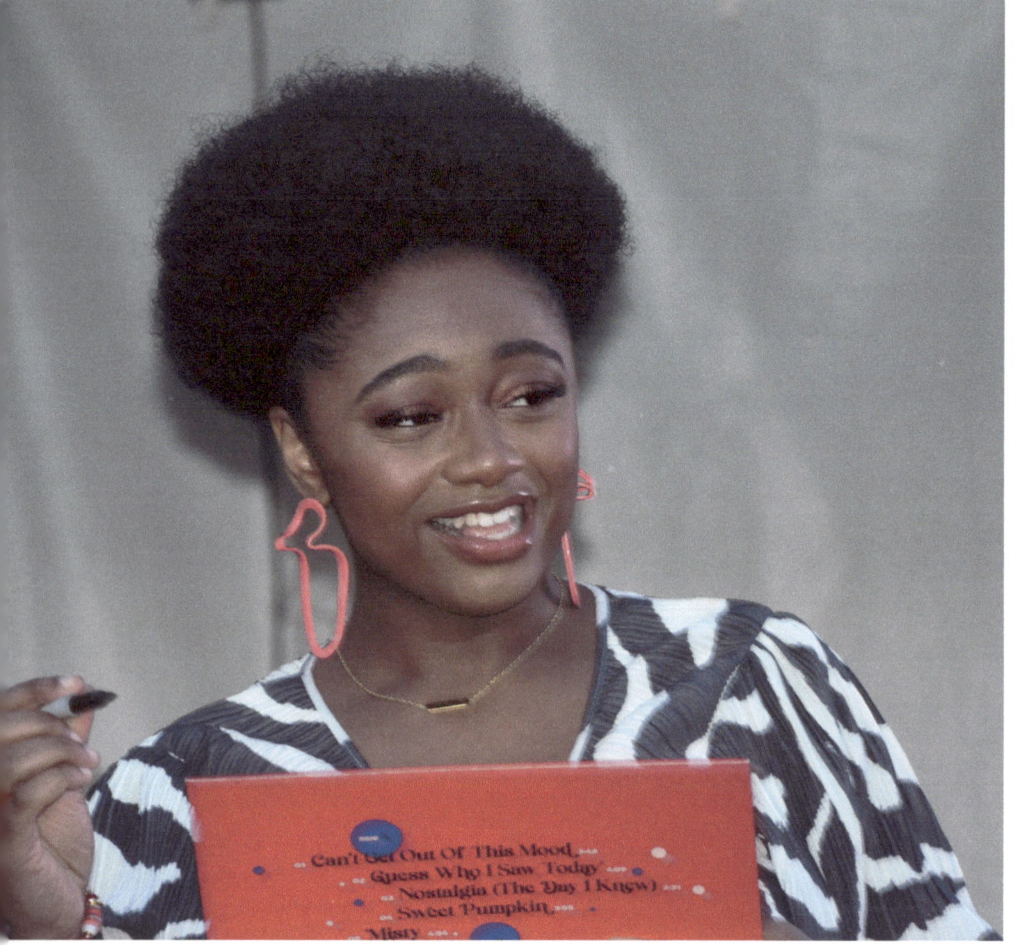

Samara Joy, 2023

Samara Joy McLendon earned two Grammy Awards in 2023 for Best Jazz Album for Linger Awhile *and Best New Artist.*

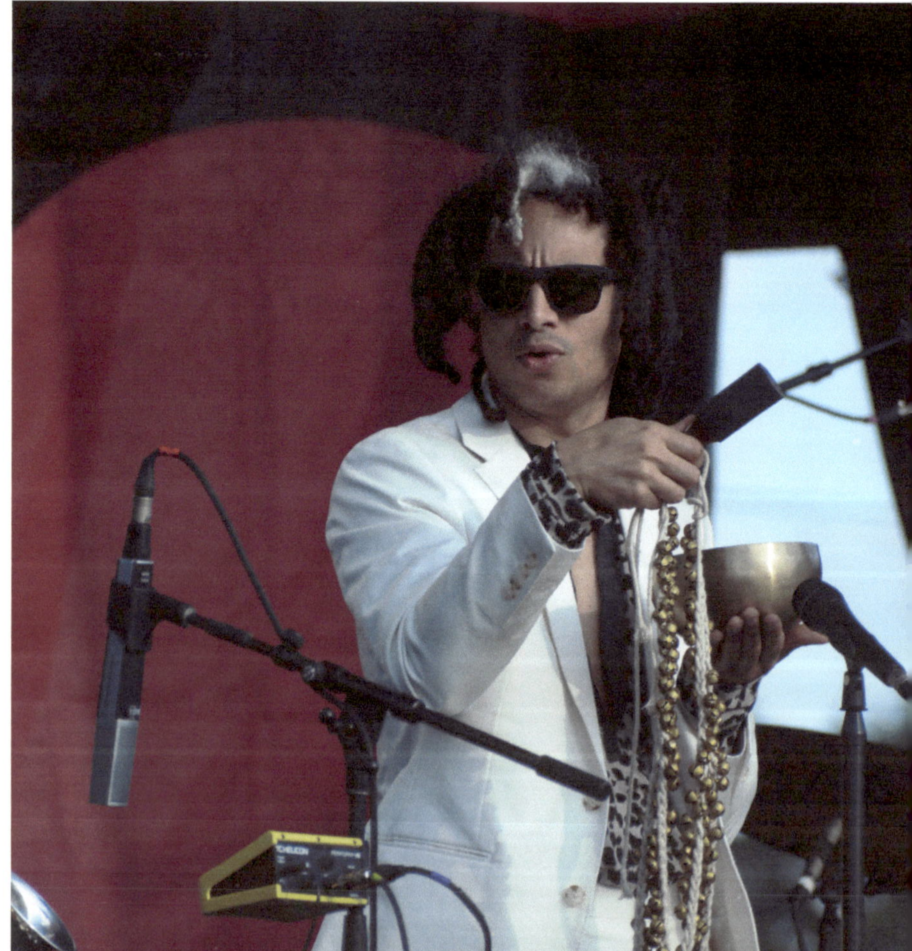

José James, 2023

Jazz and hip-hop vocalist Jose James's sound is often compared to jazz poet, singer known for his spoken word, and musician, Gil Scott-Heron. His musical influences are John Coltrane, Marvin Gaye and Billie Holiday.

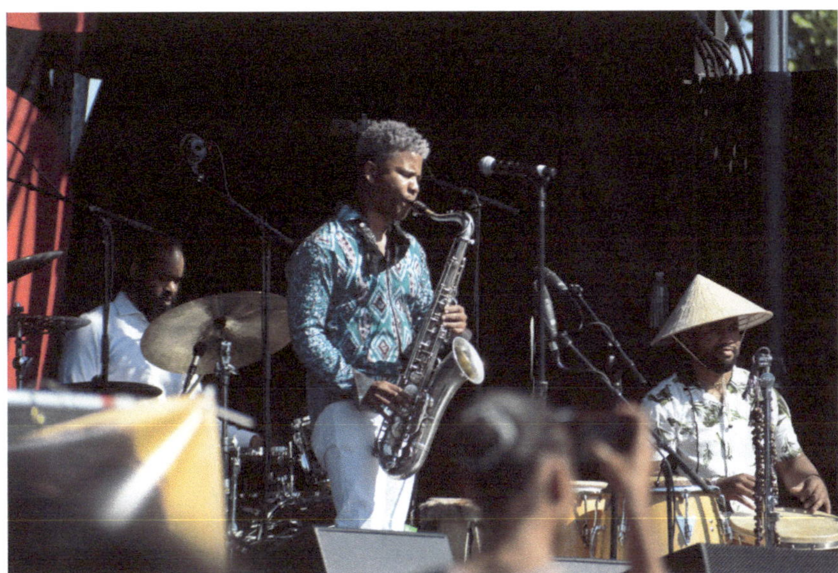

Stanley Clarke, 2023

Bassist, composer, and founding member of Return to Forever, Stanley Clarke is a five-time Grammy Award-winning artist.

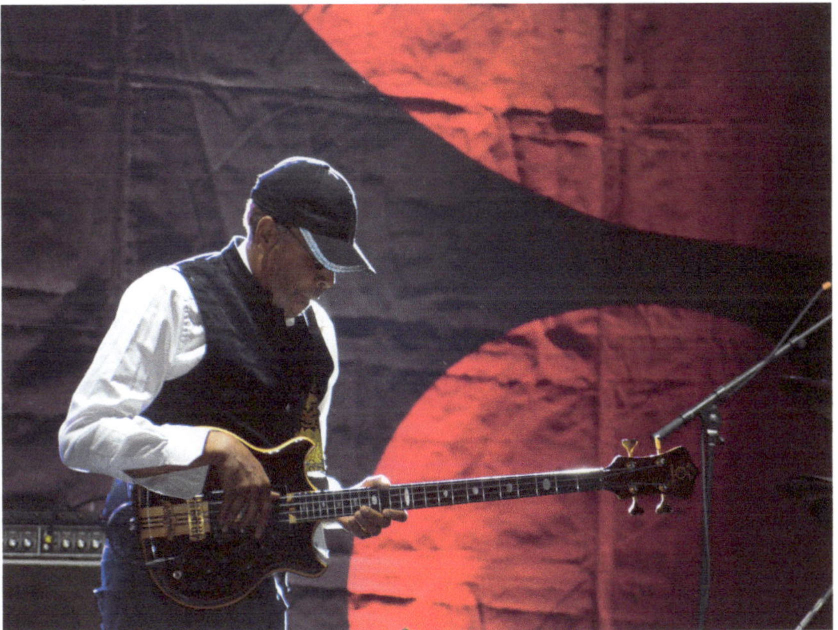

David Sánchez, 2023

Born in Puerto Rico, Sanchez began his musical career at a young age playing conga at eight and the tenor saxophone at the age of twelve.

Tony Hightower, 2023

Tony Hightower is one of Atlanta's local favorites. He is also known for many jingles including the Georgia Lottery, Kroger, and Coca-Cola.

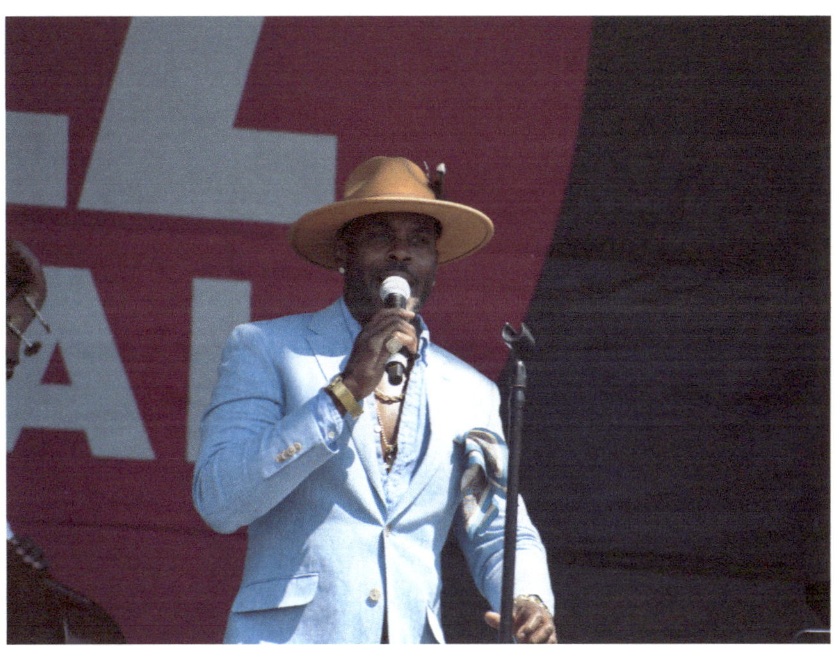

Stanley Jordan, 2015

Legendary jazz guitarist Stanley Jordan is known for his two-handed tapping style of playing.

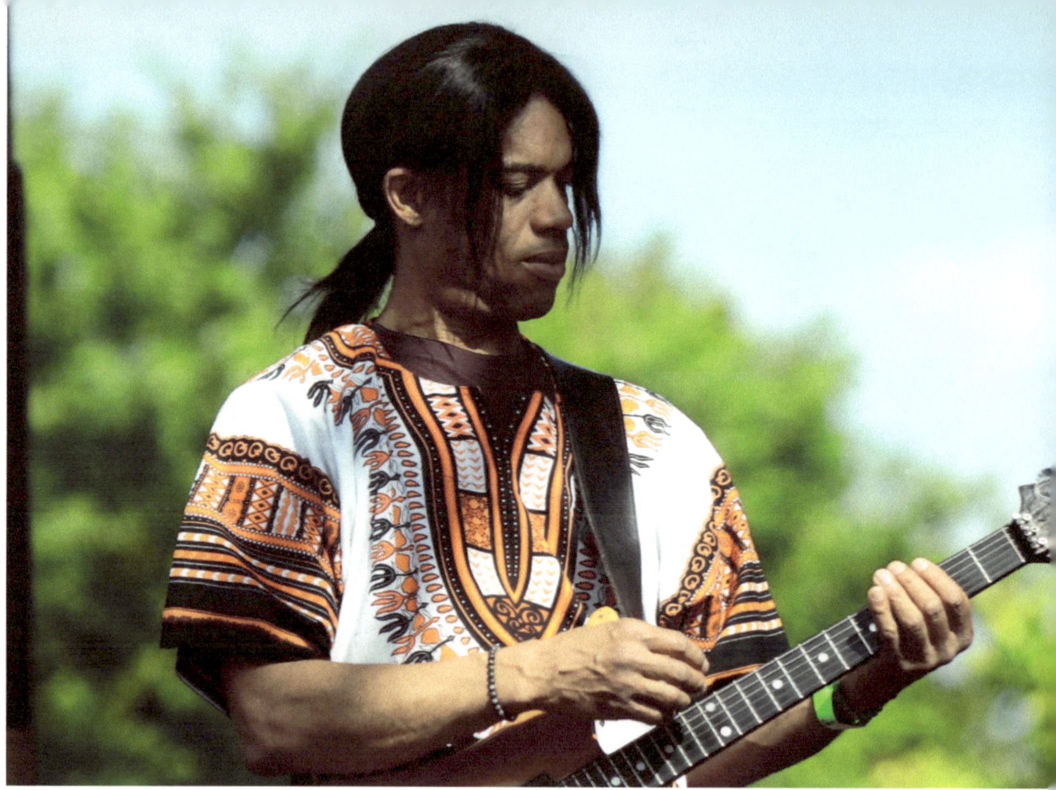

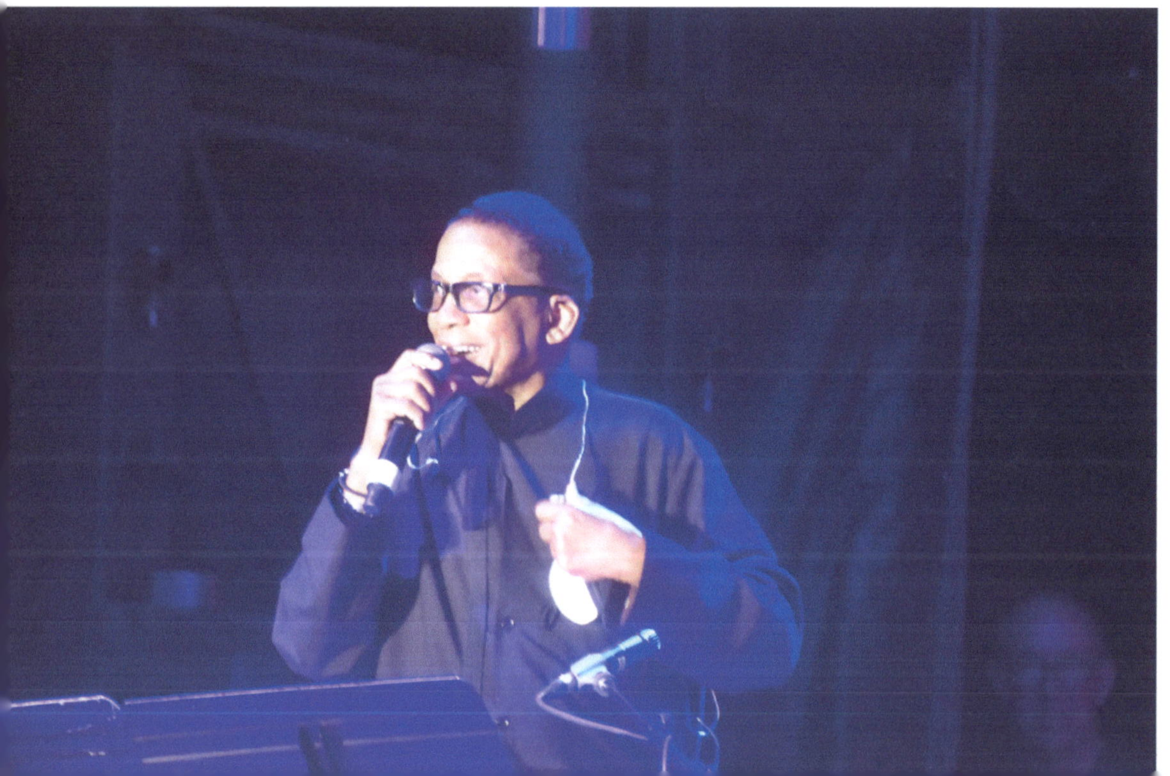

Herbie Hancock, 2022

Herbie Hancock is a winner of multiple Grammy Awards, a jazz pianist, keyboardist, bandleader, and composer. His musical groups include the Headhunters, The Miles Davis Quintet, and the Los Angeles Philharmonic. Some of his film scores include Harlem Nights, Round Midnight, *and* Death Wish.

Juneteenth Celebration 2022

Centennial Olympic Park 2022

Juneteenth is a celebration on June 19th commemorating the emancipation of enslaved people in the United States. In 2021, it was officially recognized as a federal holiday.

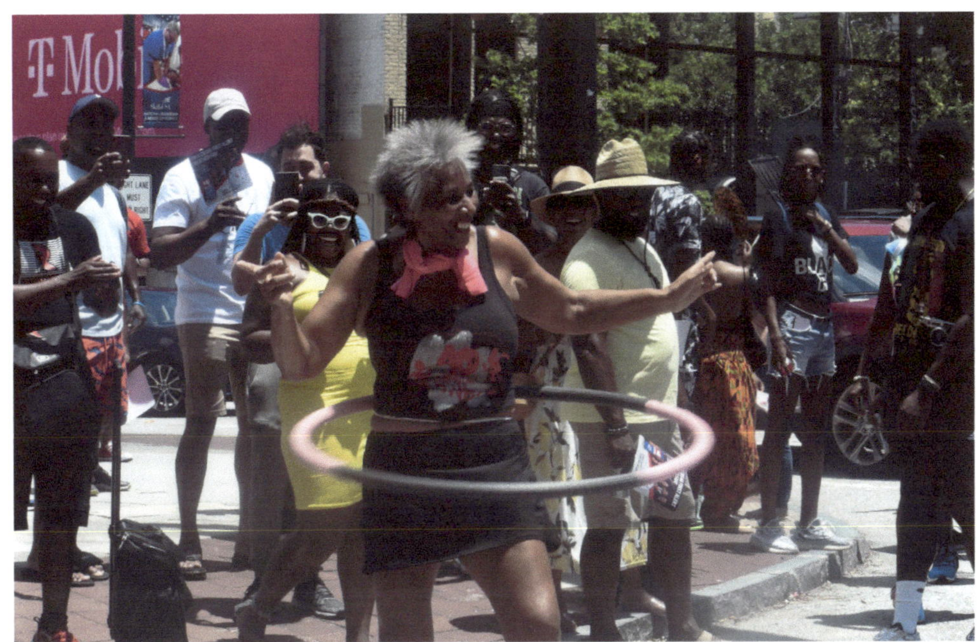

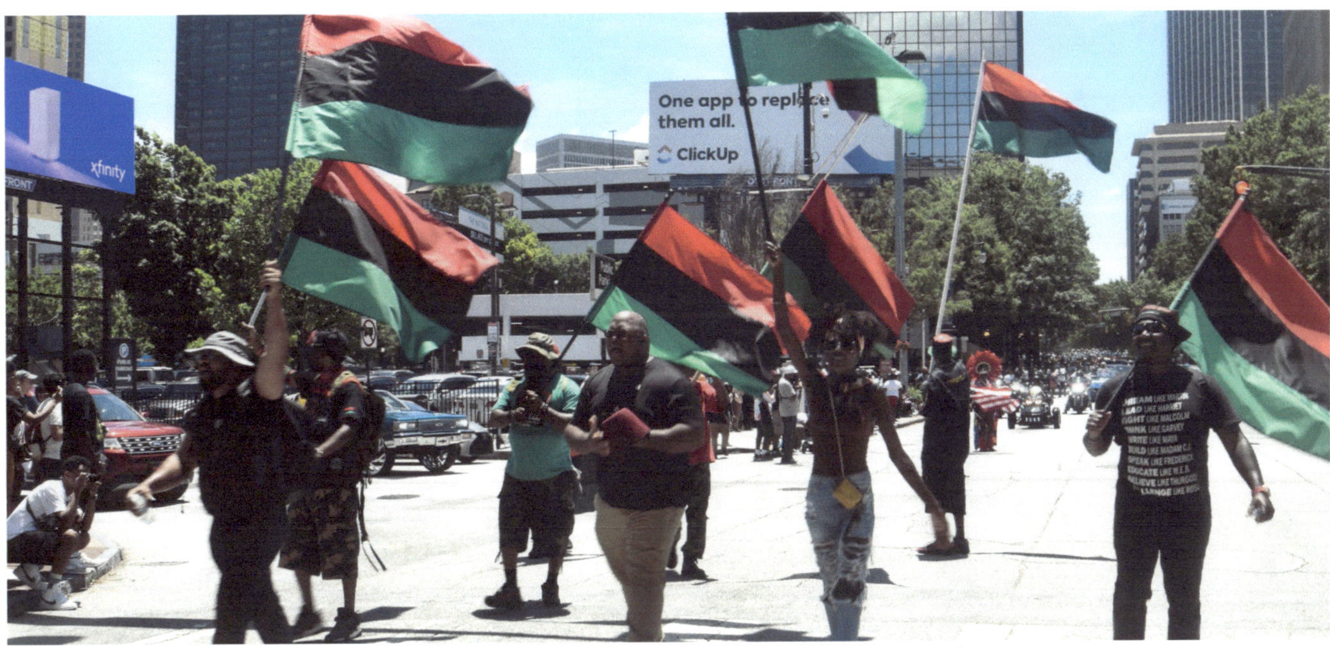

Native American Festival and Pow Wow

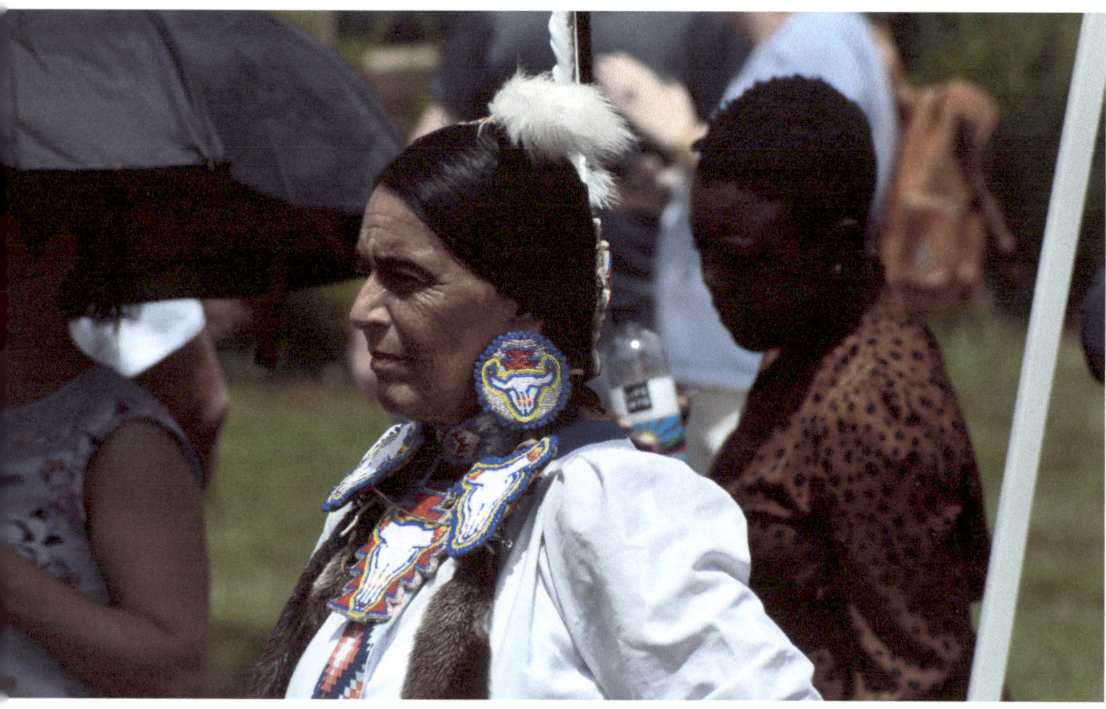

The festival in East Point, Georgia, is in honor of the Muscogee land that the city sits on.

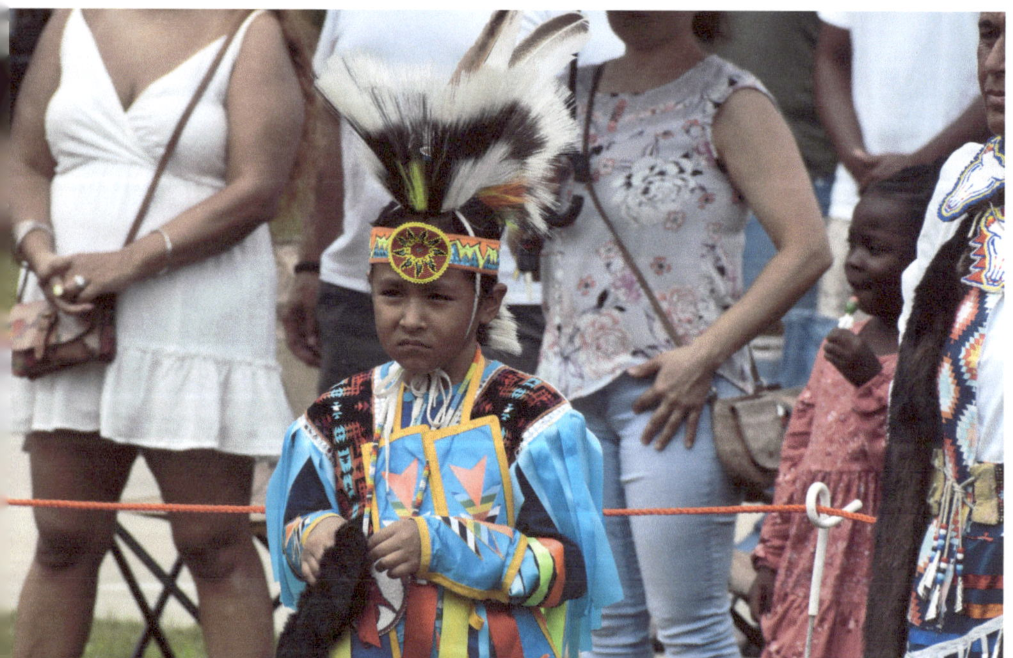

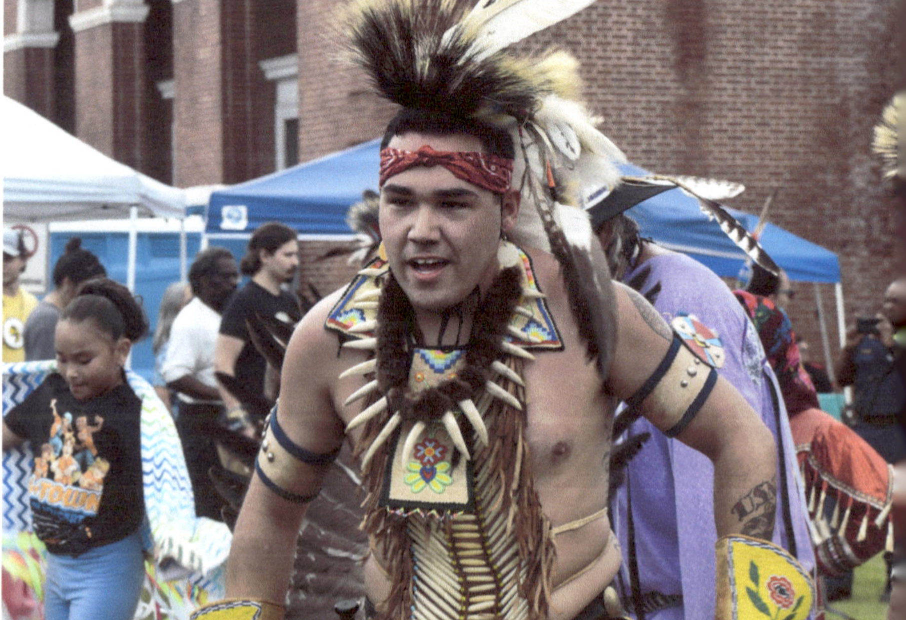

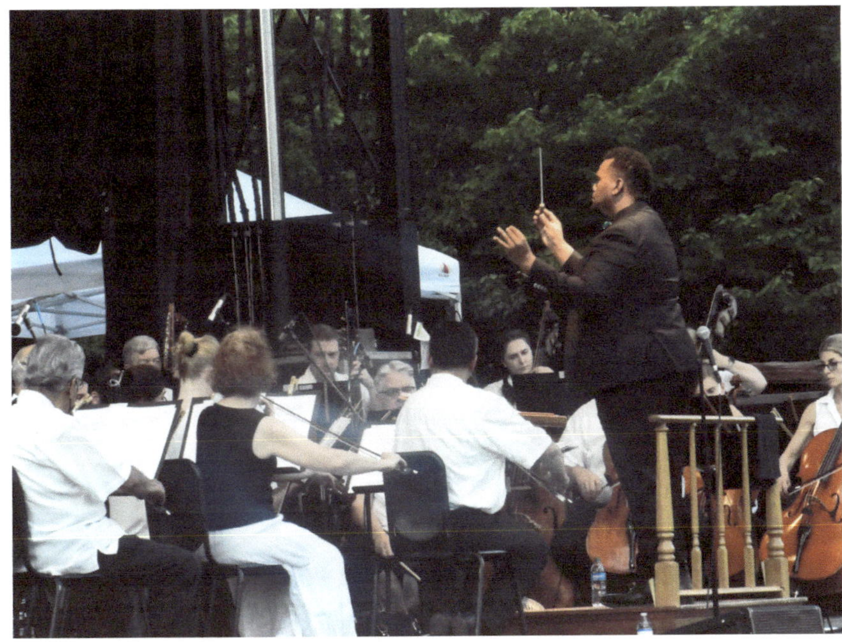

Atlanta Symphony Orchestra

Founded in 1945, the Atlanta Symphony Orchestra serves as the cornerstone of musical excellence in Atlanta.

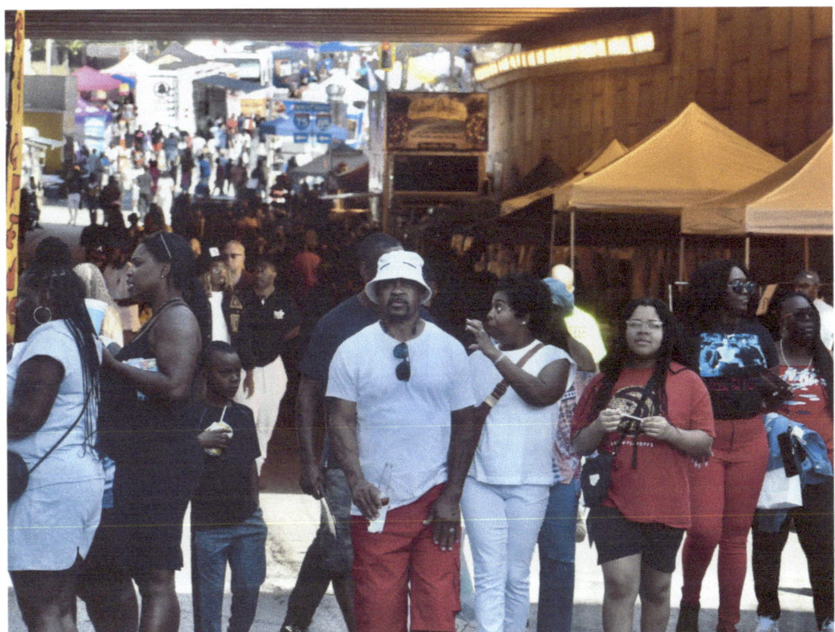

Sweet Auburn Music Festival

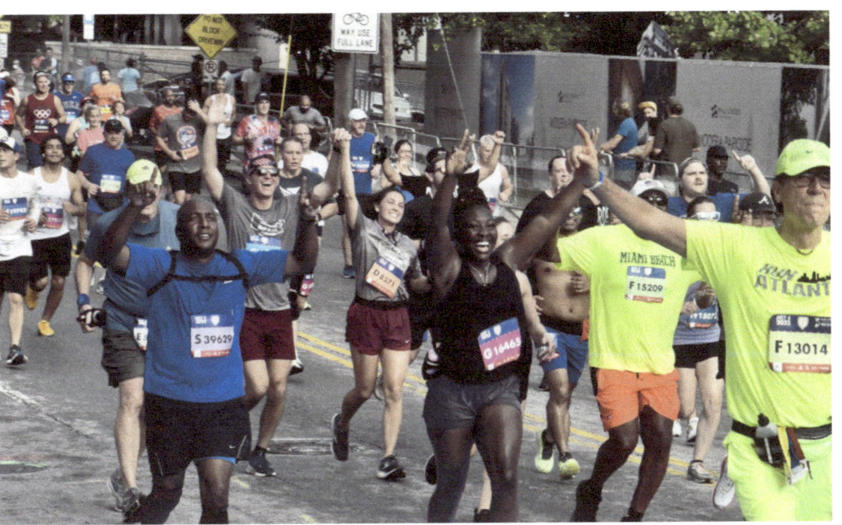

Peachtree Road Race

Runners partake each year in this tradition on Independence Day, since July 4, 1970.

Dragon Con

Dragon Con (held every Labor Day weekend in Atlanta) represents the culture of sci-fi, comics, gaming, and so much more.

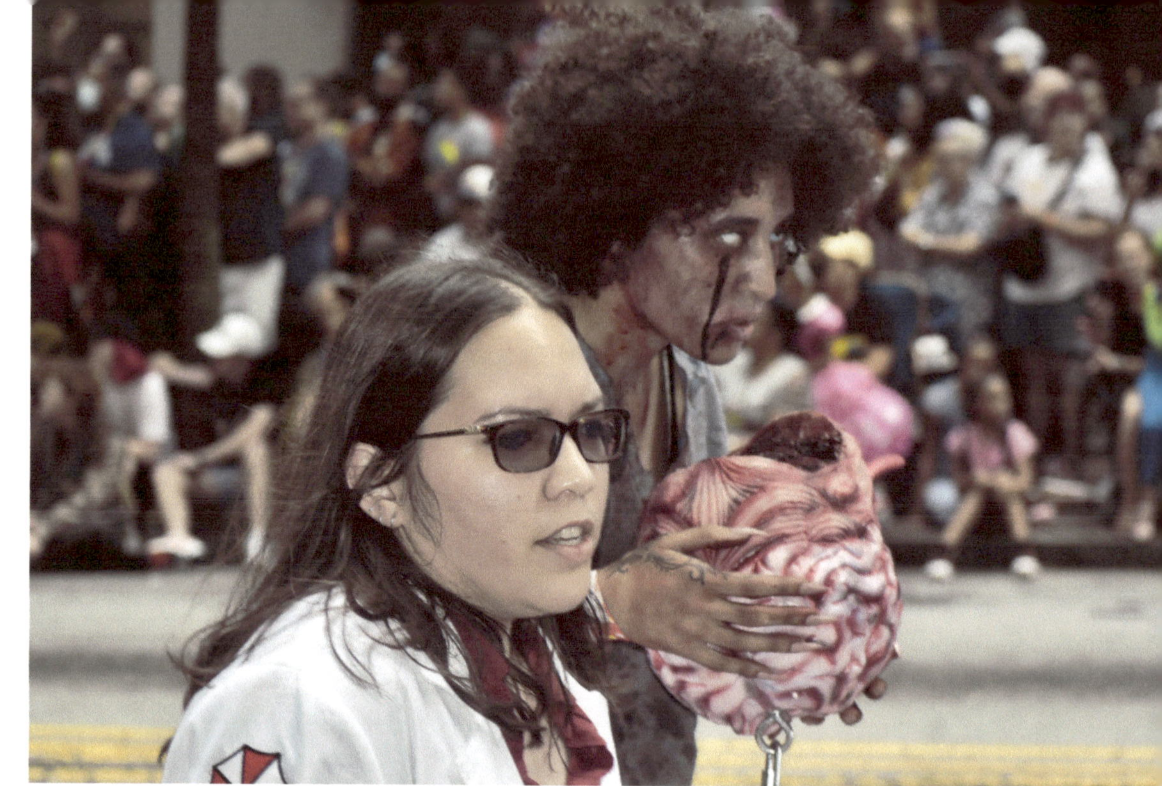

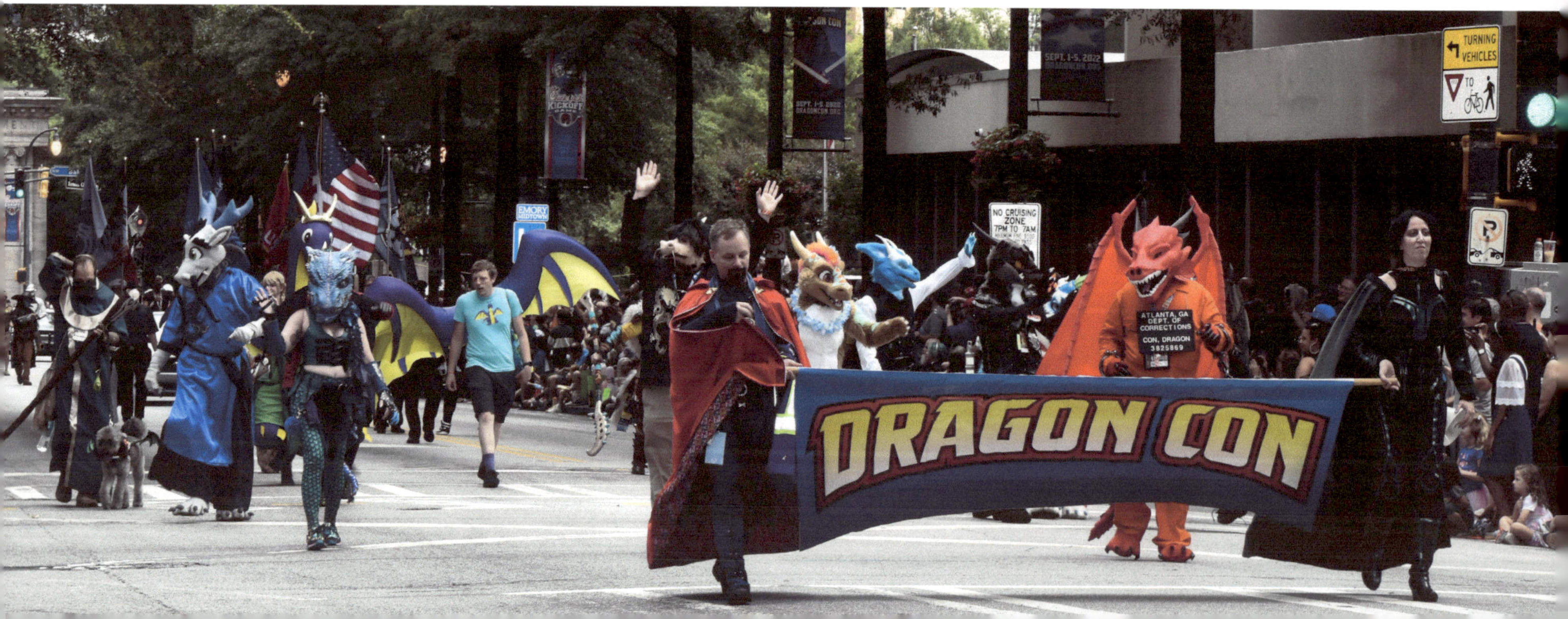

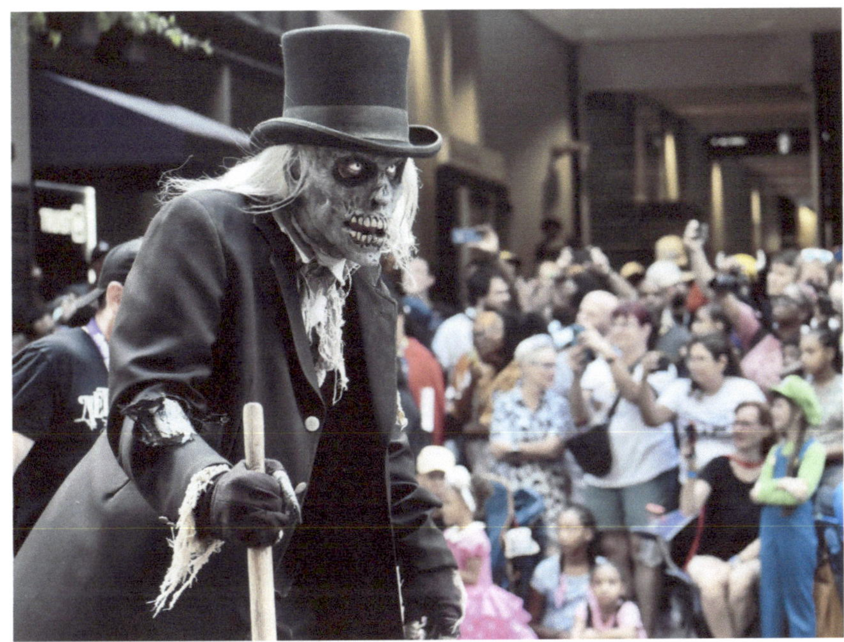

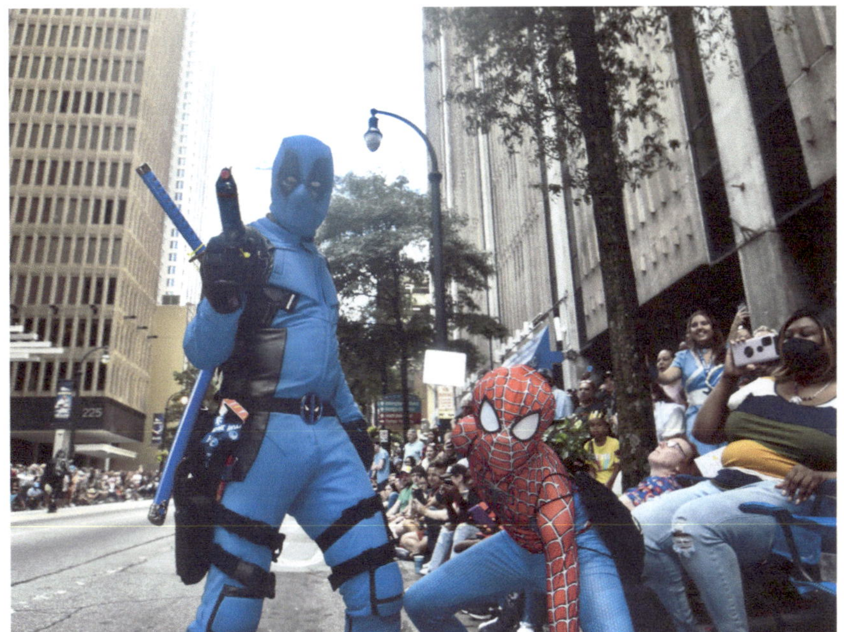

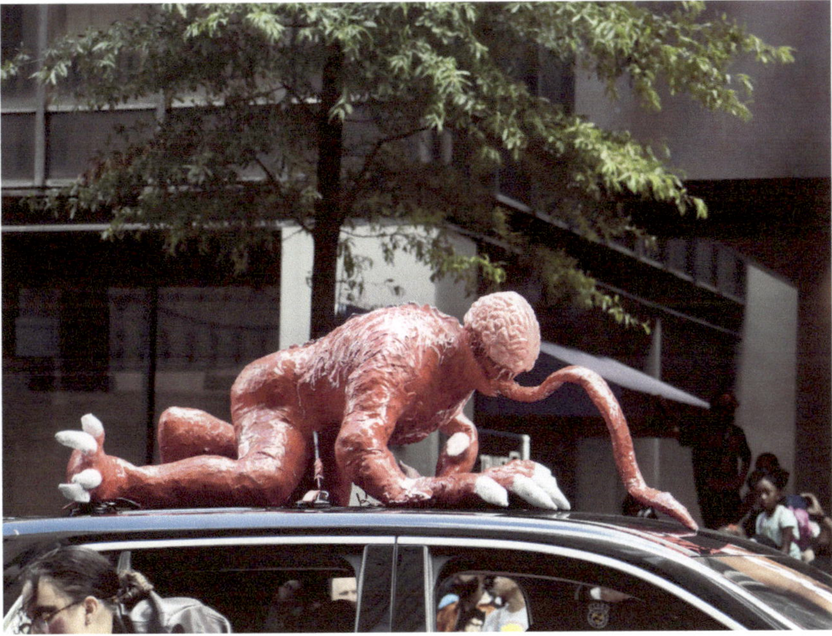

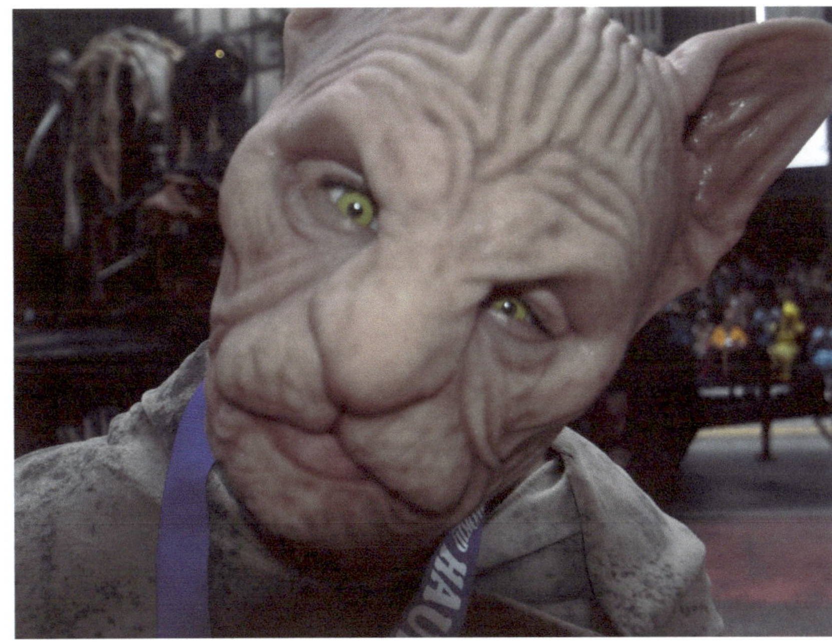

Chalktober Festival

Marietta Square

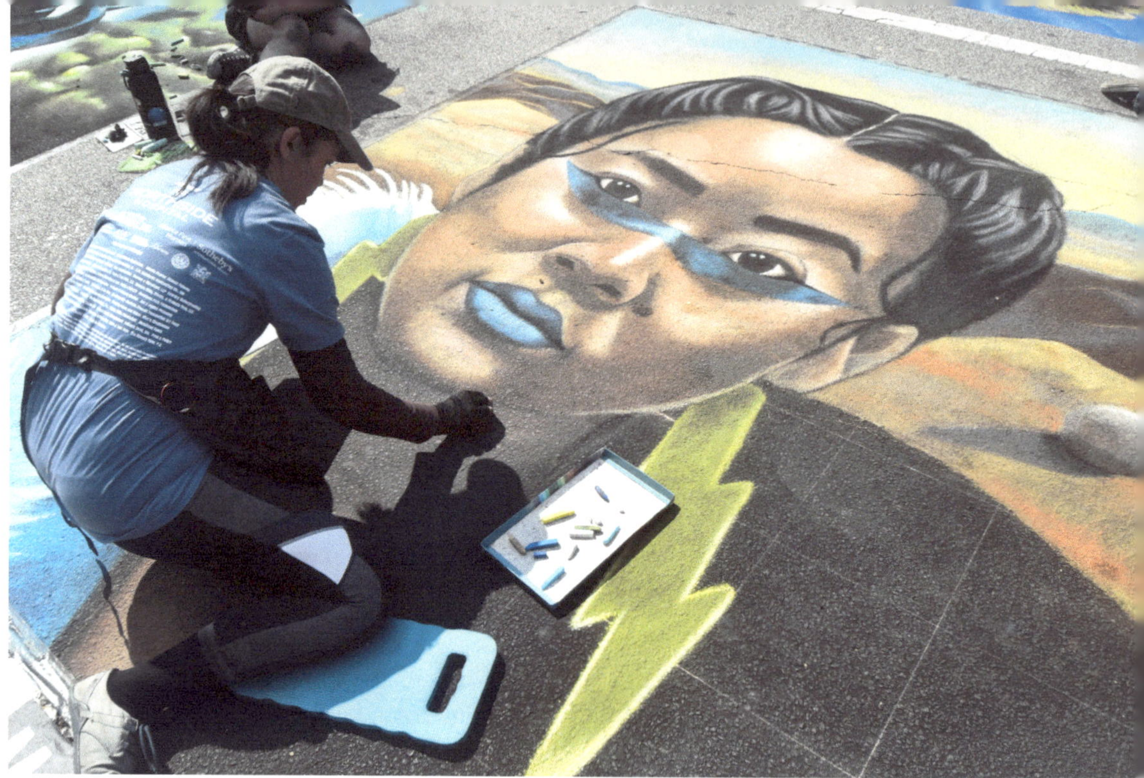

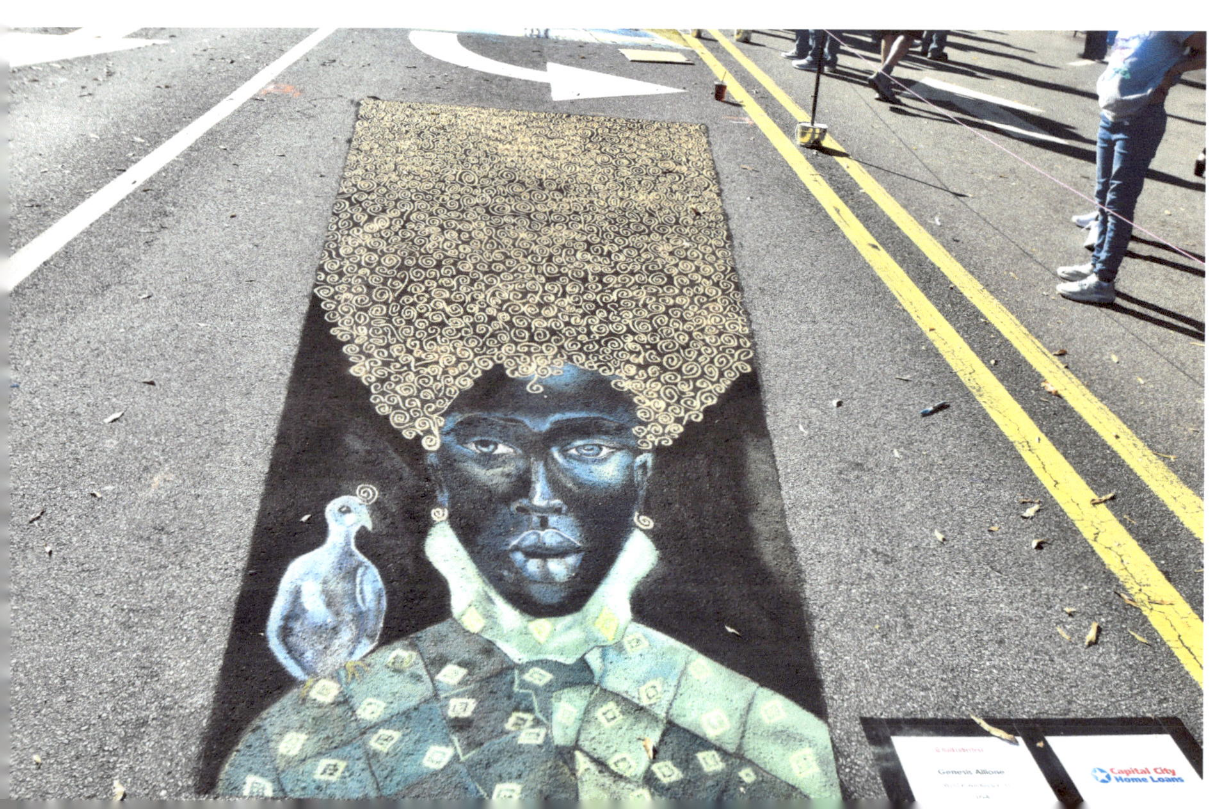

House in the Park

House in the Park held in Grant Park is a cornucopia of soul and energetic sounds, an orchestra of House music musicians featuring artists, DJs that are local, regional and international. This annual one day event gathers cultures, bridges communities, and is a unifying cross-cultural movement.

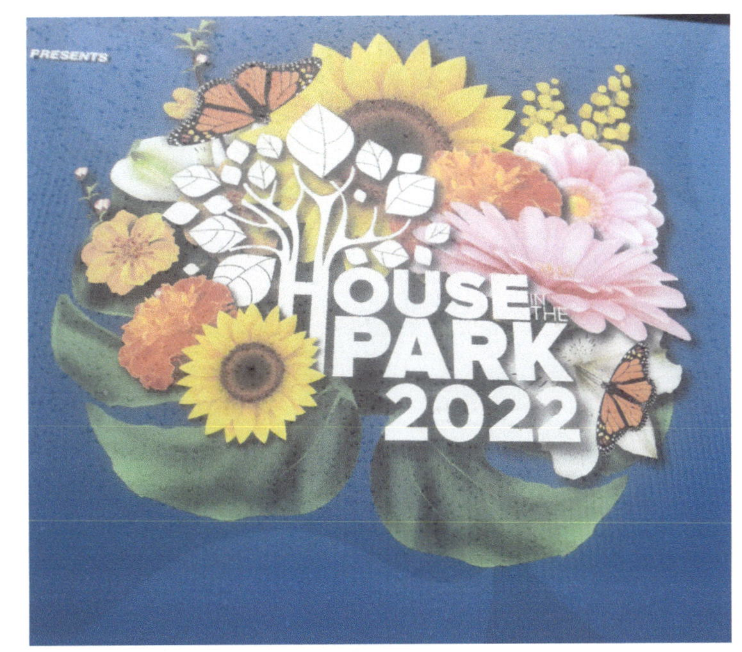

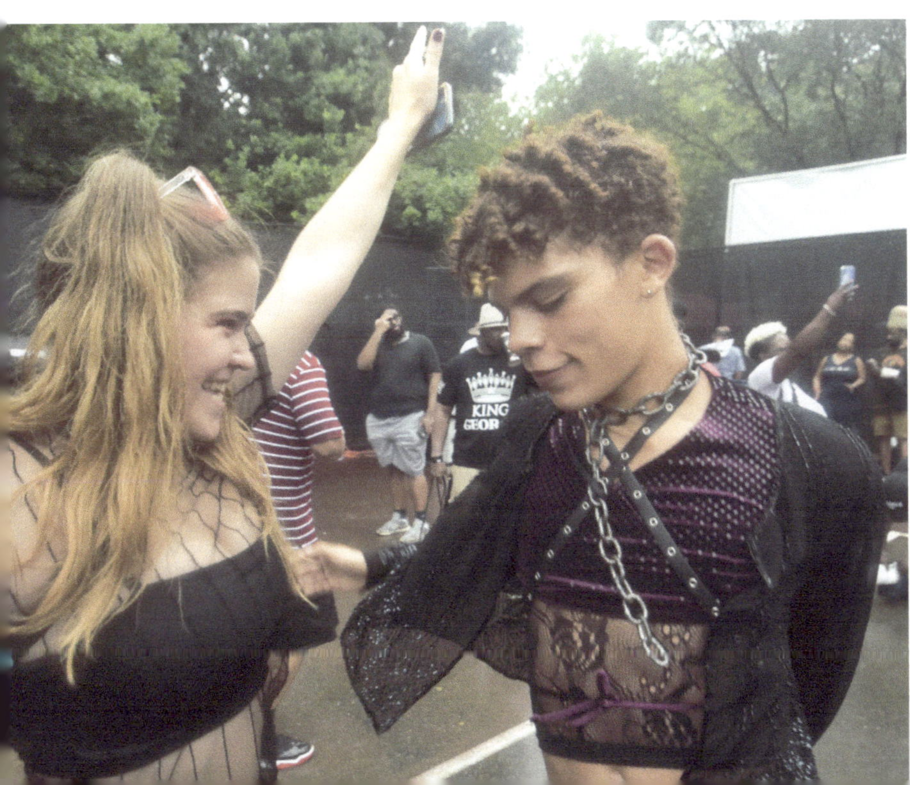

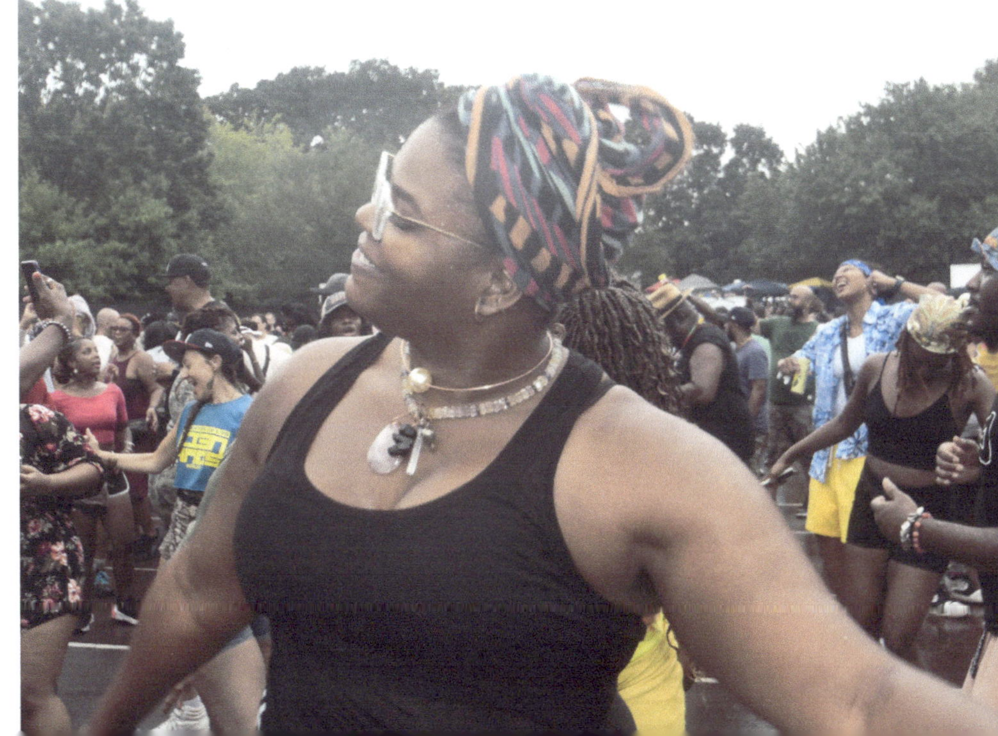

Murals Highlighting Atlanta

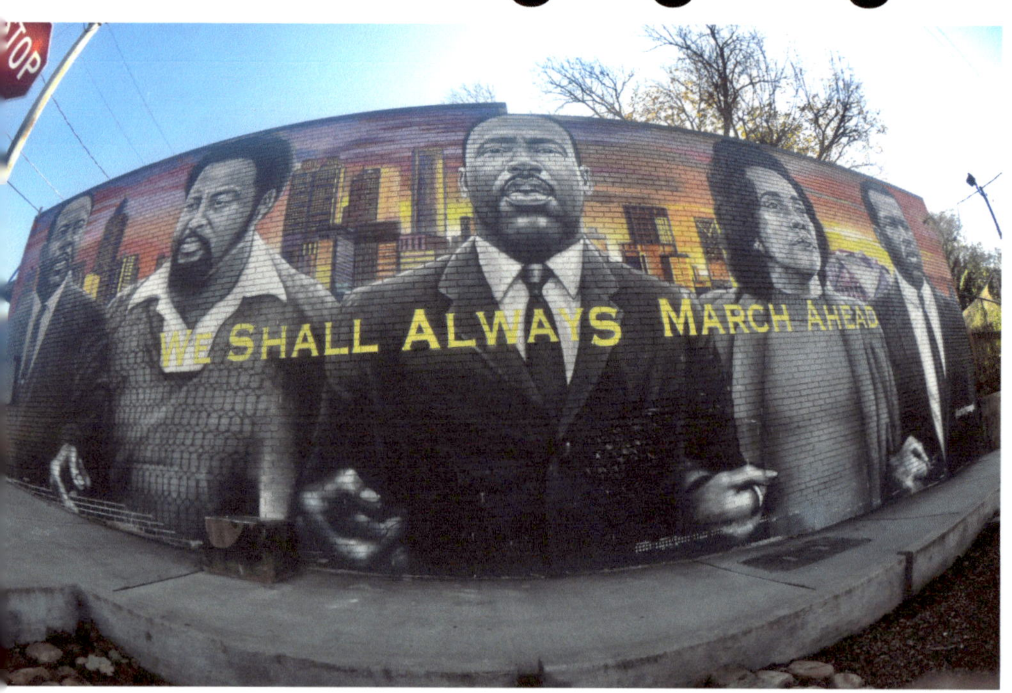

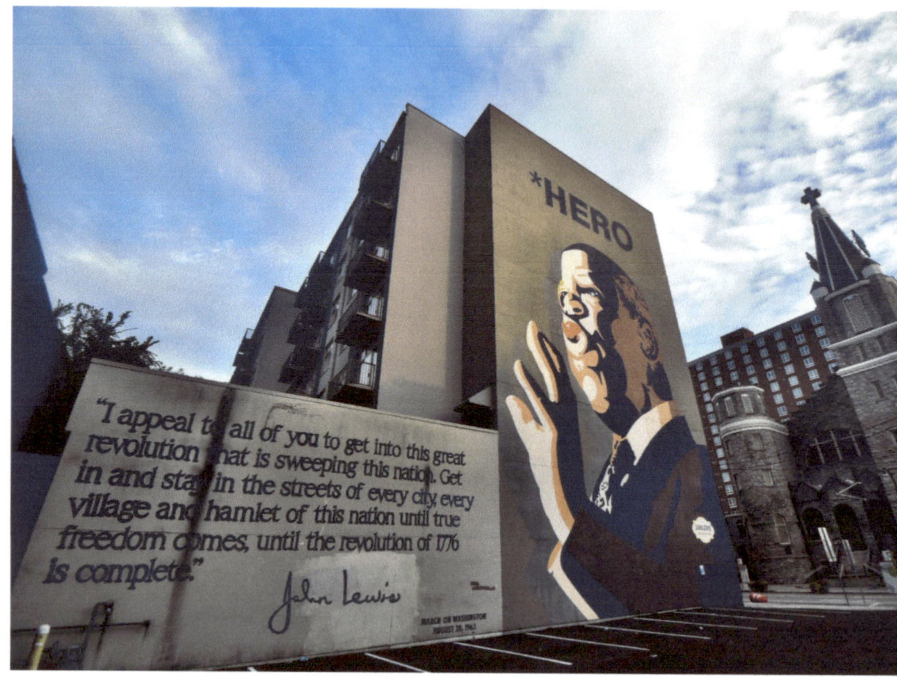

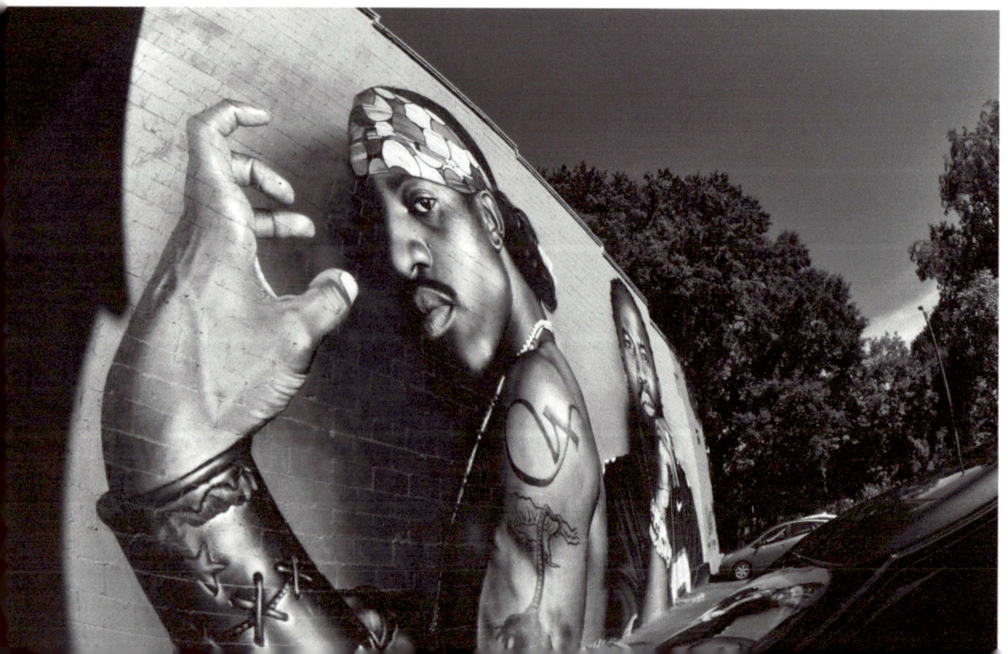

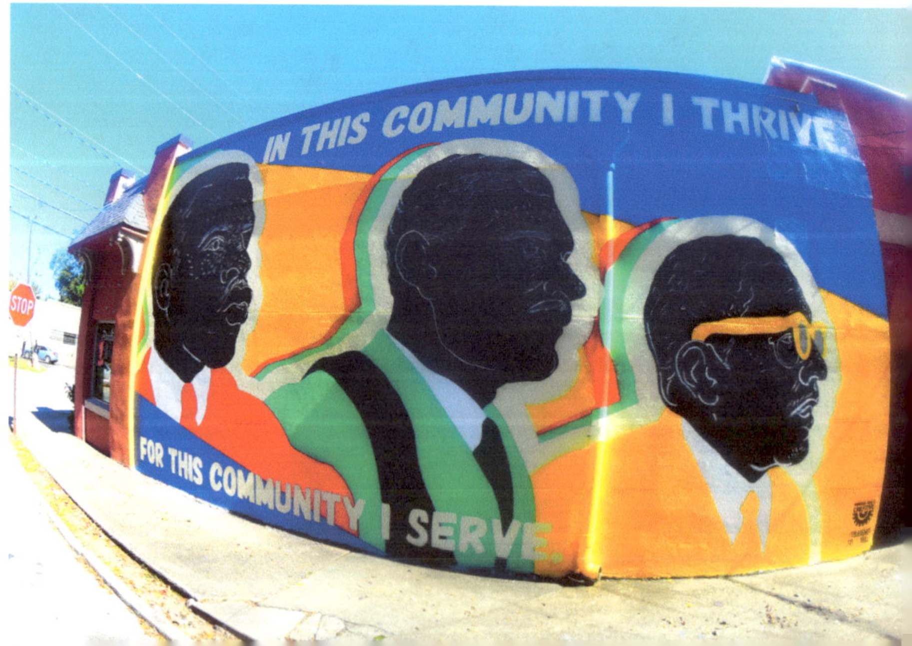

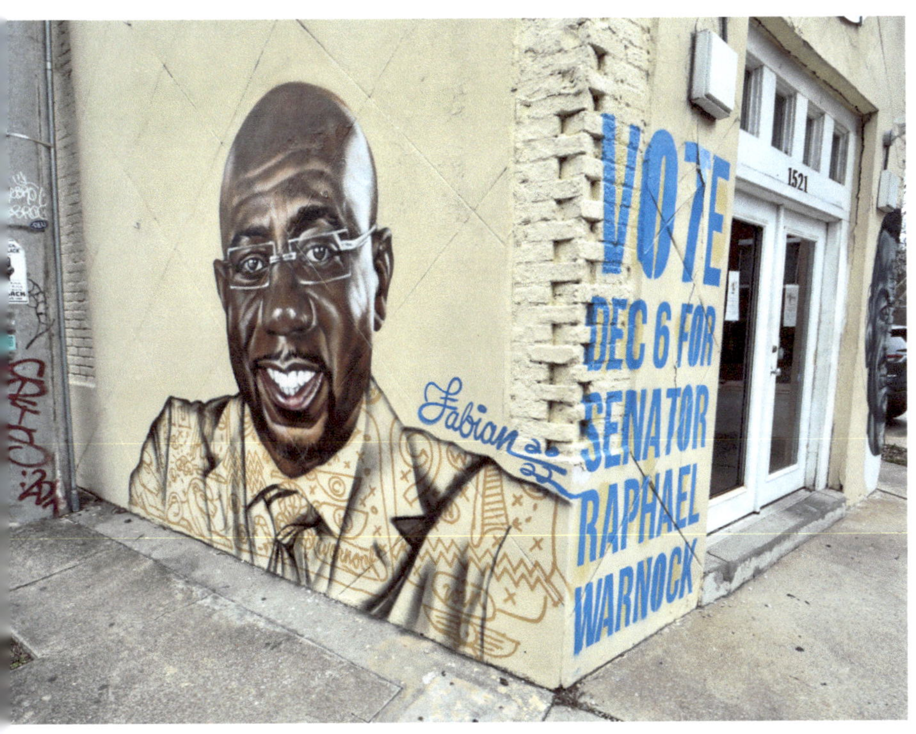
VOTE
DEC 6 FOR
SENATOR
RAPHAEL
WARNOCK
Fabian
1521

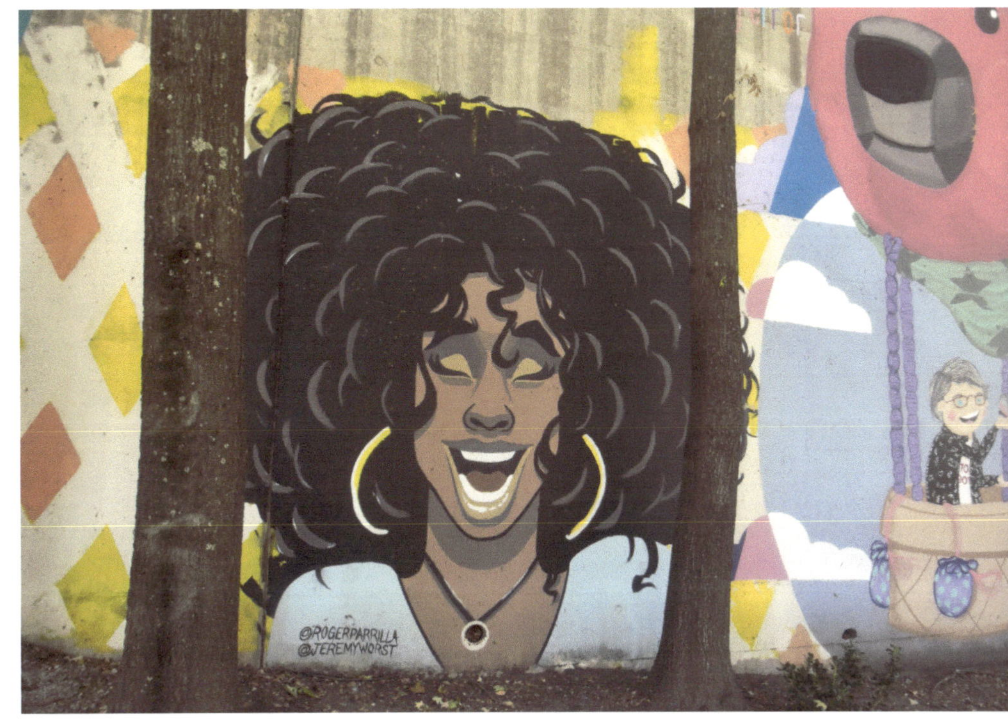
@ROGERPARRILLA
@JEREMYWORST

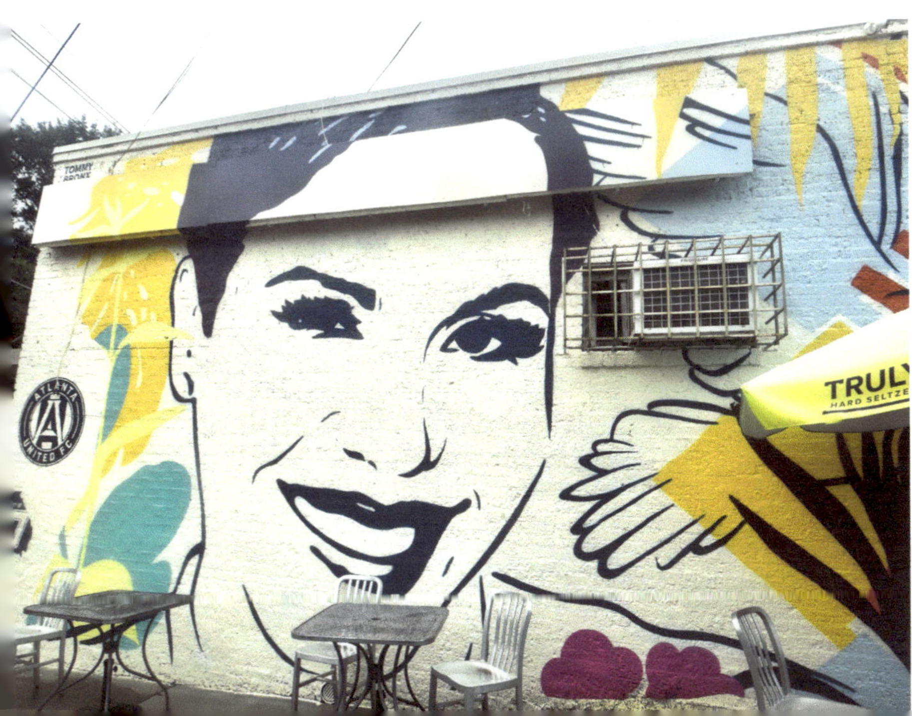
TOMMY
TRULY
HARD SELTZER
ATLANTA
UNITED FC

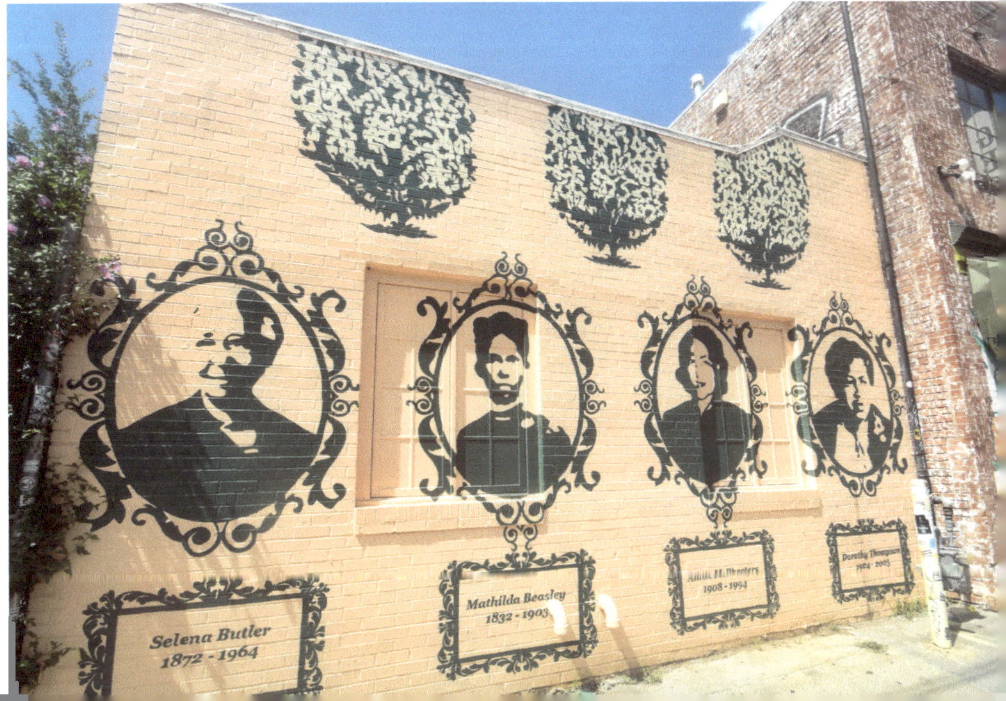
Selena Butler
1872 - 1964
Mathilda Beasley
1832 - 1903

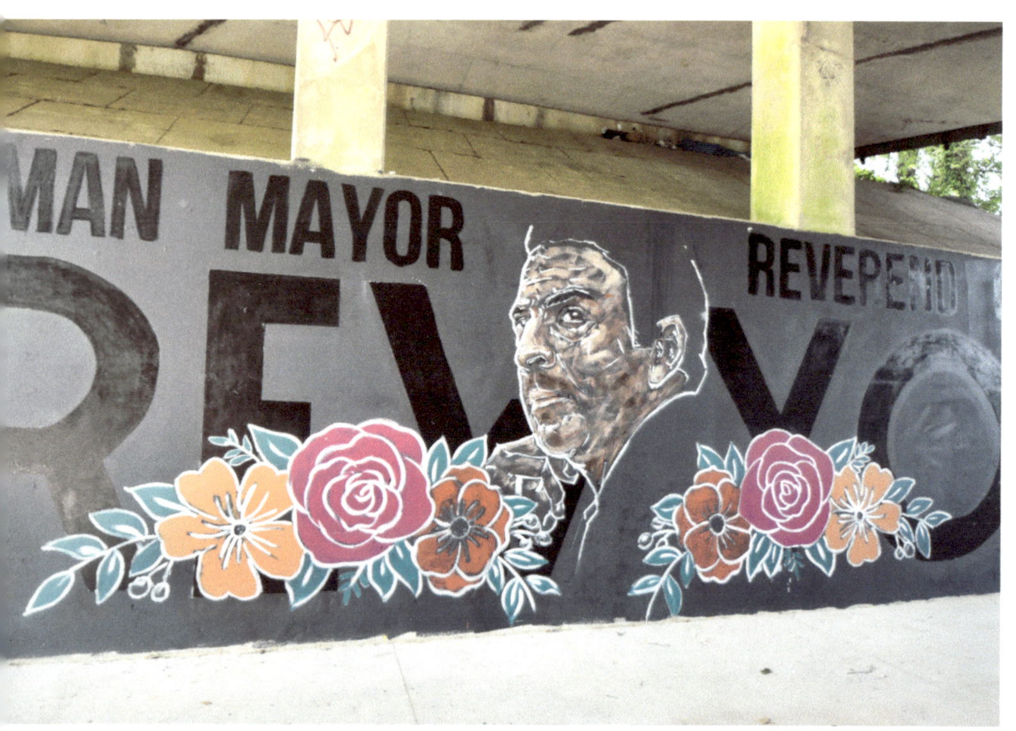
MAN MAYOR
REV
REVEREND

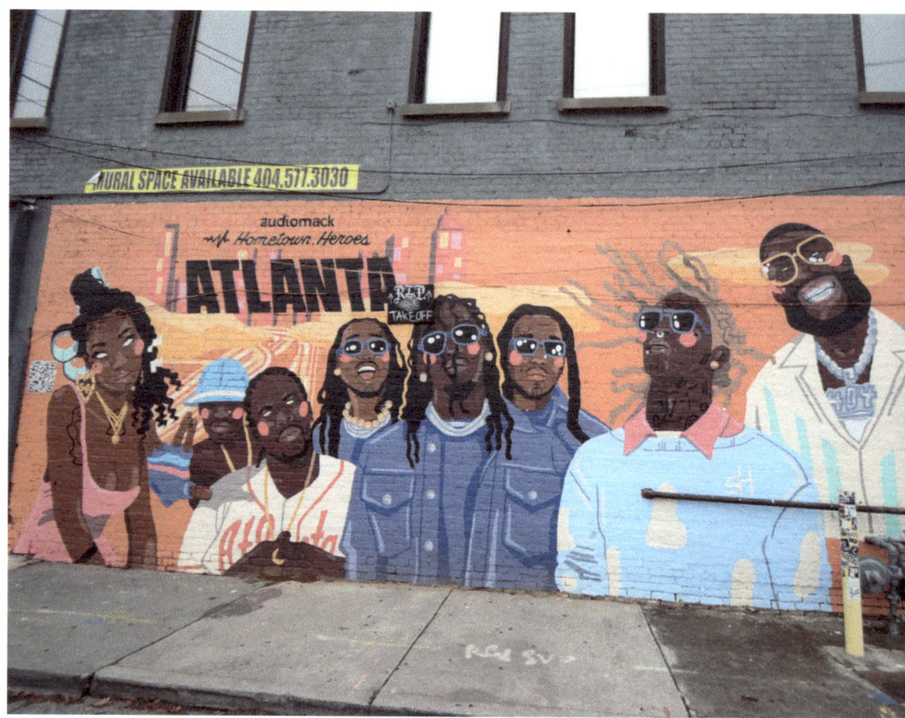
MURAL SPACE AVAILABLE 404.577.3030
audiomack
w/ Hometown Heroes
ATLANTA
R.I.P.
TAKEOFF

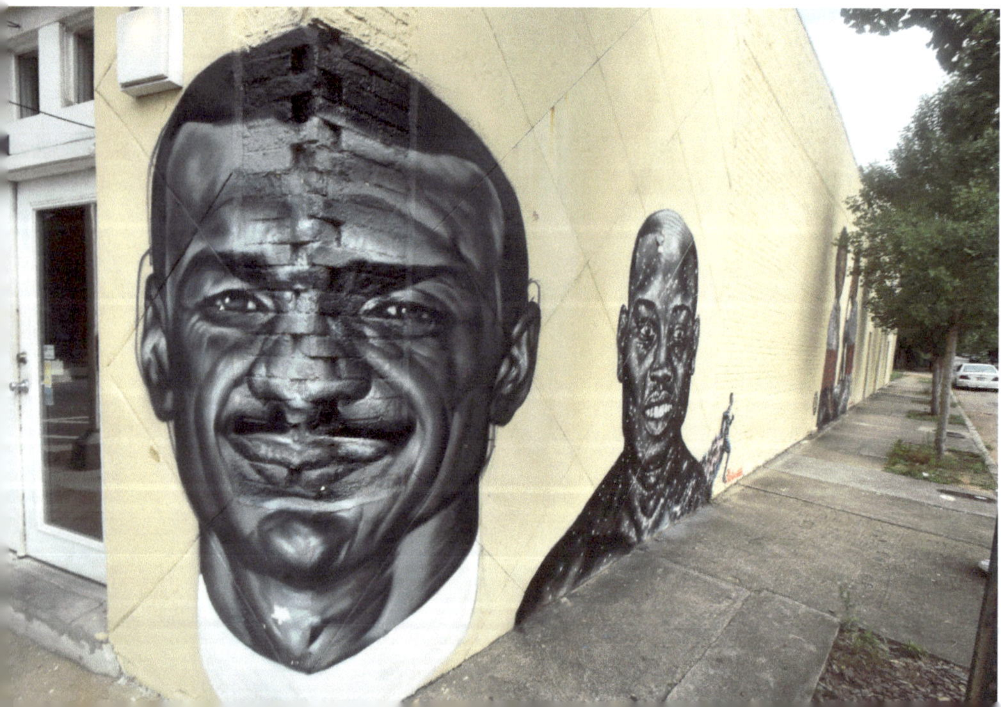

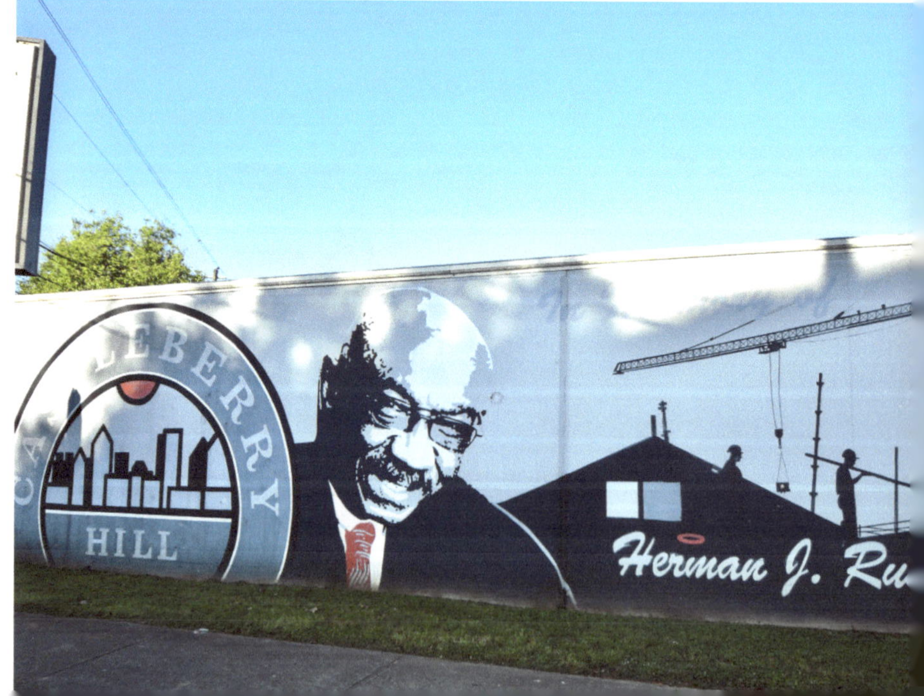
CASTLEBERRY
HILL
Herman J. Ru

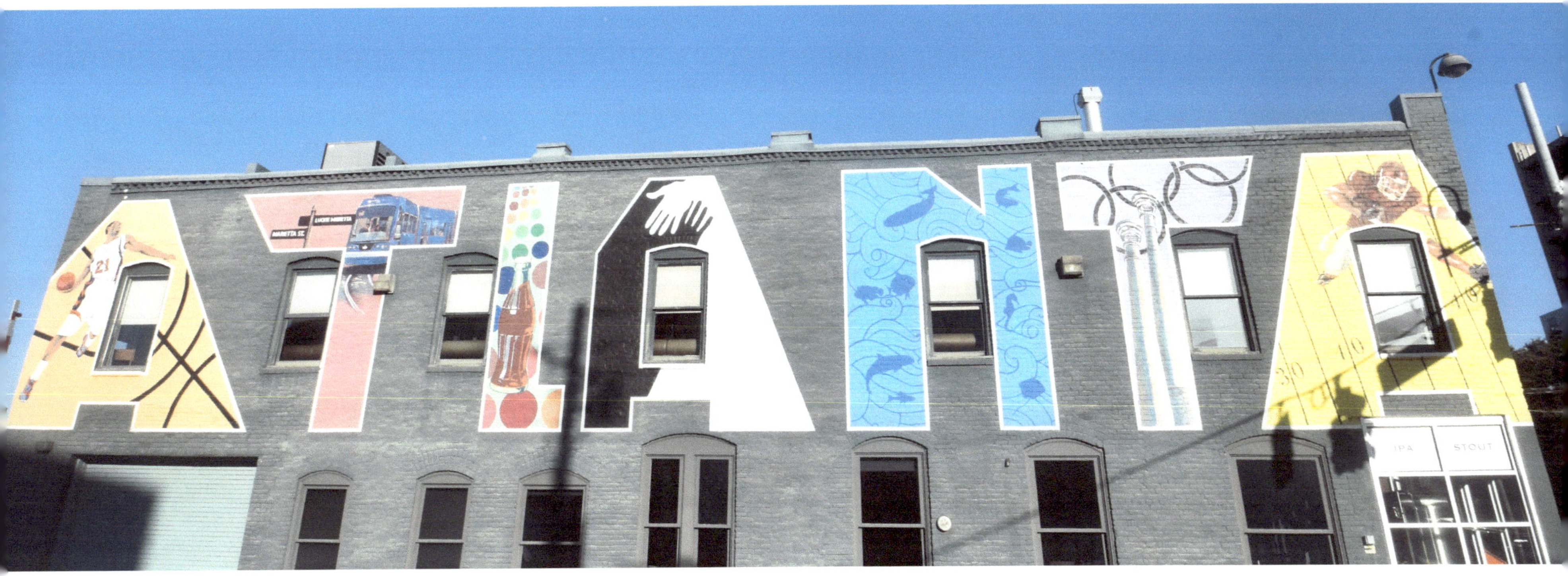

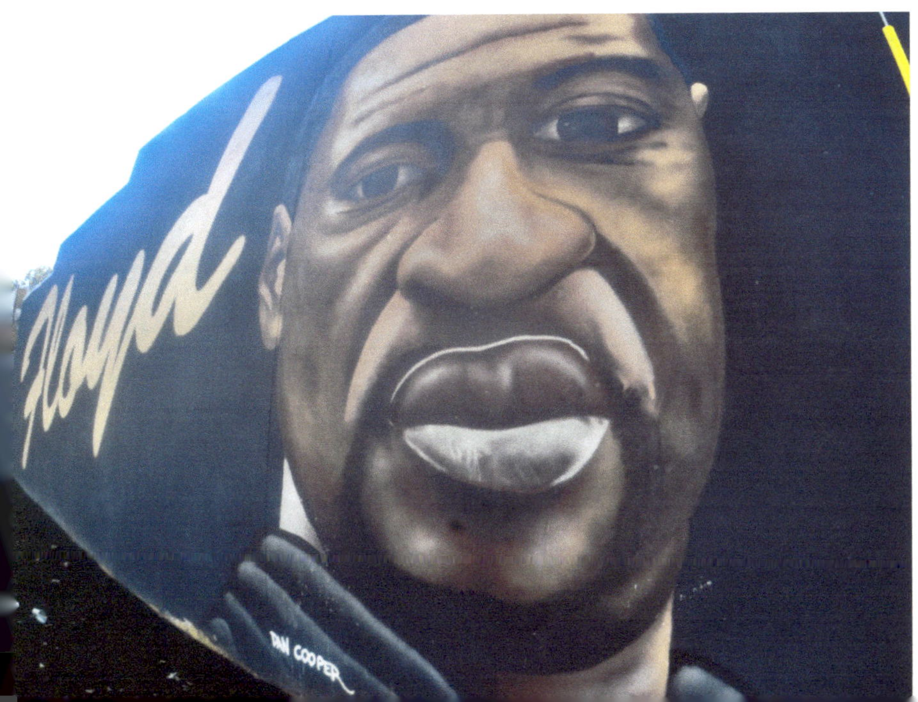
Floyd
TAN COOPER

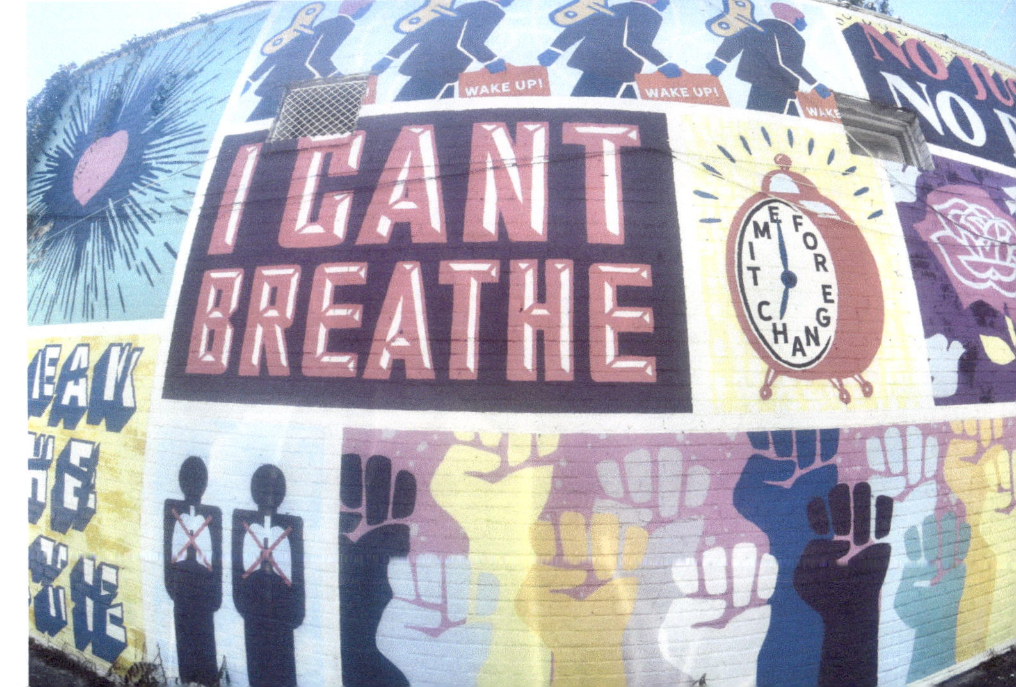
WAKE UP!
WAKE UP!
WAKE
NO JU
NO J
I CANT
BREATHE
TIME
FOR
CHANGE

A Poignant View from Jackson Street Bridge

On Monday, April 20, 2020, at 8:54 a.m., the roads were saturated from a moderate rainfall. What would have been a bustling freeway on an ordinary day, was now silent and vacant. On this day at the beginning of the pandemic, there was not one car in sight.

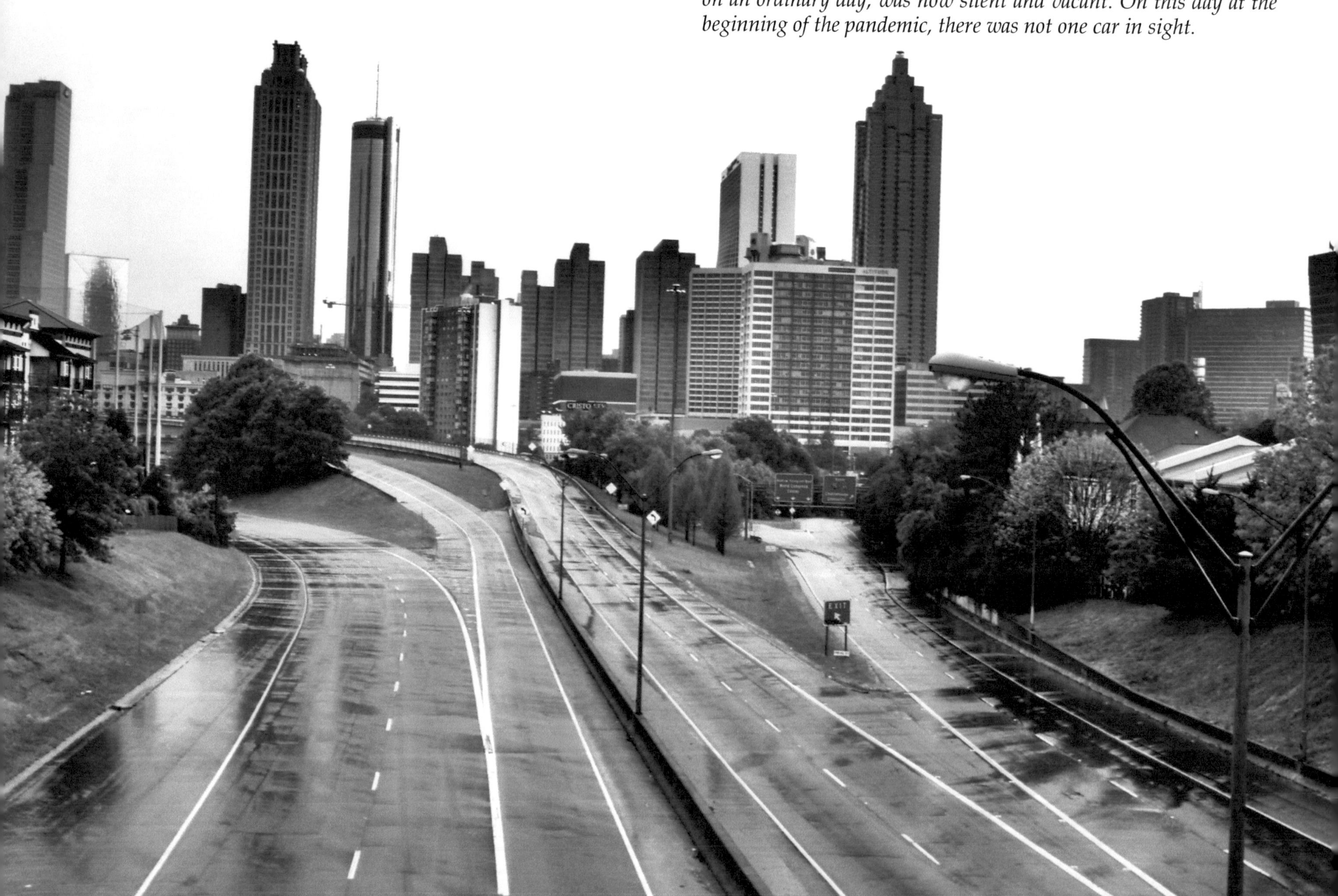

The Pandemic

Toilet Paper for Sale

One of the many items that were scarce during the pandemic.

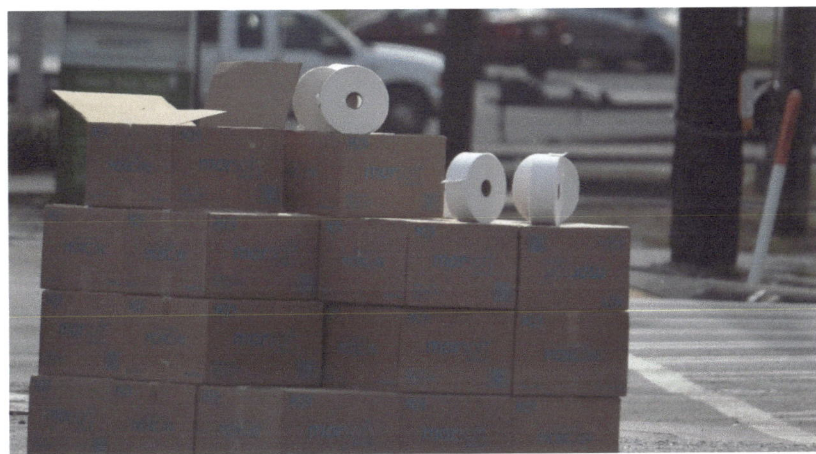

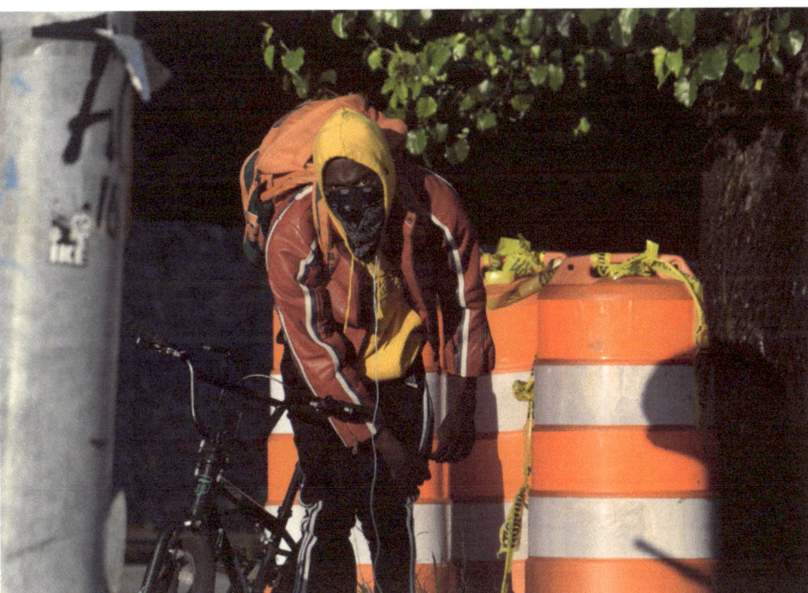

The Blue Angels and Thunderbirds Honoring Essential Workers Over Centennial Park

Exhilarating! Without the aid of a tripod, just a steady hand and an even steadier balance, I captured speed and in-flight formation, while essential workers were honored in this unprecedented time in history.

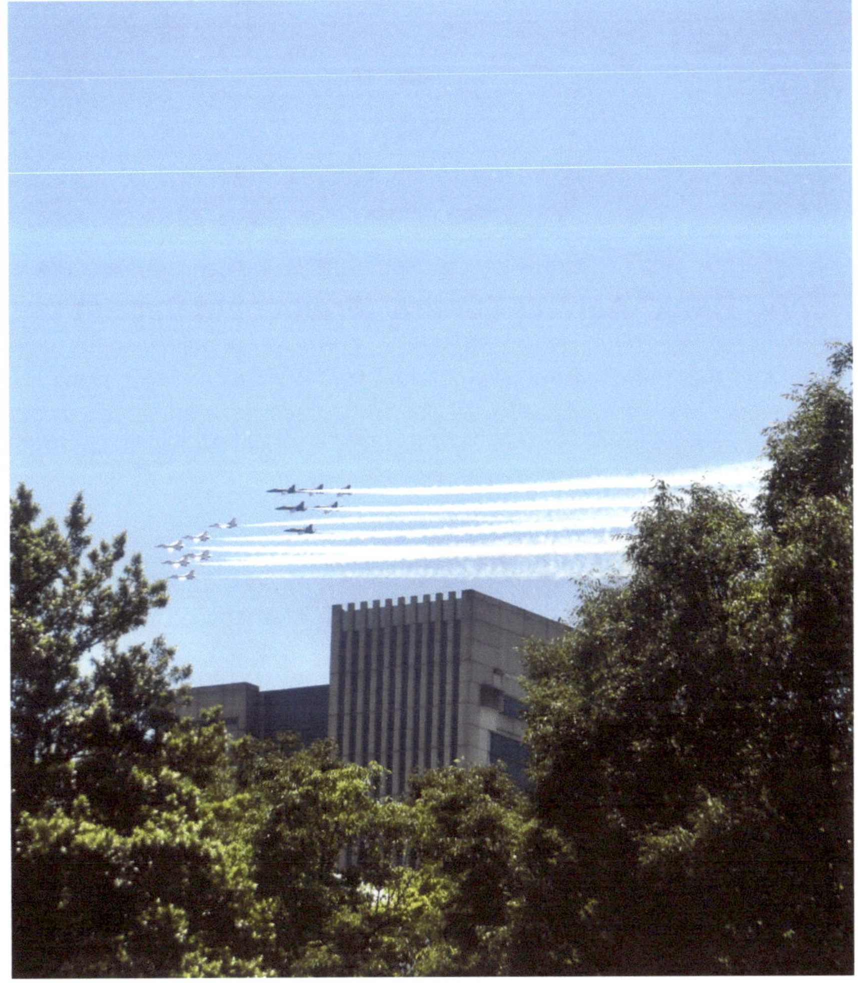

Rest in Peace—The Heroes

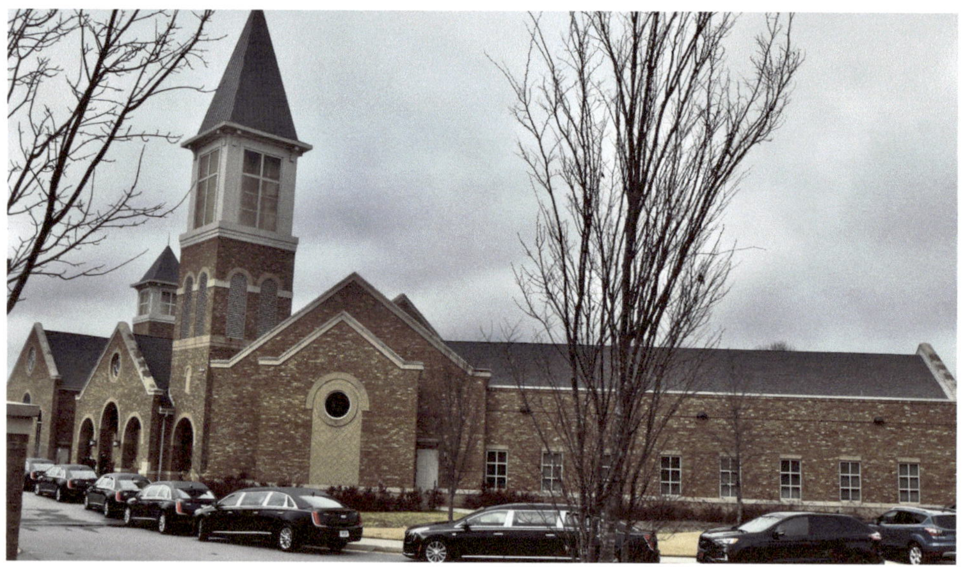

Henry "Hank" Aaron's Funeral (Friendship Baptist Church)

Baseball legend Henry "Hammerin' Hank" Louis Aaron overcame racial bigotry and hatred and was inducted into the Baseball Hall of Fame in 1982. He is remembered as the player who broke Babe Ruth's home run record. In 2002, he was awarded the Presidential Medal of Freedom by President George W. Bush, the highest honor given to a civilian by the American government.

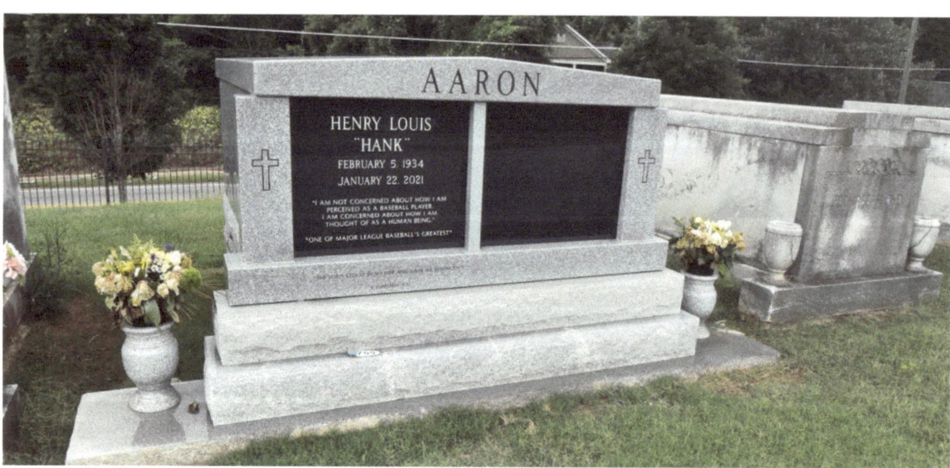

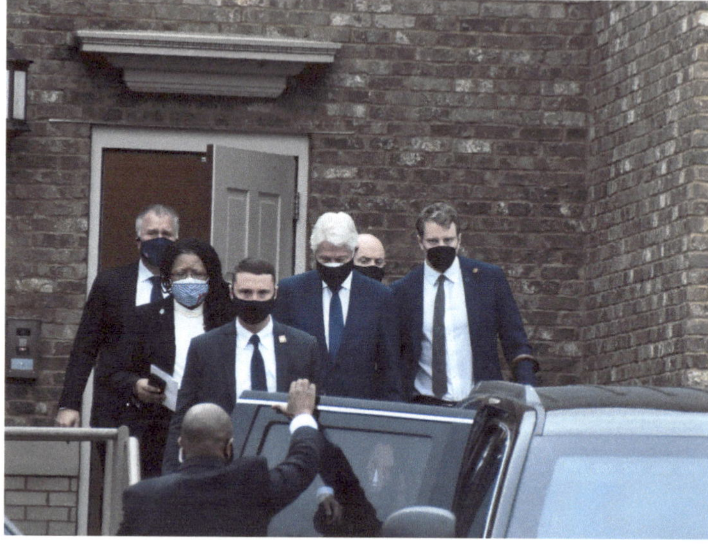

Former President Bill Clinton

Former President Clinton in attendance at Hank Aaron's funeral held at Friendship Baptist Church.

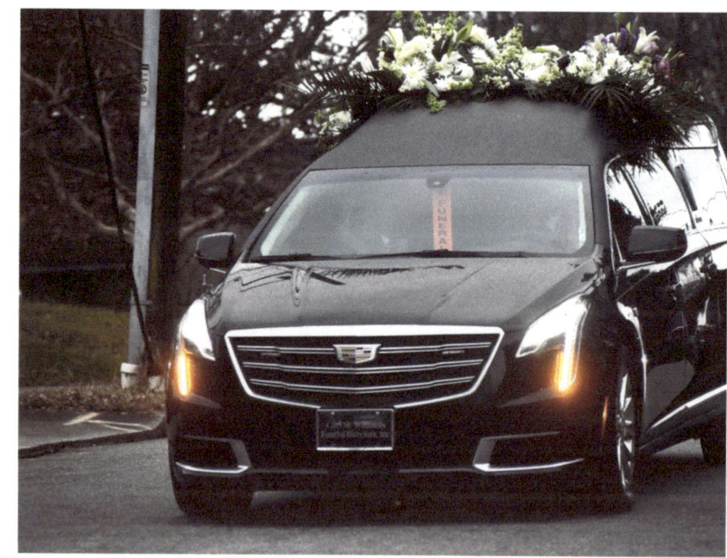

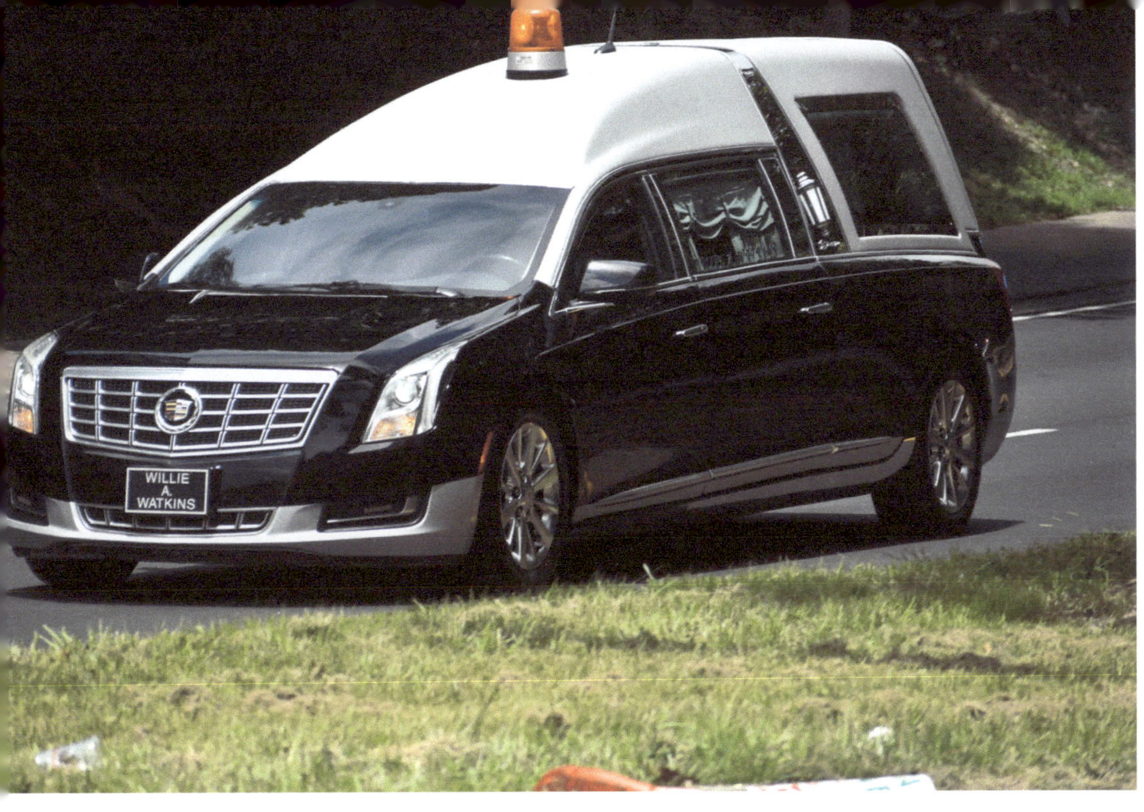

Congressman John Lewis

Congressman John Lewis was a Civil Rights icon, one of the "Big Six" leaders of the movement in the 1960s, and a freedom fighter for more than sixty years. He was also awarded the NAACP Spingarn Medal, and the sole John F. Kennedy "Profile in Courage Award" for lifetime achievement. He coined the phrase "Good Trouble."

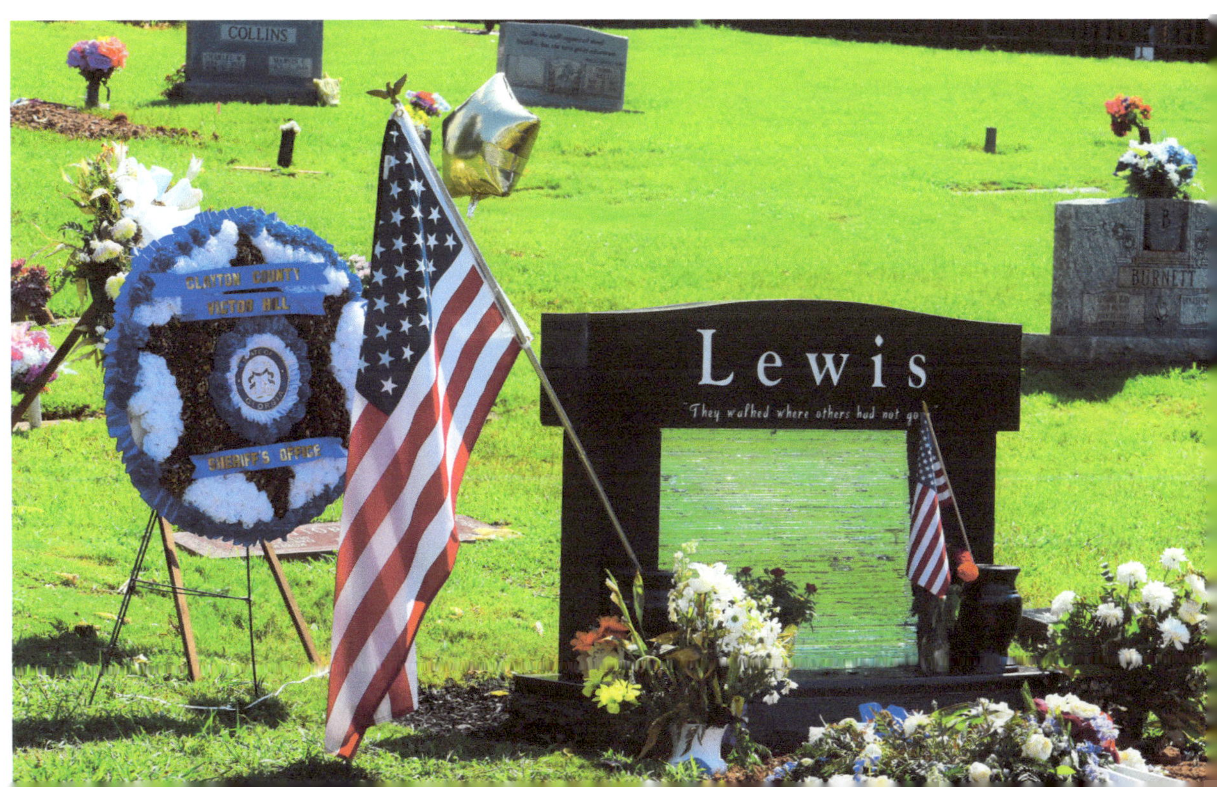

Unhoused

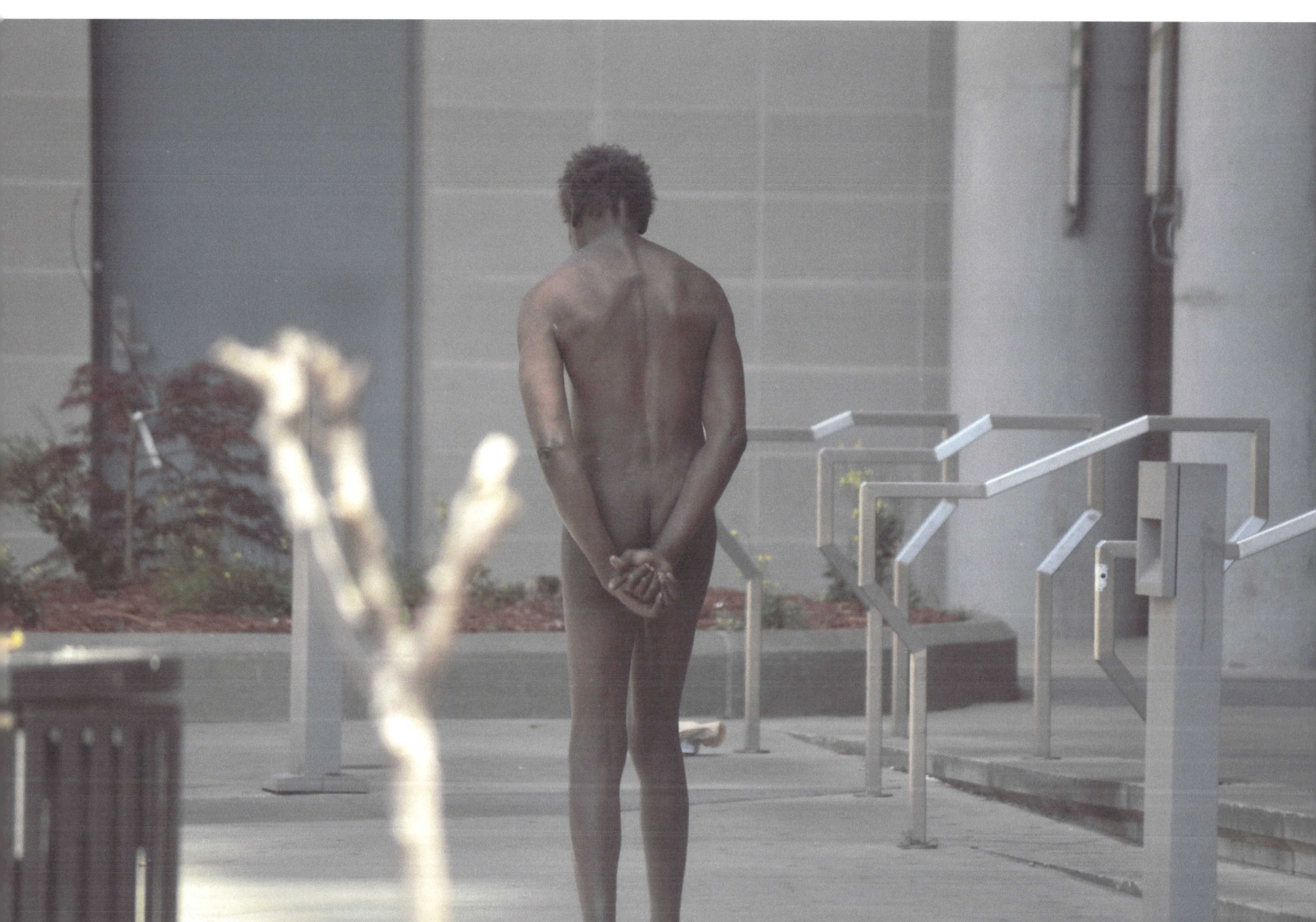

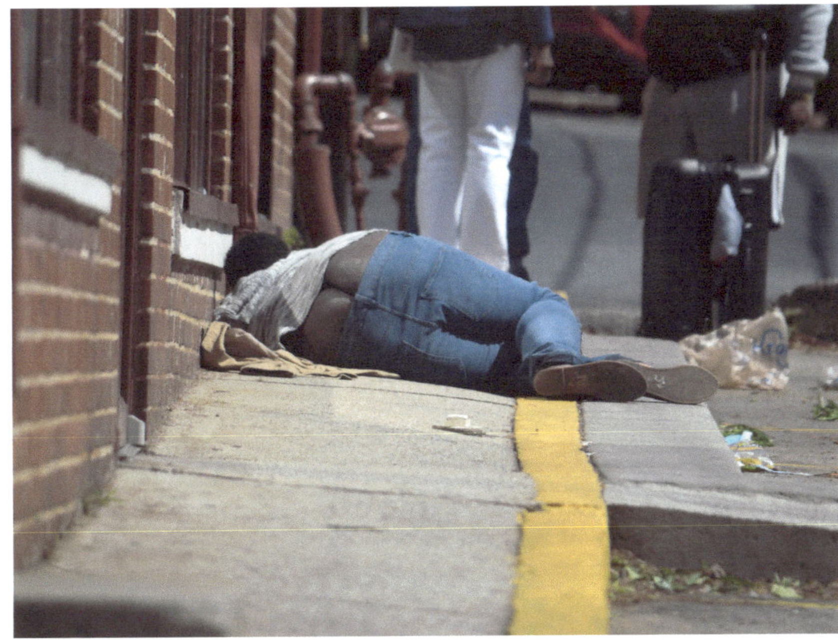
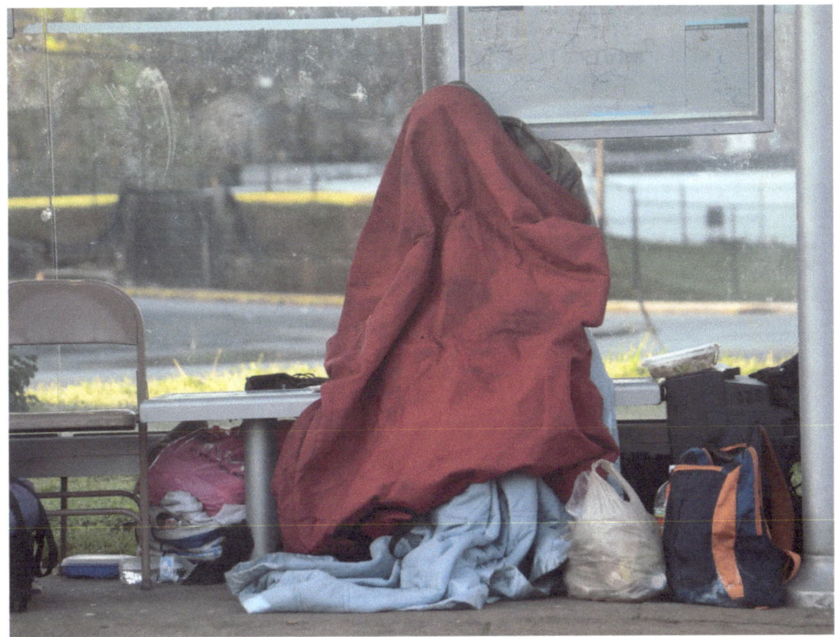
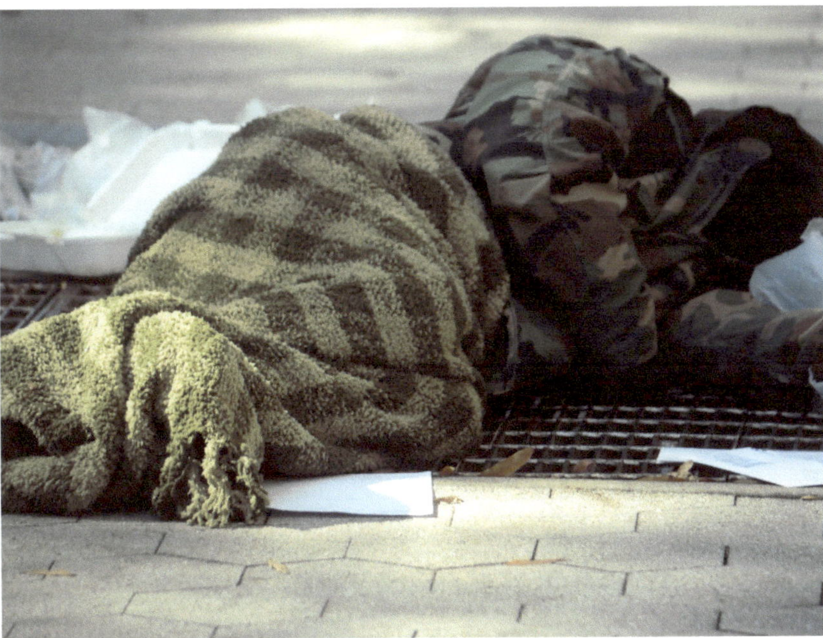
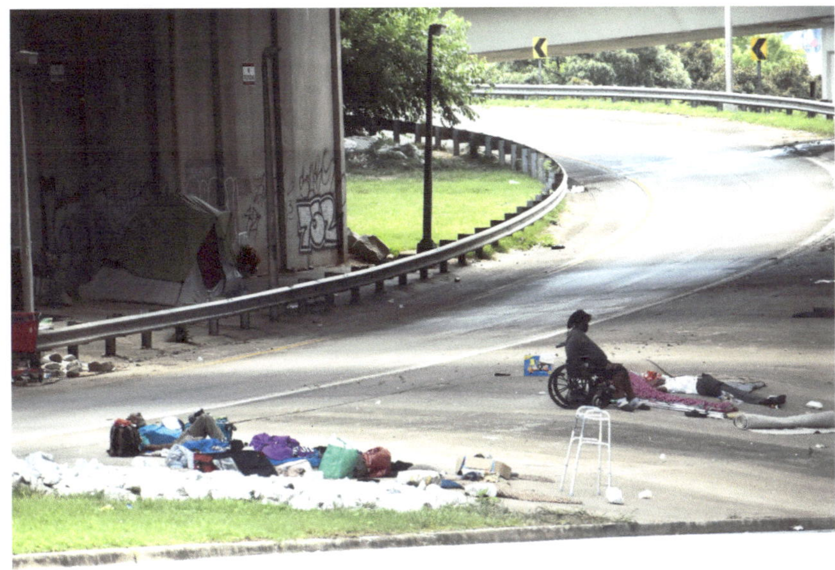

Civil Unrest

Celebration of the 2020 Presidential Election.

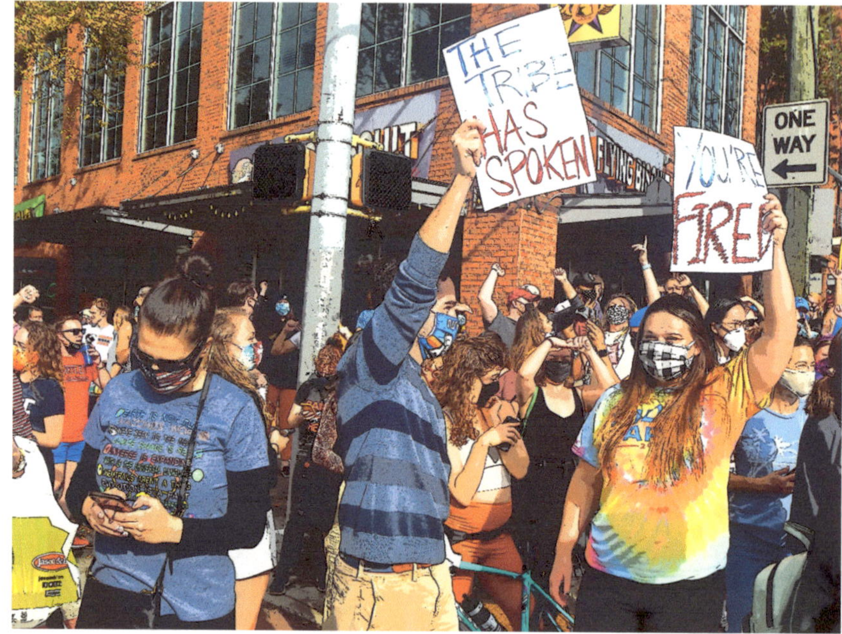

Arms Raised, Fists Clenched, Solidarity, Black Lives Matter

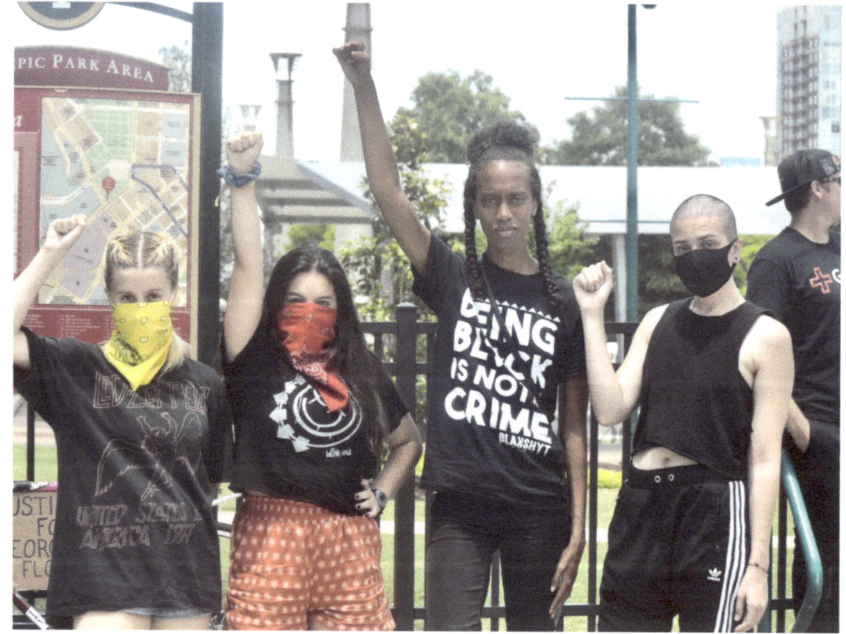

The Omni Hotel after the Murder of George Floyd

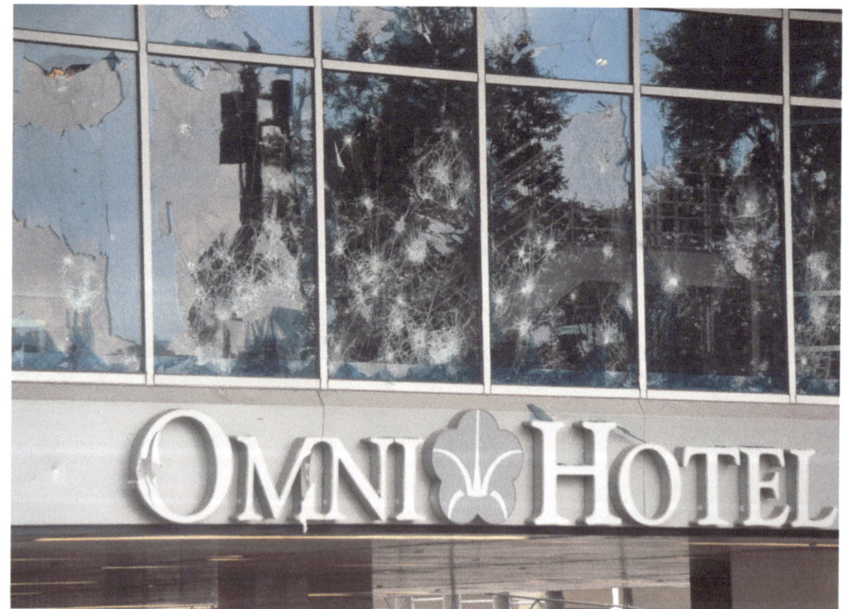

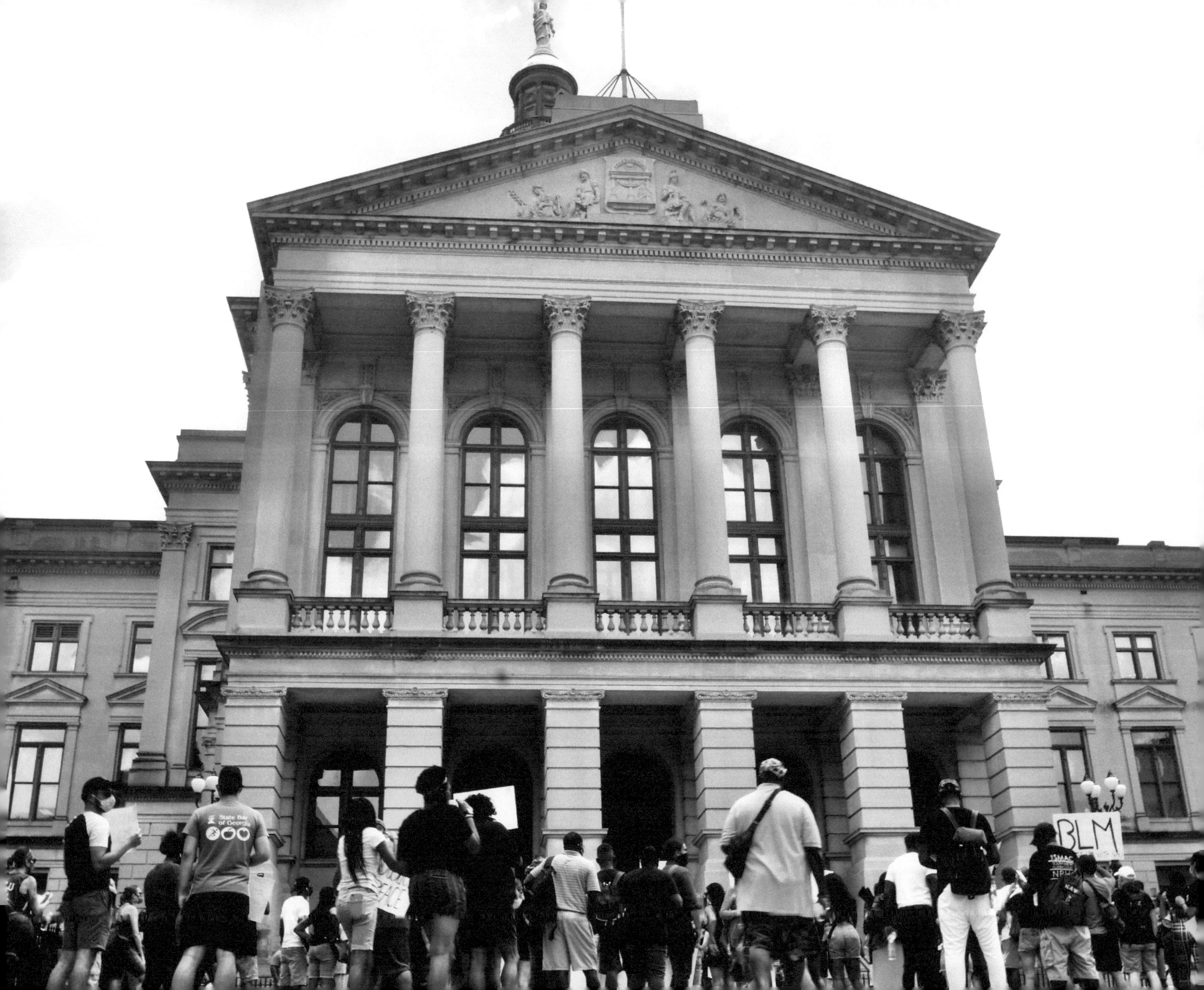

State Bar of Georgia
BLM

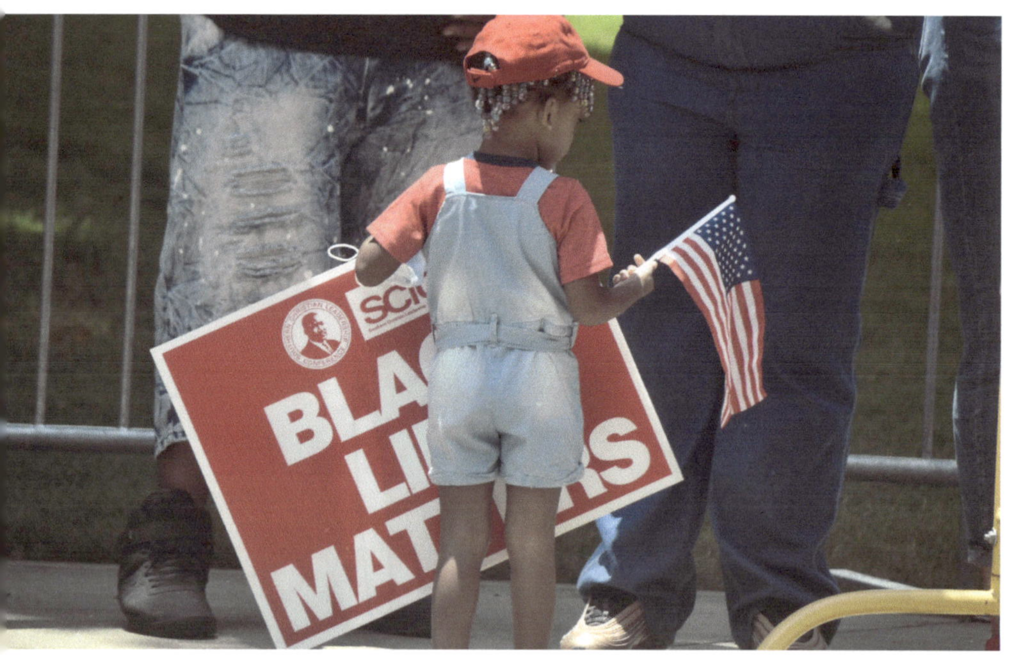

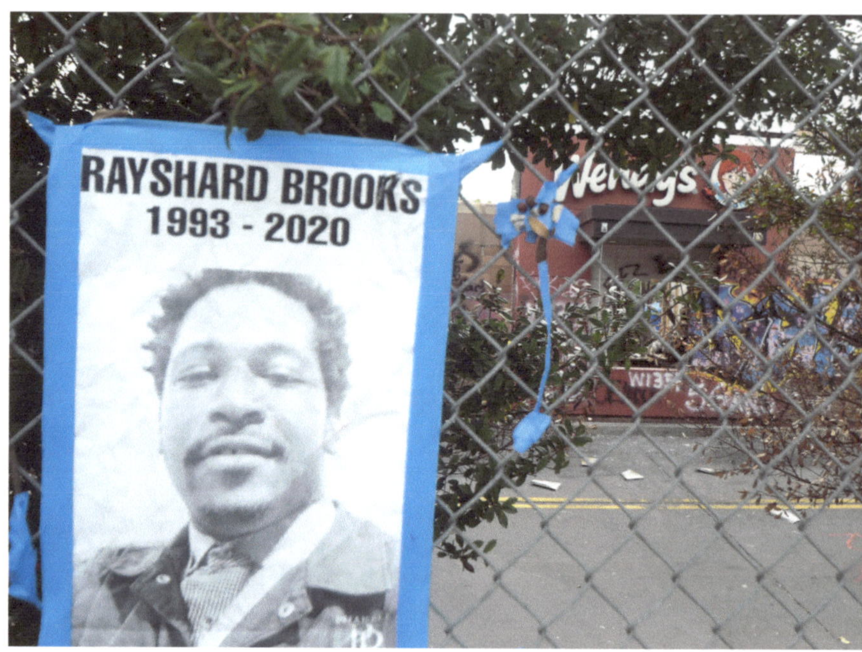

Rayshard Brooks Funeral

A Wendy's restaurant was burned after the murder of Rayshard Brooks.

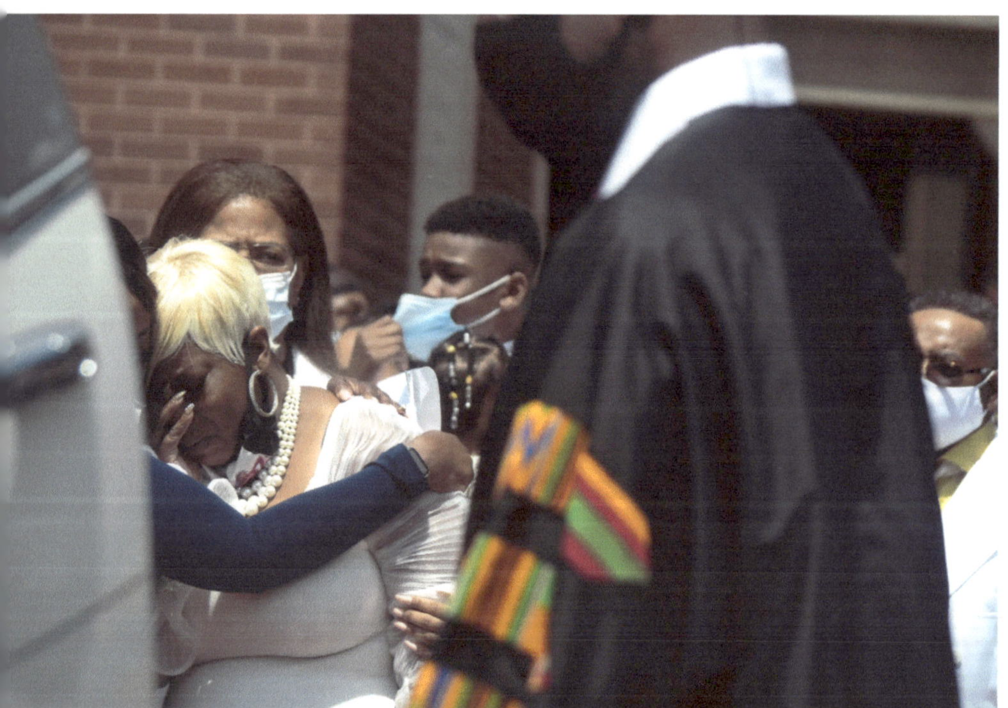

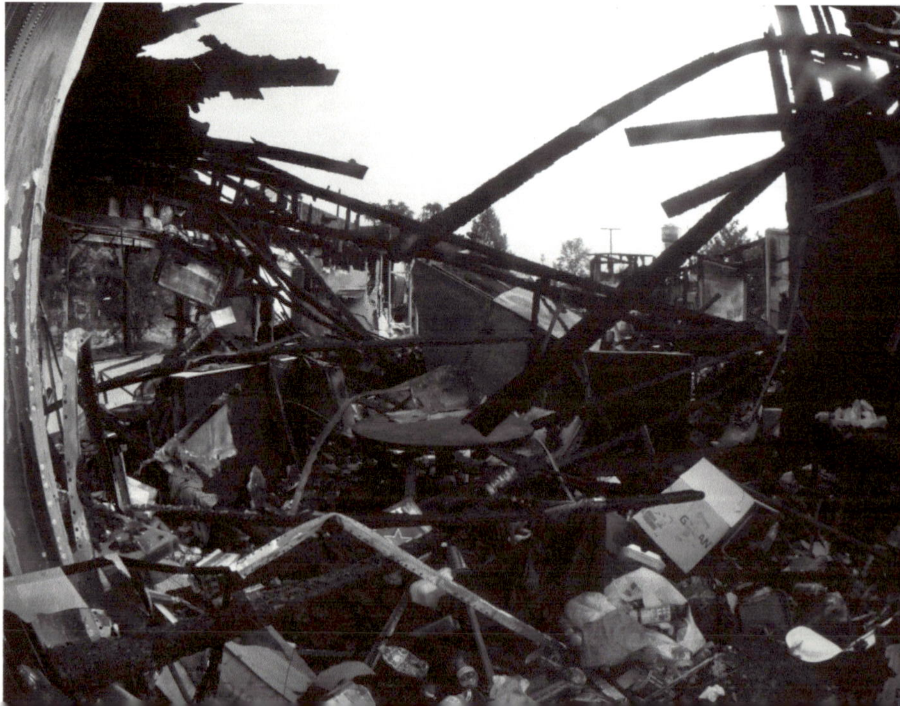

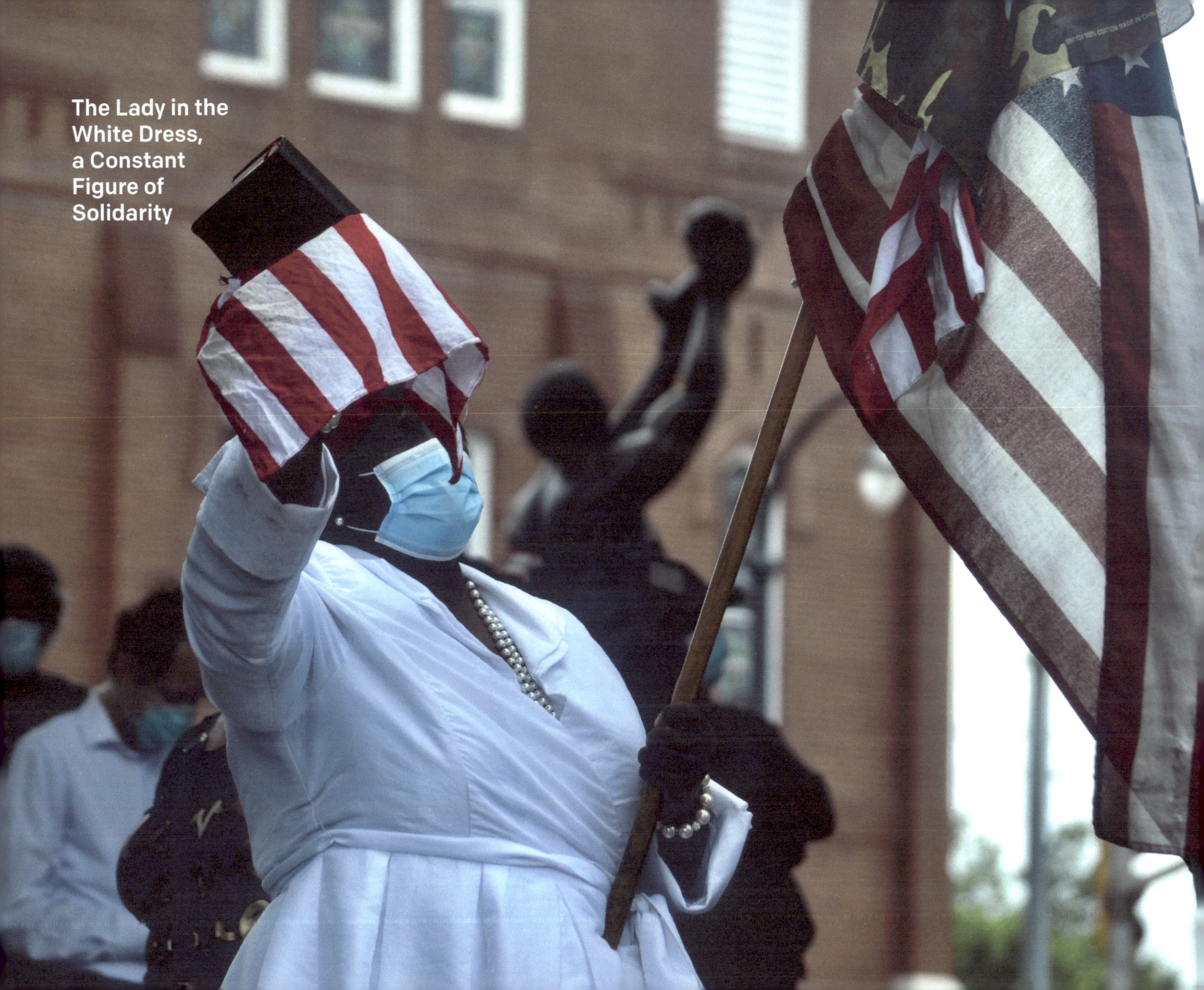

The Lady in the
White Dress,
a Constant
Figure of
Solidarity

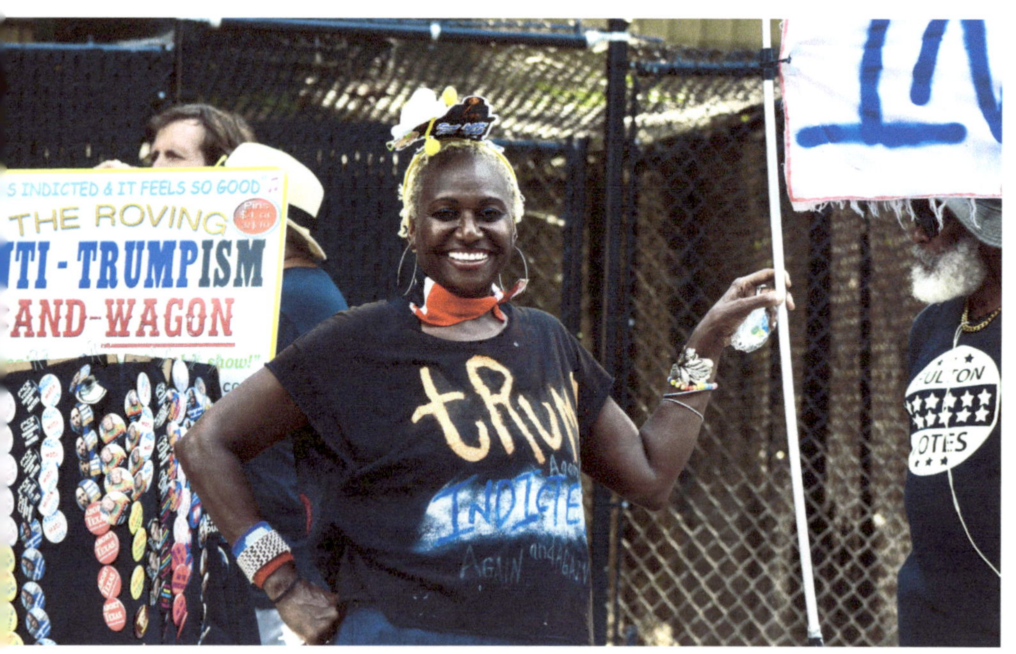
IS INDICTED & IT FEELS SO GOOD!
THE ROVING
TI - TRUMPISM
AND-WAGON
tRUMP
INDICTED
Again and again
FULTON
OTES

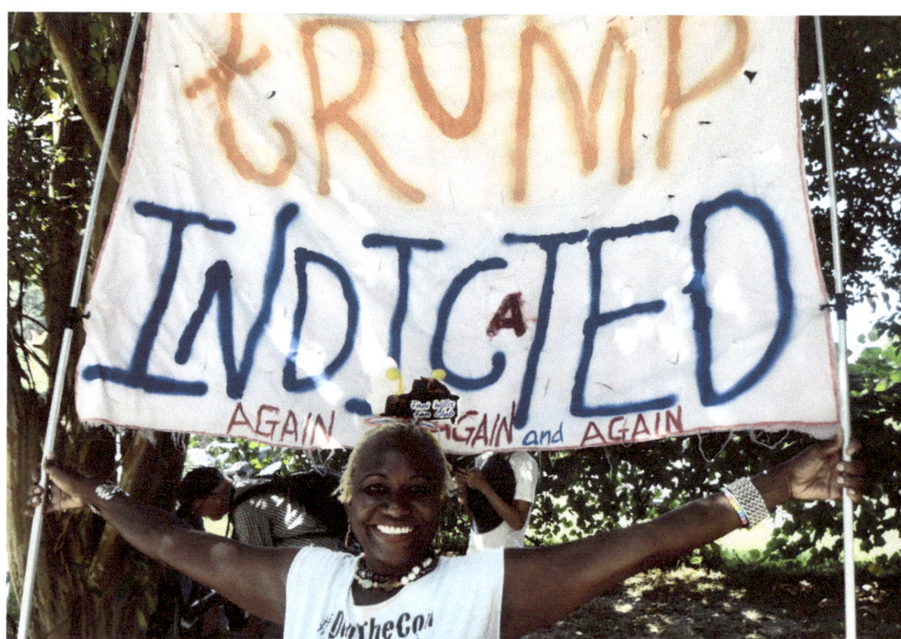
TRUMP
INDICTED
AGAIN and AGAIN and AGAIN

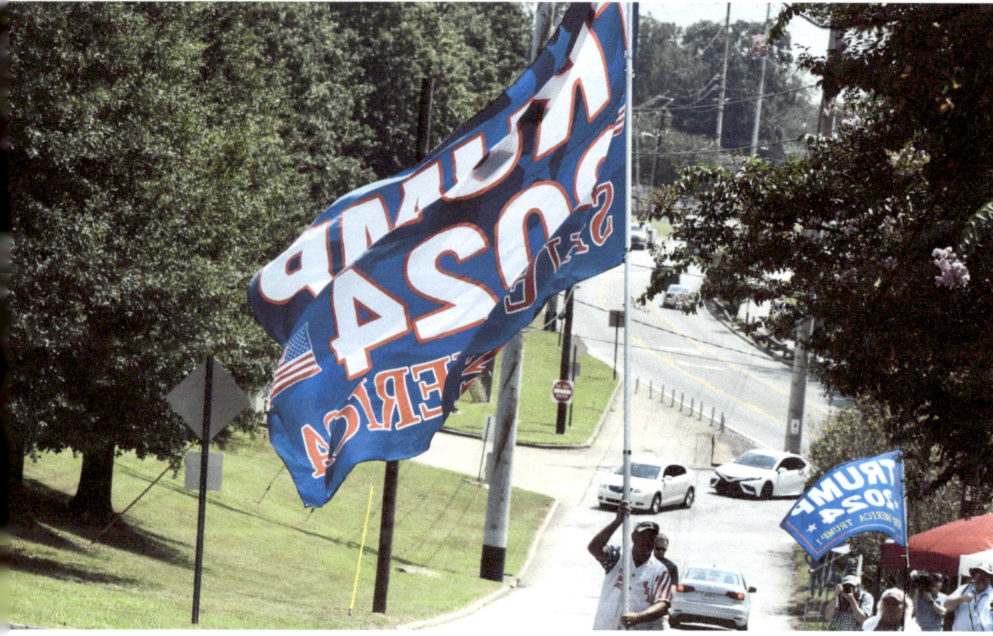
TRUMP
2024
AMERICA
TRUMP
2024

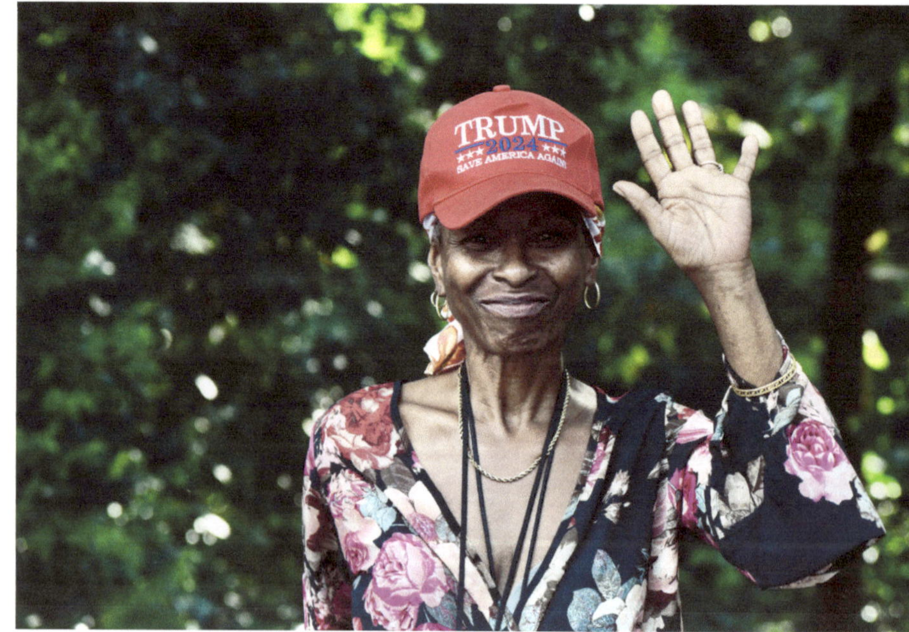
TRUMP
2024
SAVE AMERICA AGAIN

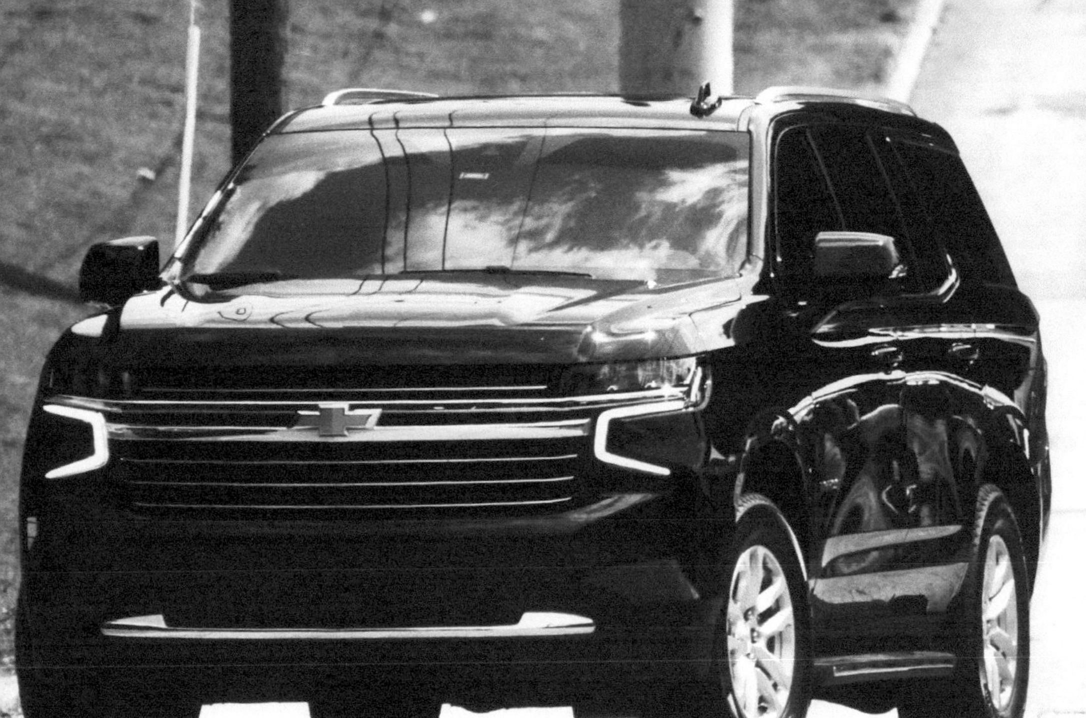

**Rudy Giuliani arrives
at Fulton County Jail**

**Fulton County Courthouse, the Beginning
Days of a Media Frenzy following the 2020
Election Fraud Case**

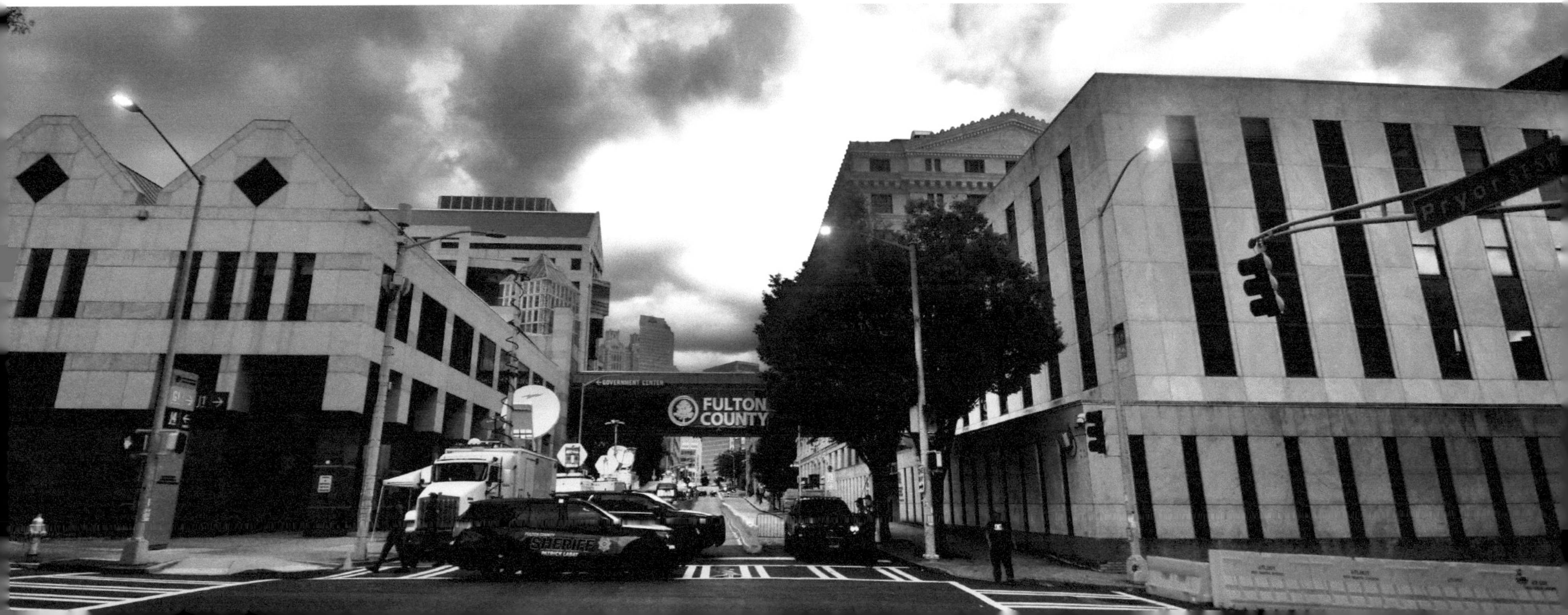

Iconic People

Monica Jones Kaufman Pearson

Monica Jones Kaufman Pearson is the first woman and the first African American to anchor the evening news in Atlanta, Georgia. Monica established a distinguished career in journalism for over thirty-seven years. She held the same position at the same station (WSB) longer than any other television personality.

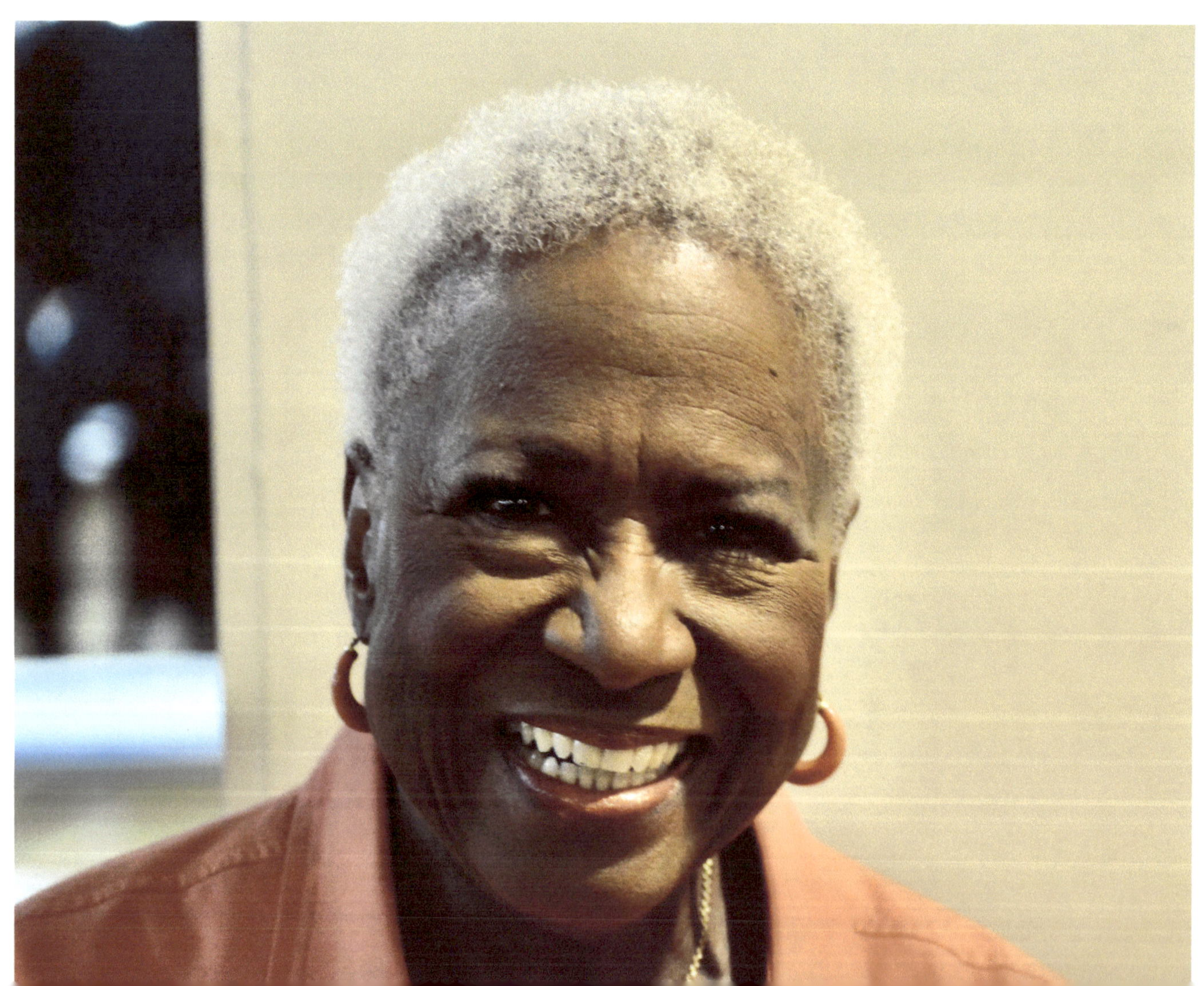

Stacey Abrams

Stacey Yvonne Abrams is a political leader, lawyer, voter's rights advocate, and New York Times *best-selling author of* Lead from the Outside, Our Time is Now *and* While Justice Sleeps. *She has also penned eight romance novels under the pen name Selena Montgomery.*
Stacey became the first African American woman and the first Georgian to deliver a response to the State of the Union. In 2022, she ran again against Gov. Brian Kemp for a second attempt and lost, after first losing to him in 2018.

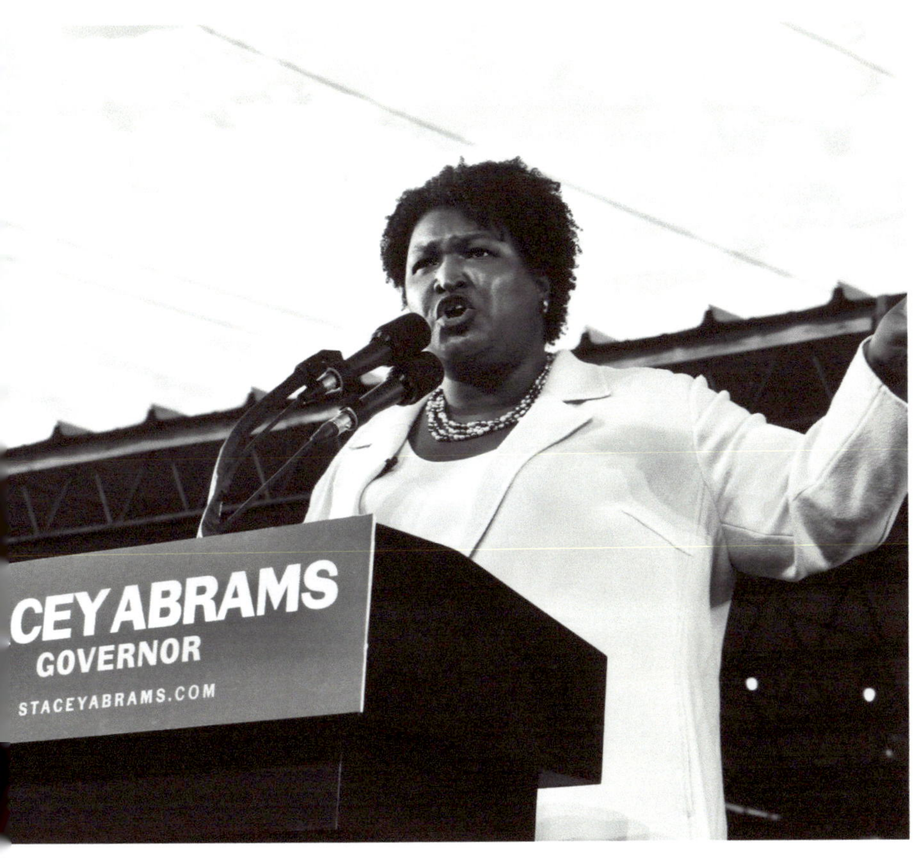

Andre Dickens

Atlanta's sixty-first mayor, Andre Dickens is an Atlanta native, and earned a bachelor's degree in chemical engineering at Georgia Tech and a master's in public administration from Georgia State University.

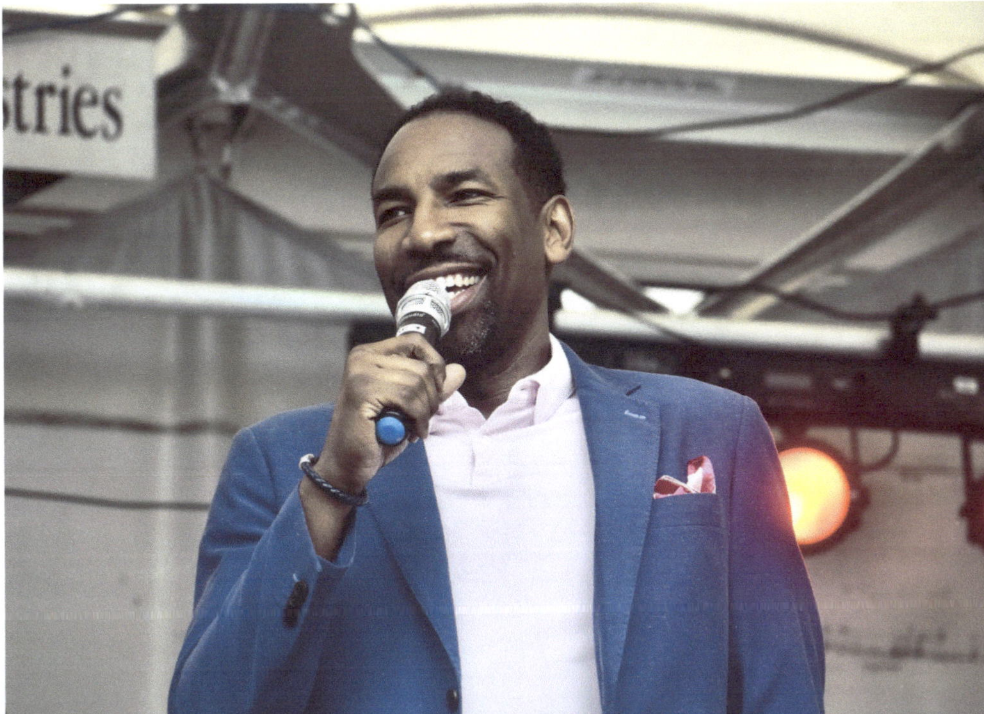

Andrew Young, Former Mayor of Atlanta and Former Ambassador to the United Nations under the Jimmy Carter Administration

Atlanta's fifty-fifth mayor was a key strategist whose negotiations led to the passage of the Civil Rights Act of 1964 and Voters Rights Act of 1965. In 1972, Young was elected to Congress, becoming the first African American representative from the Deep South since Reconstruction.

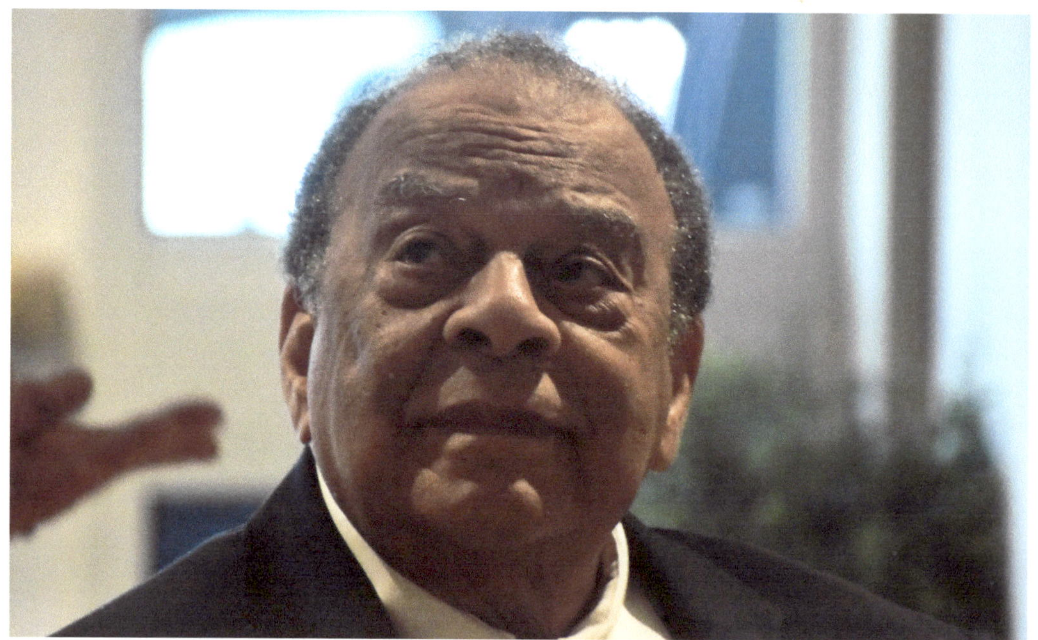

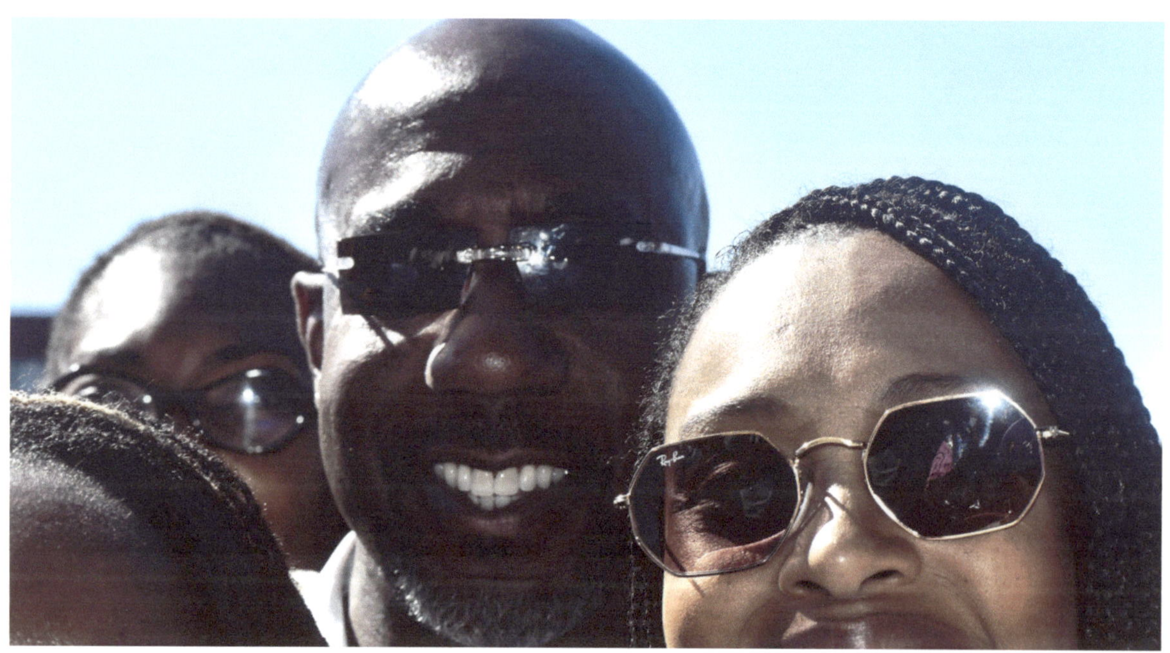

Senator Raphael Warnock

Senator Raphael Warnock is the senior pastor of Ebenezer Baptist Church. He is the first African American to represent Georgia in the Senate, and the first African American Democrat elected to the Senate in a southern state.

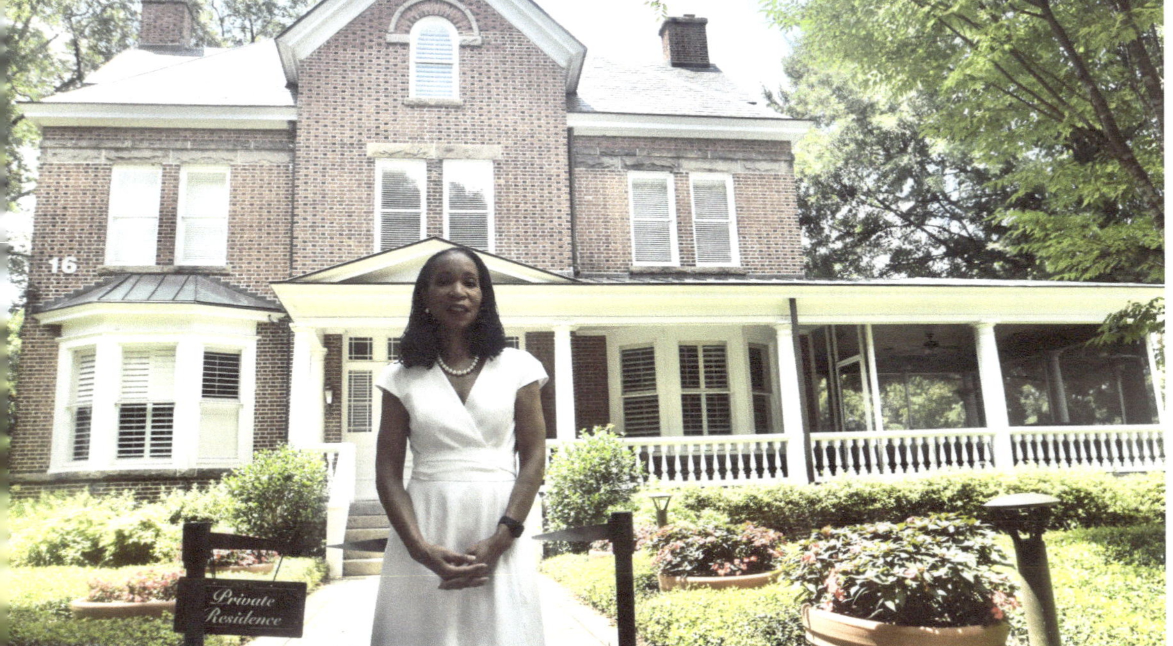

**Spelman College President,
Dr. Helene D. Gayle**

Senator Jon Ossoff

Senator Jon Ossoff became the youngest member of the Senate elected, and the first Jewish Senator elected to represent the state of Georgia. Senator Ossoff is seen here campaigning at Morehouse College.

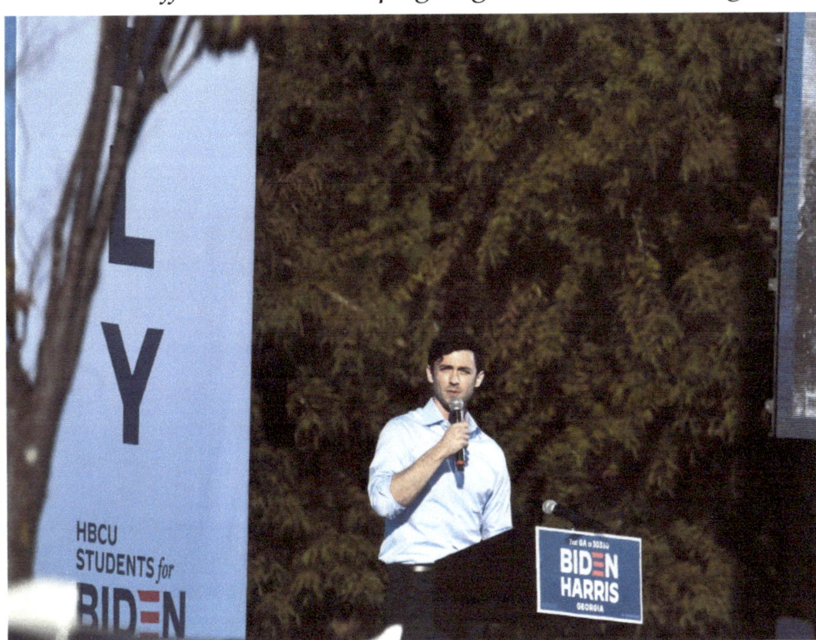

Vice President Kamala Harris

Kamala Harris, the first female vice president of the United States, visits Morehouse College campaigning for the 2020 Presidential election.

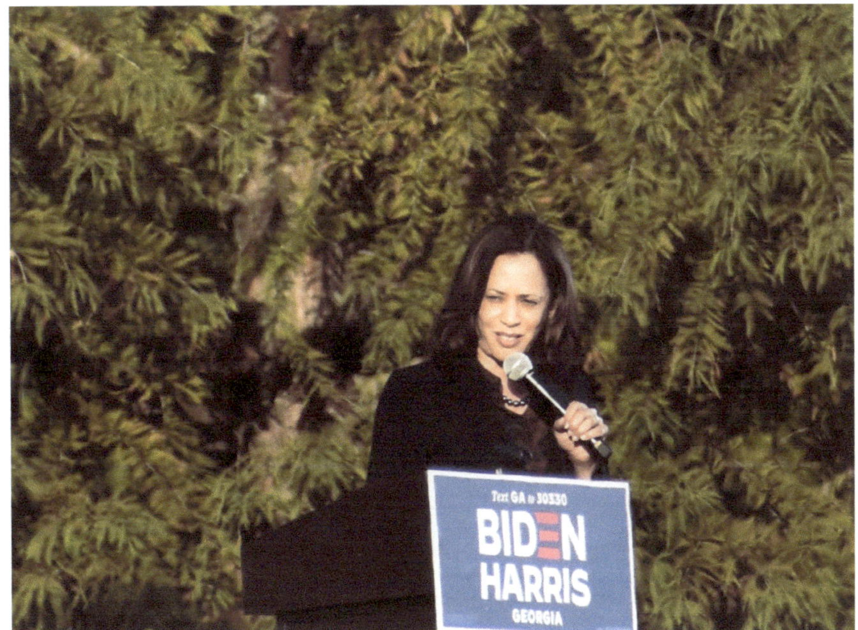

The Future of Atlanta—Entrepreneurs

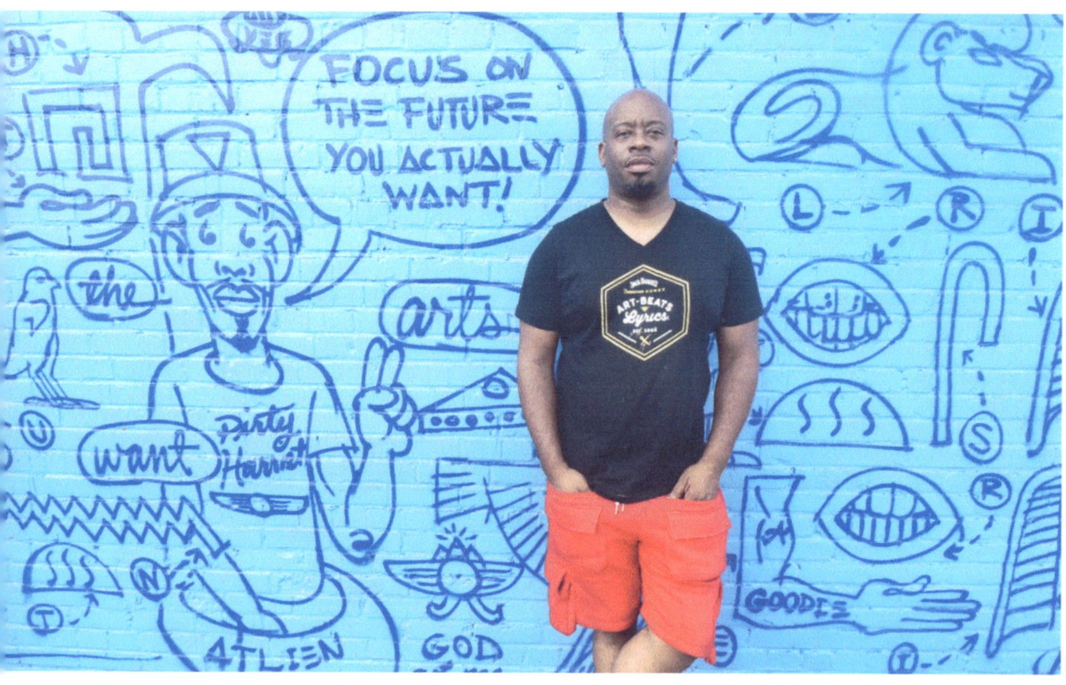

Contemporary Artist and Muralist, Fabian Williams

After working for thirteen years in the advertising industry with a long list of clients from Nike to Warner Bros. to HBO, Fabian made a decision to move to a purely expressive practice, where he had the freedom to express more political and socially relevant contemporary themes.

Willie Hall
Owner and Operator of WH Flooring

Willie Hall's inspiration was sparked by reading Reginald Lewis's biography, who was the first African American to build a billion-dollar company.

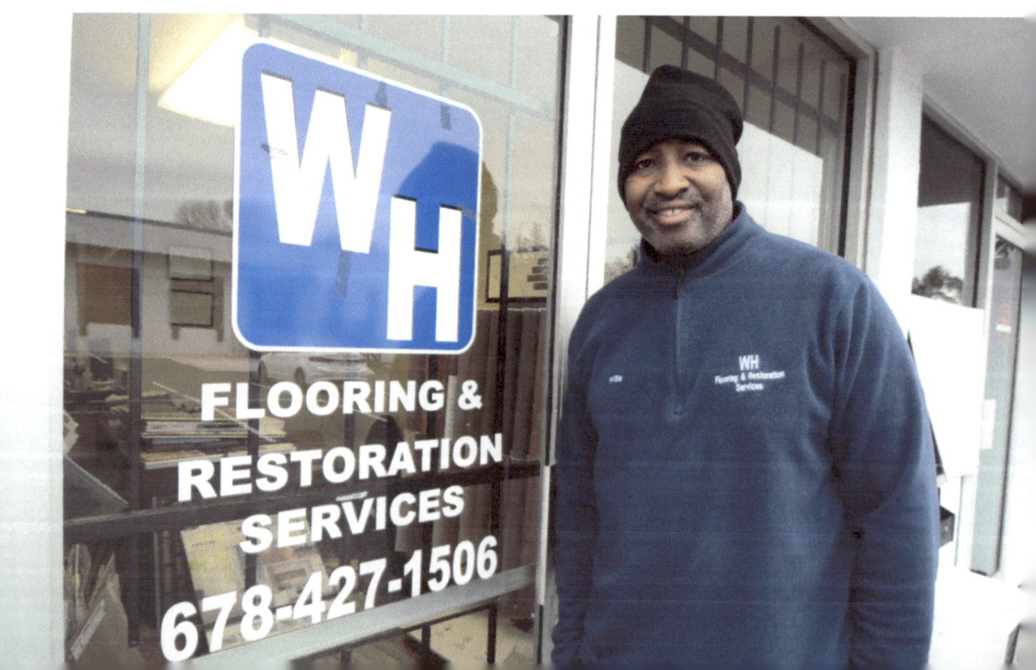

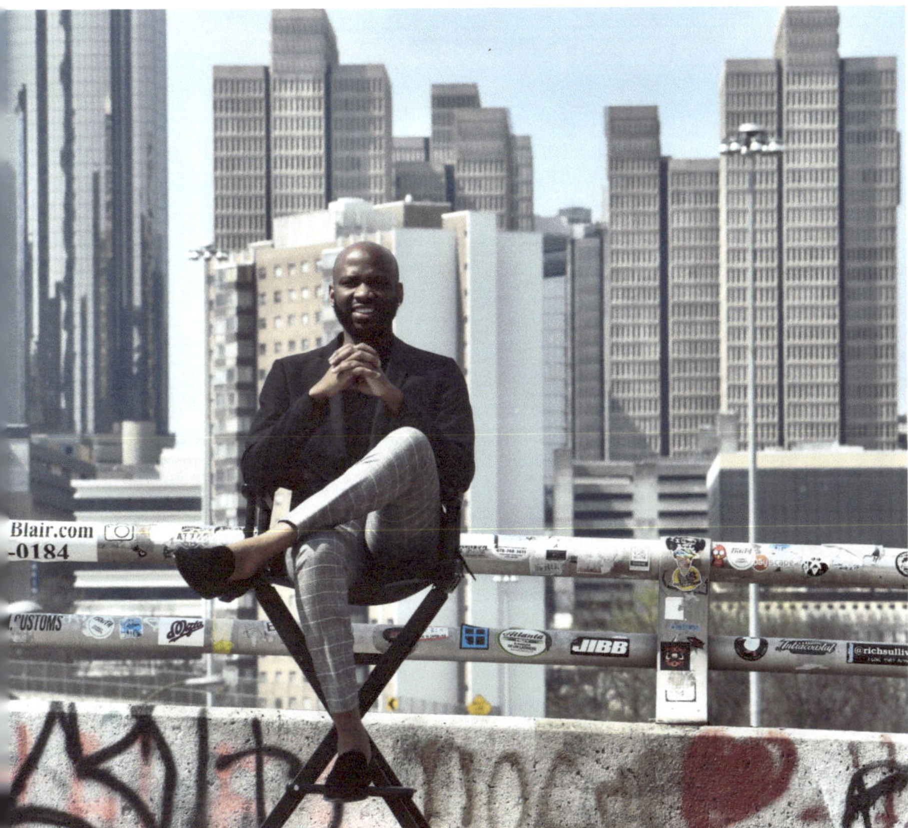

Jeremy Cormier, Director and Playwright

Jeremy is the Chief Executive of Jeremy Cormier Presents, an entertainment company based in Atlanta, Georgia. He has worked with well-known celebrities such as Janet Jackson, Shirley Murdock, Jennifer Holliday, and a host of others. In his spare time, he is often found contributing to his community through service projects and volunteering at his church (Impact).

Jamie Bowman
Owner of BLENDED Smoothie and Juice Bar

Prior to the inception of BLENDED, Jamie worked in the music and entertainment industry for many years. It was her parents' failed health and passing that was the catalyst for her desire to change her eating habits and to help others on their journey to wellness.

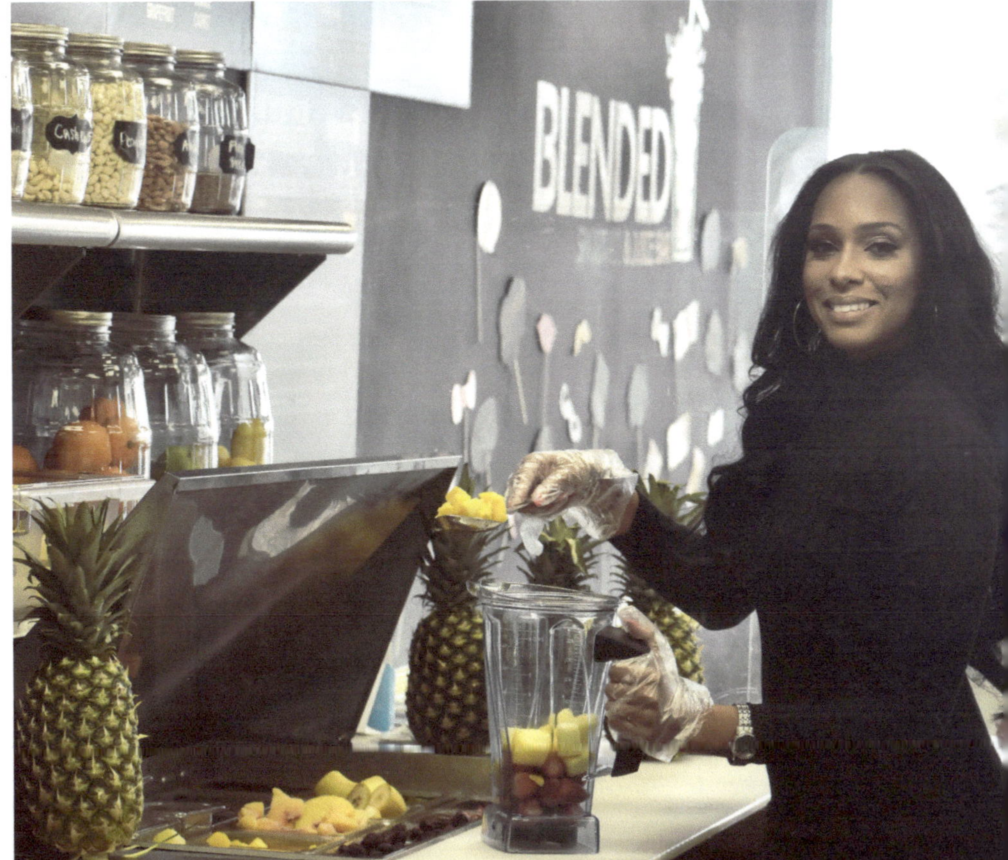

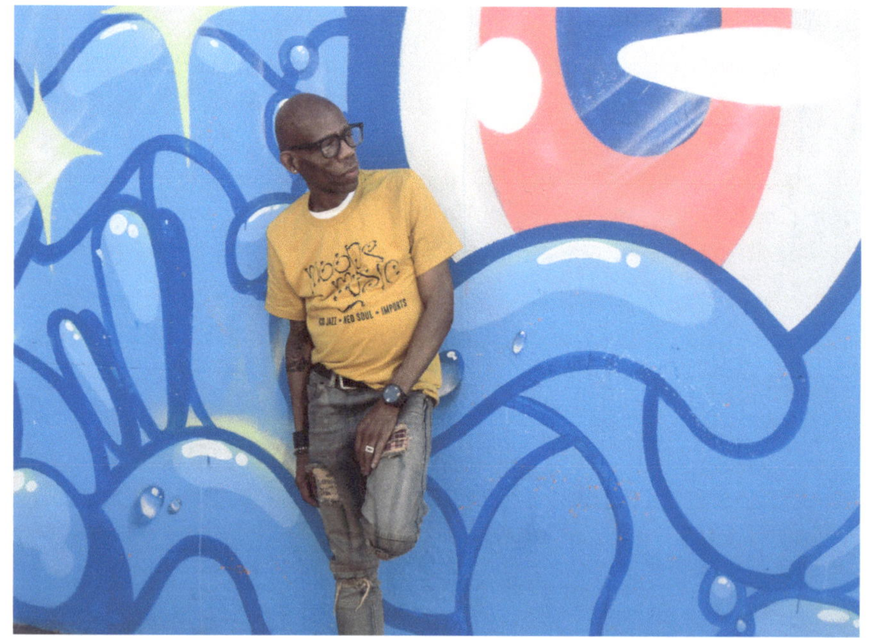

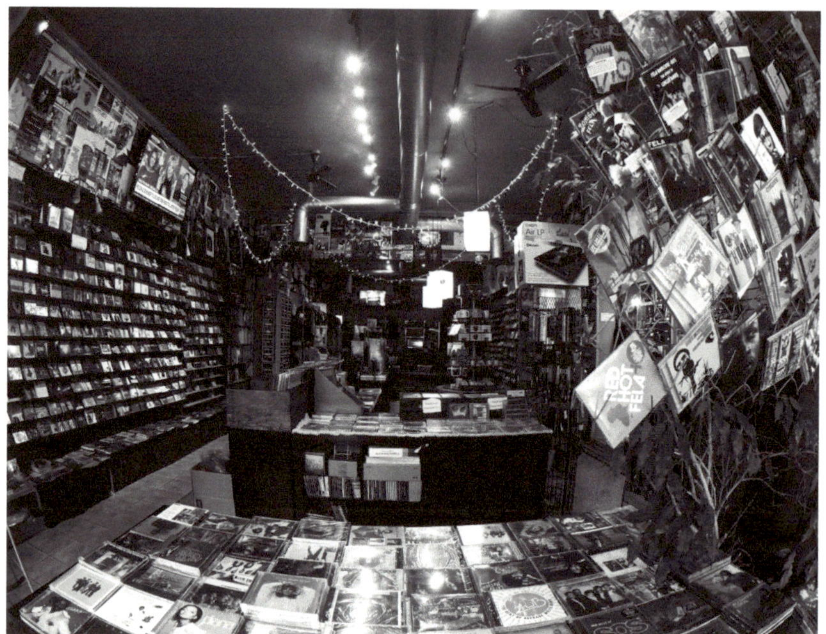

Darryl Harris
Owner of Moods Music and Soul Village

Moods Music is a musical staple located in the heart of Atlanta's Historic Little Five Points. It was birthed from Darryl's love of music in the year 2000.

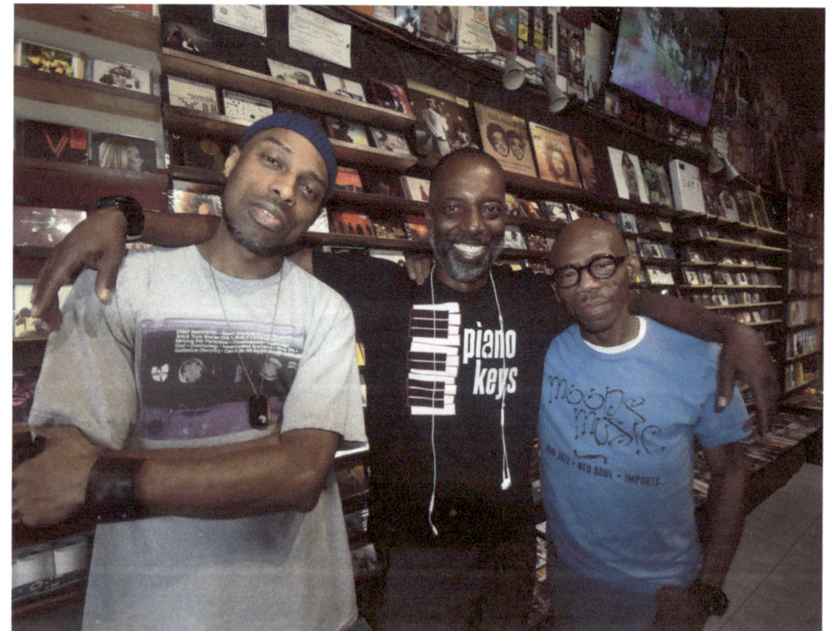

The Dynamite Dave Soul, DJ Kemit, and Darryl Harris (A Wealth of Musical Talent Serving the Atlanta Community)

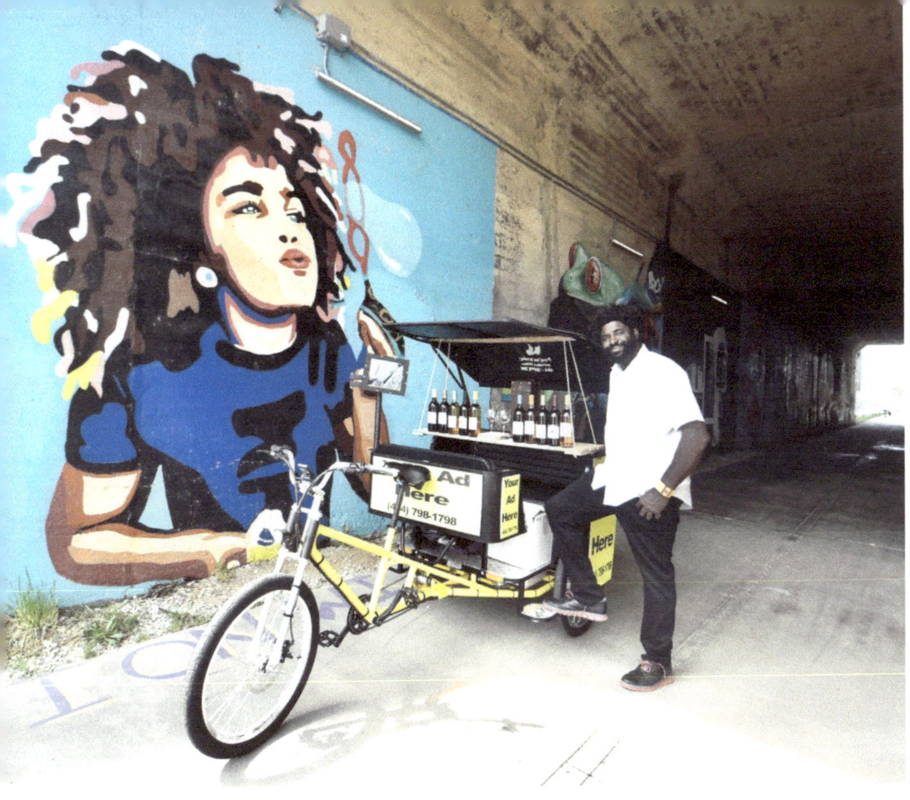

Jay the Dreamer
Gifted and Talented Entrepreneur

Jay White is a multitalented entrepreneur whose talents span from so many different angles. Jay's businesses spans from Pedicabs Atl as well as making Uncommon Wine, to creating fifty millionaires by the end of 2023.

Cherie Collins
Jeweler and Founder of Nappy Rutz

Cherie creates some of the funkiest and eclectic earwear that are in line with the vibe of the city. Nappy Rutz specializes in enhancing ones beauty by way of handcrafted accessories. Visit nappyrutz.com for some of the boldest accessories.

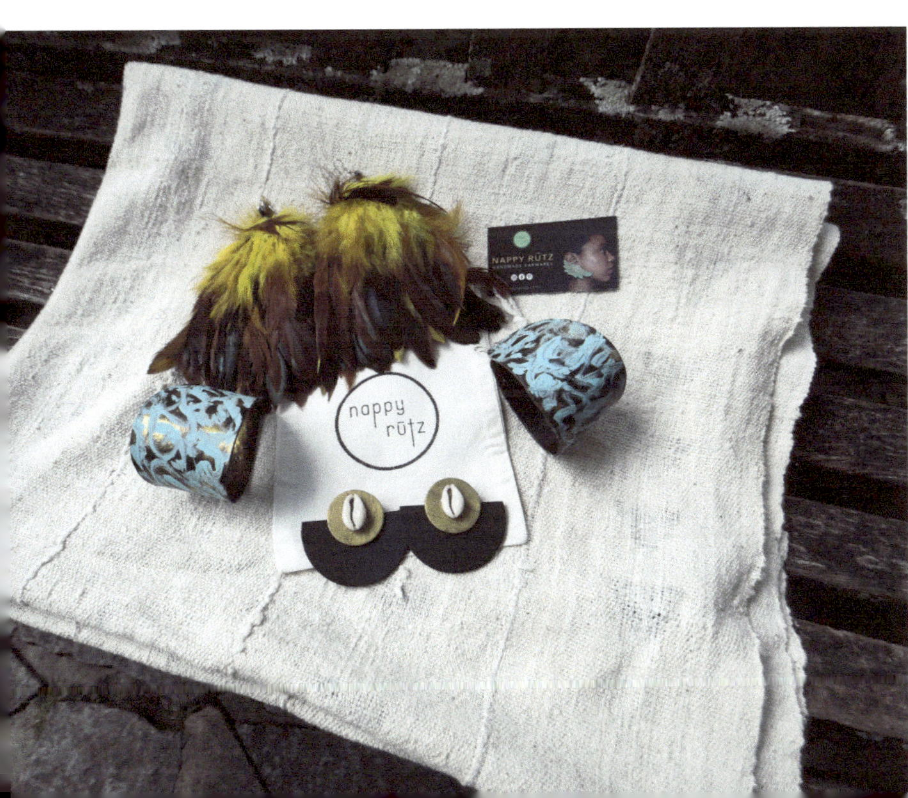

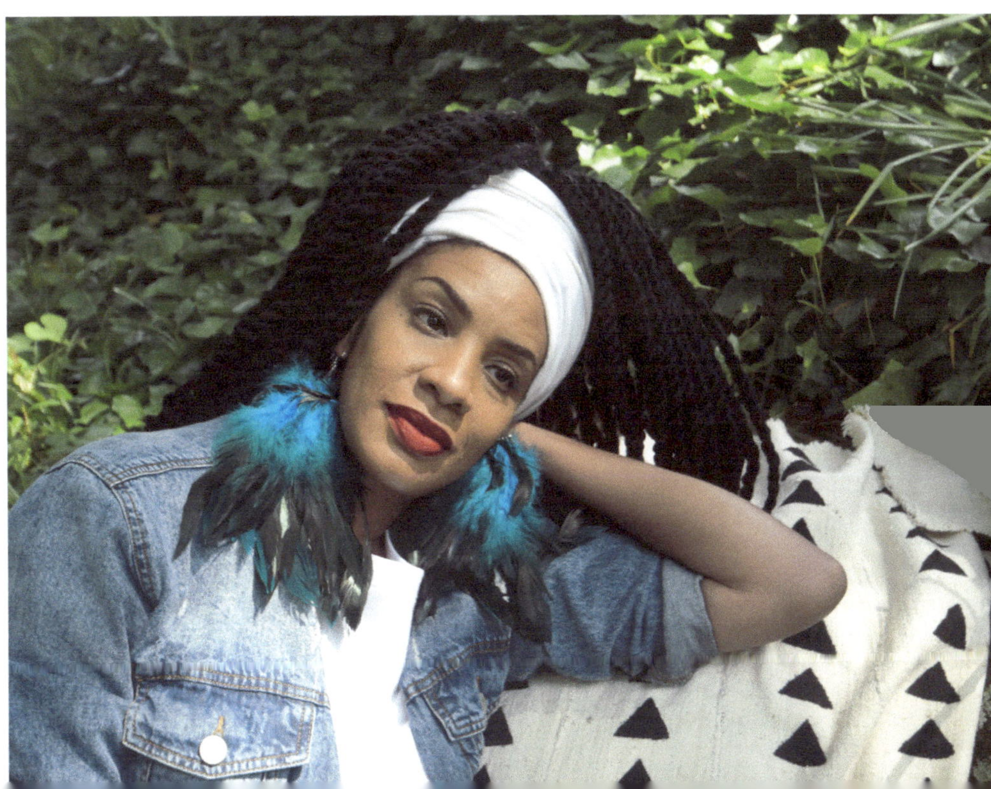

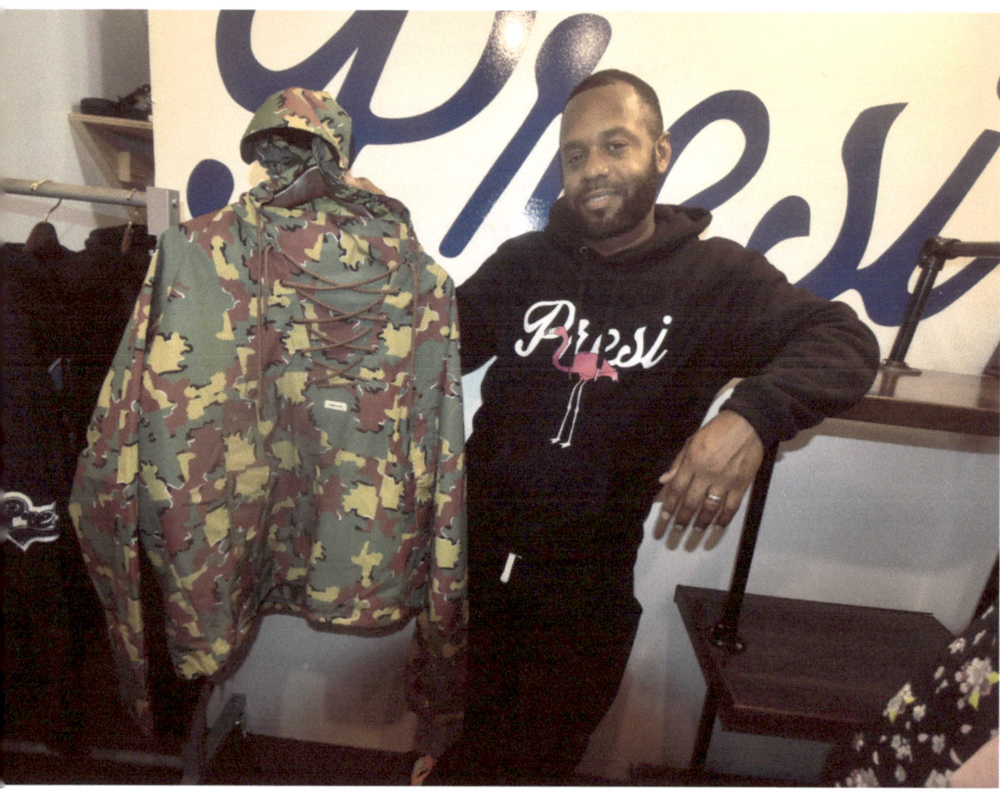

Giscard Walters, PRESI Clothing Designer
Giscard created PRESI as a brand for ordinary people who aspire to do ordinary things.

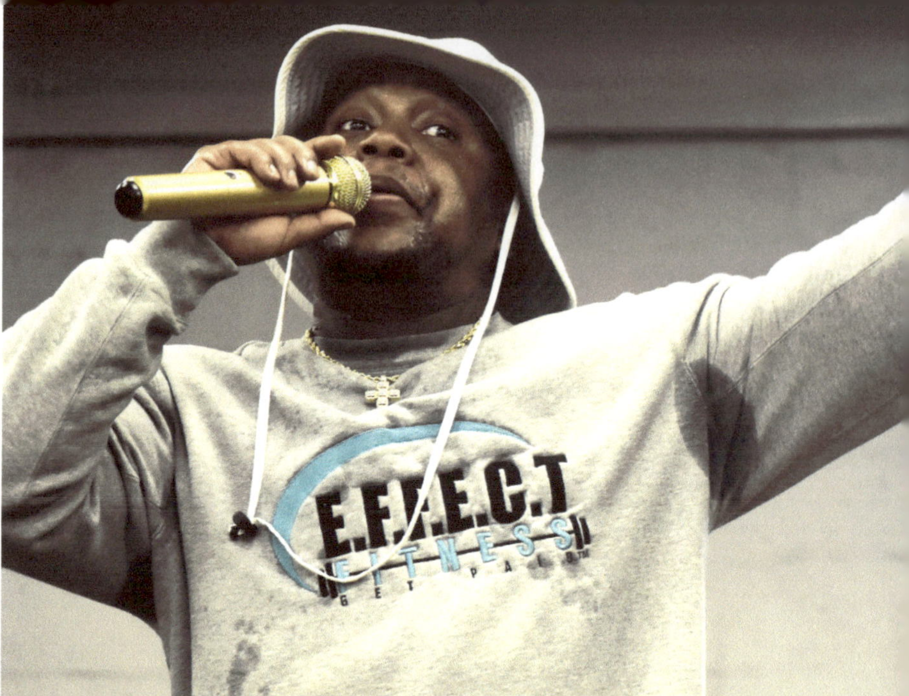

Dooley
Owner and Fitness Motivator of E.F.F.E.C.T Fitness
"It's about that time" is what you'll hear at the beginning of eac workout session. If you don't have the energy, Dooley will, with n doubt, inspire you to get motivated.

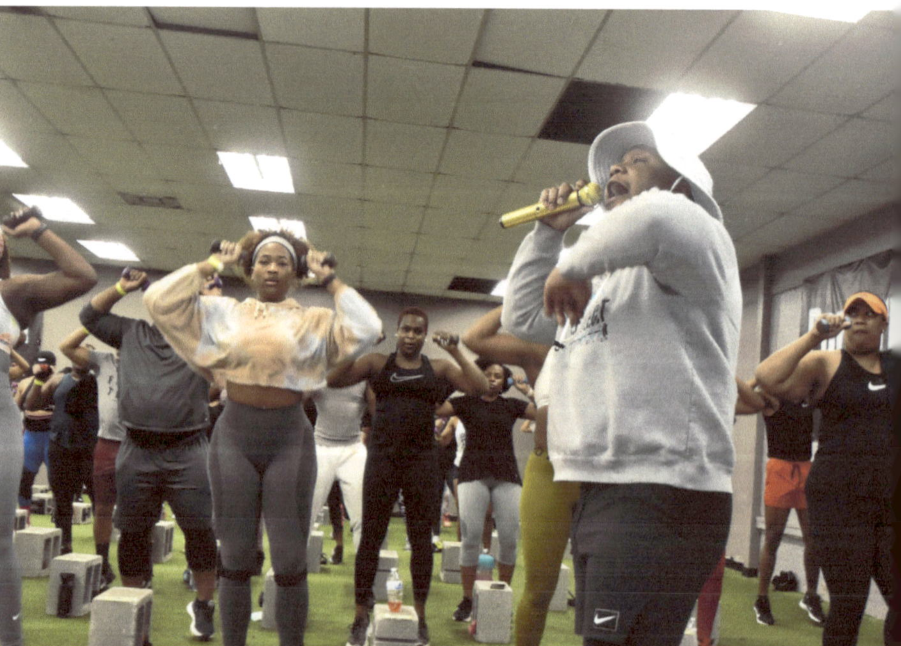

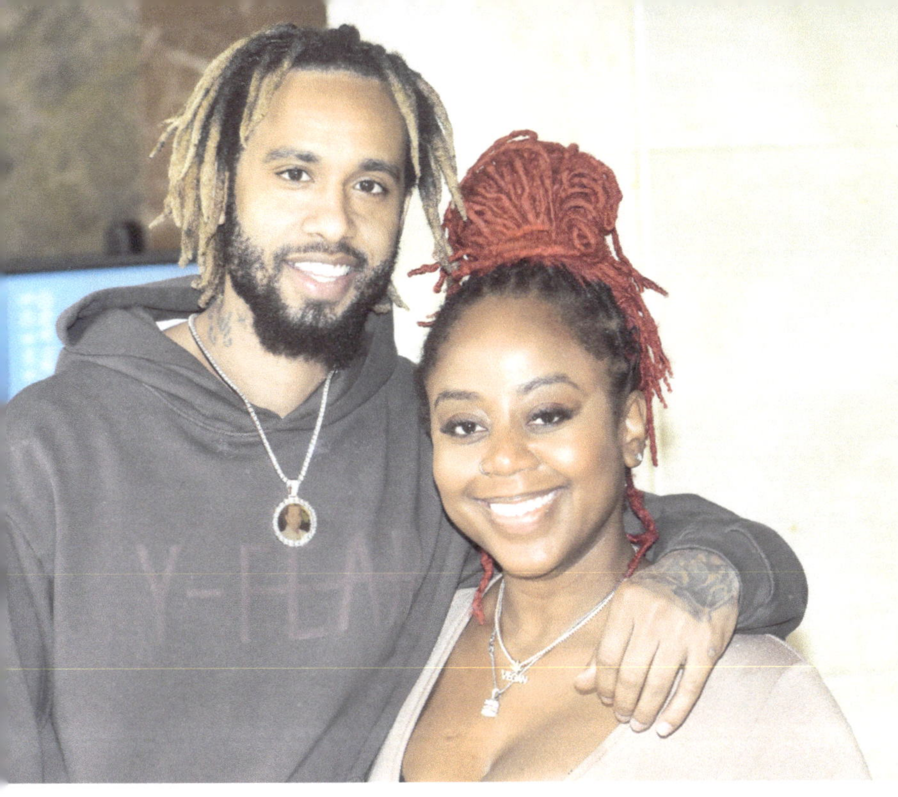

Aisha "Pinky" Cole Hayes
Owner and Founder of Slutty Vegan and Bar Vegan

Slutty Vegan is a plant-based burger restaurant chain that began as a food truck and since has expanded across the metro area, and now several states, with multiple locations. Pinky has a passion and desire to give back to the community and has done so in countless ways through her Pinky Cole Foundation. She is now married to Derrick Hayes, owner of Big Dave's Cheesesteaks.

Derrick Hayes—Owner and Founder
of Big Dave's Cheesesteaks

Hayes, as an inquisitive child, would spend lots of quality time in the kitchen with his grandfather. It was those precious moments that inspired him and sparked a desire to create great food, and later Big Dave's Cheesesteaks.

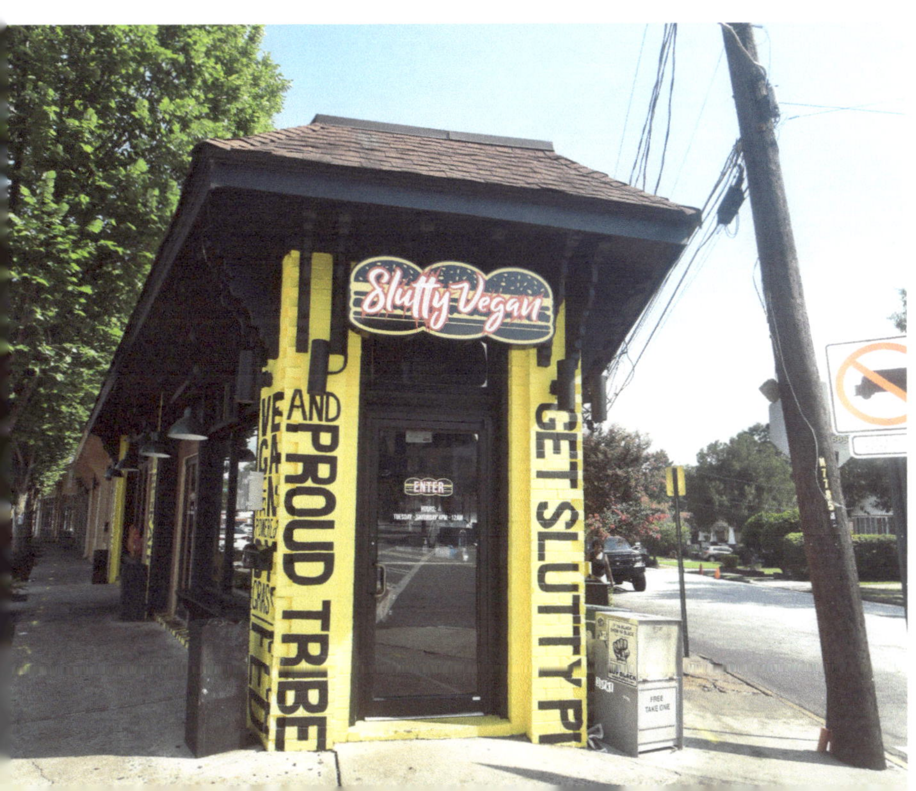

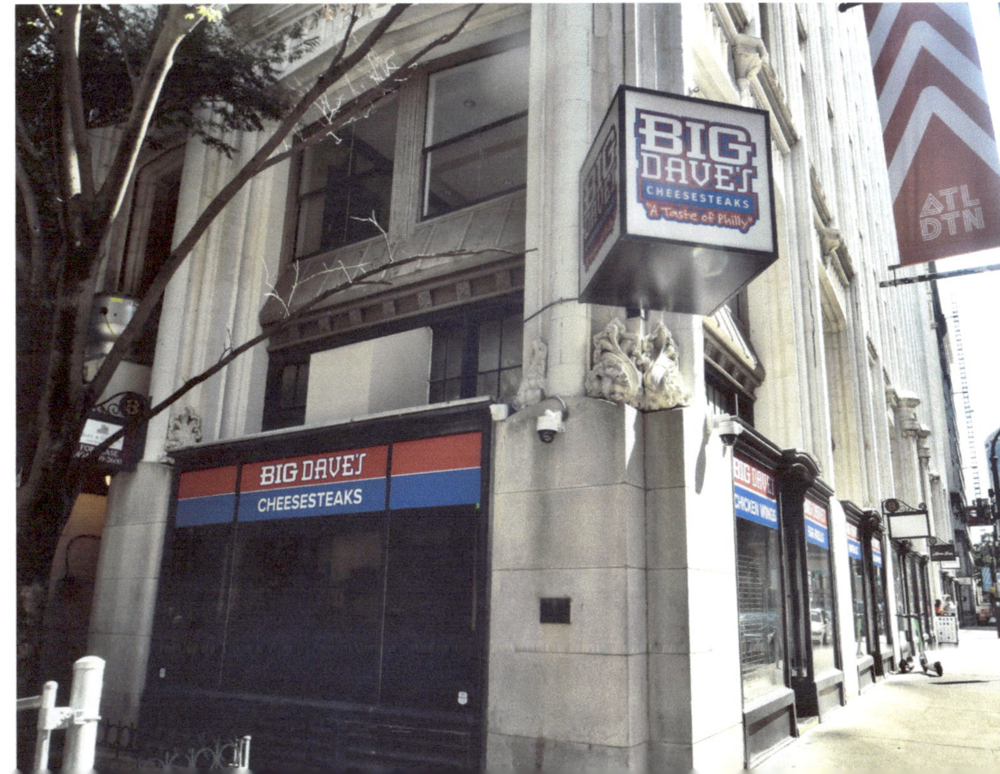

Atlanta Remembers

Gravesites of Notable Atlantans featured are located at several cemeteries in the Atlanta area including Oakland, Westview, South View, and Lincoln.

Westview Abbey Mausoleum & Chapel

Westview Abbey Mausoleum & Chapel, built in 1943, houses 11,444 entombments and spaces to hold cremated remains. Twenty-seven stained glass panels adorn the Spanish gothic style chapel and depict Jesus Christ's life from the nativity through crucifixion and resurrection.

Joseph Madison High

Joseph Madison High was the founder of Atlanta department store, J. M. High Company. His family mansion on Peachtree Street was donated by his wife, Harriet "Hattie" Harwell Wilson High and is now known as the High Museum of Art.

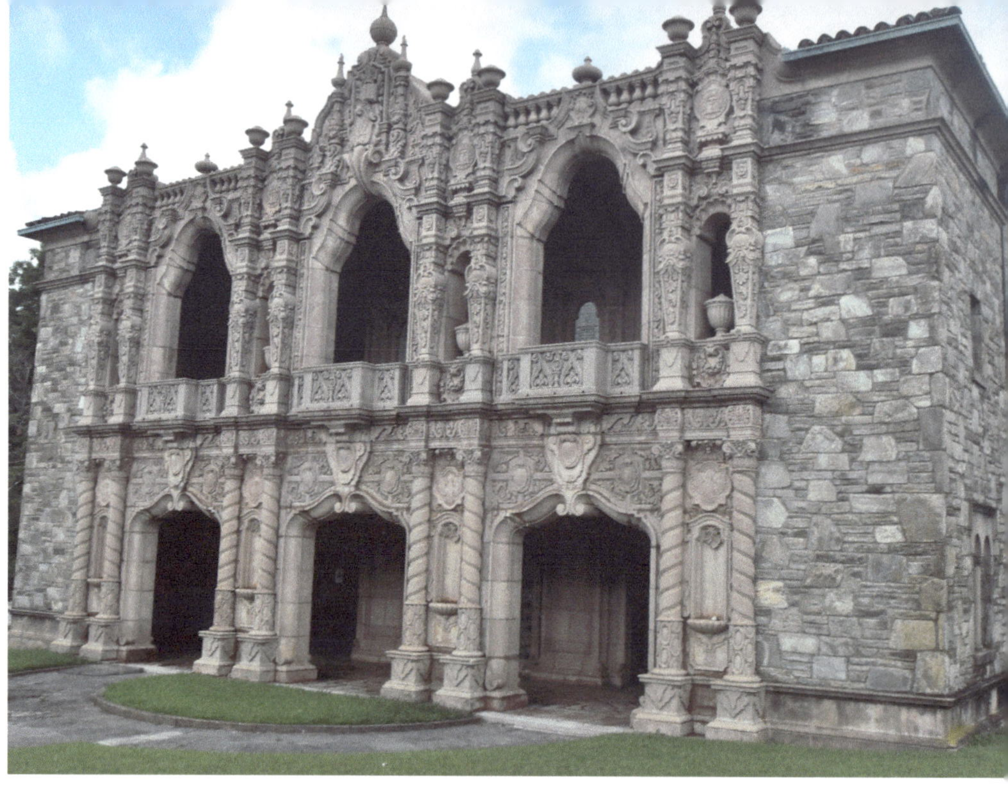

Founder of the Coca-Cola Company.

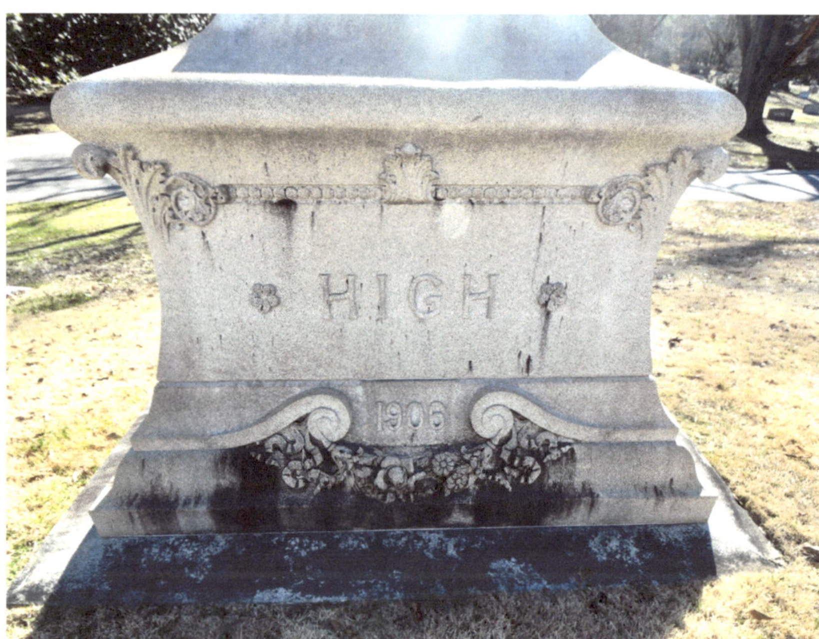

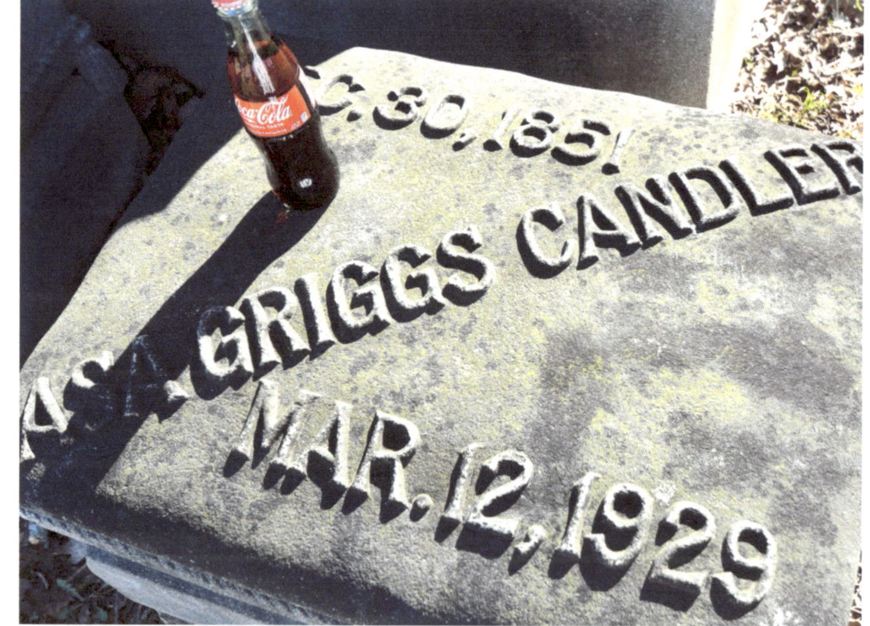

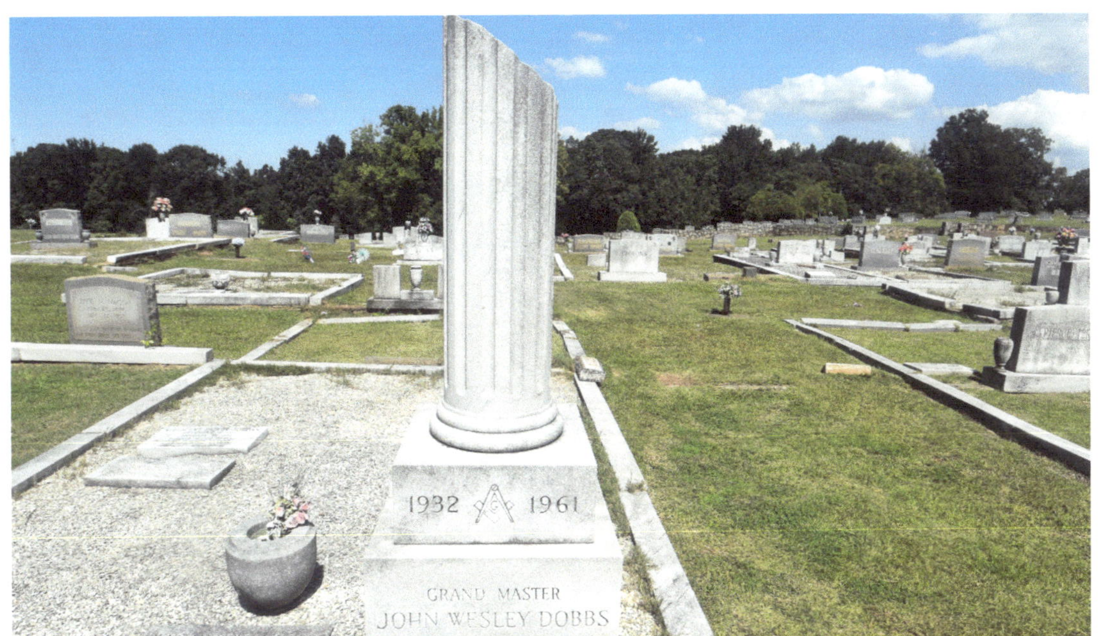

John Wesley Dobbs

John Wesley Dobbs founded the Georgia Voters League, the Atlanta Civic and Political League, and cofounded the Atlanta Negro Voters League. He was the grandfather of Atlanta's first African American mayor, Maynard Jackson Jr.

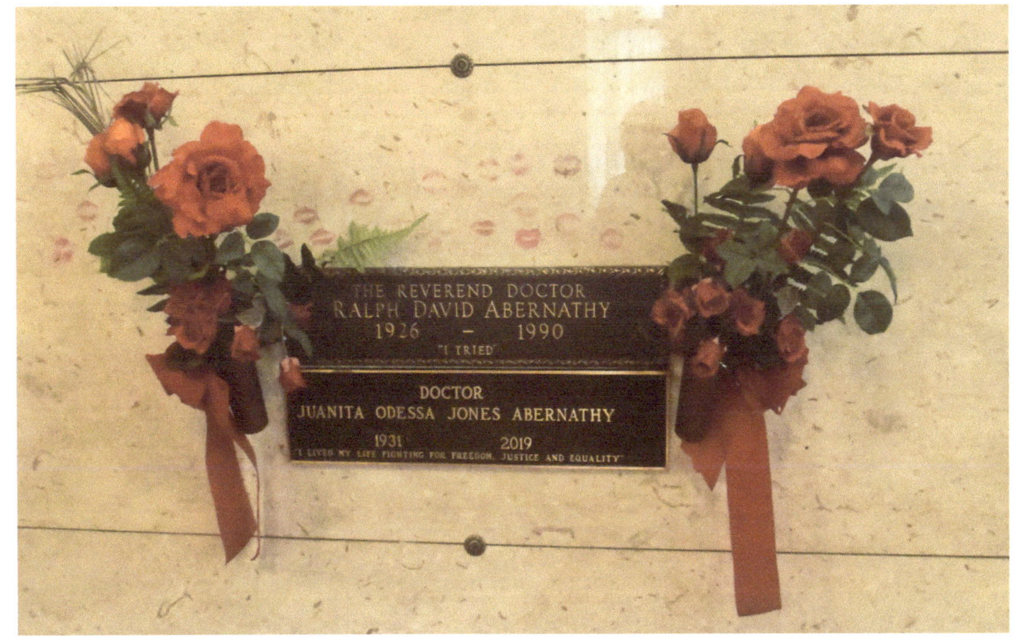

Reverend Doctor Ralph David Abernathy

Reverend Dr. Ralph David Abernathy was a Baptist pastor and central figure and leader of the Civil Rights Movement. He was the closest friend and advisor to Dr. Martin Luther King Jr.

Henry Grady

A journalist and editor of the Atlanta Journal Constitution. *Grady Hospital was named after him.*

Robert Winship Woodruff

Many educational and cultural landmarks in Atlanta bear his name, including the Woodruff Arts Center, Woodruff Park, and the Robert W. Woodruff Library.

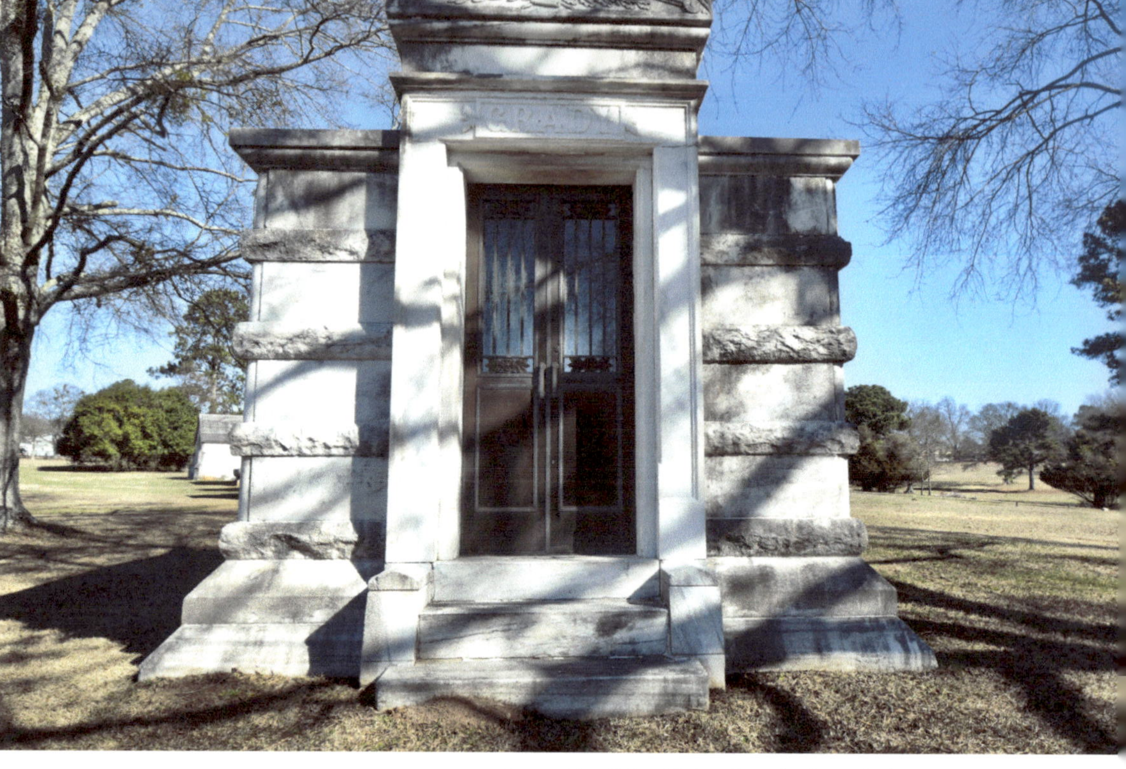

Cordy "C. T." Tindell Vivian

Civil Rights Leader

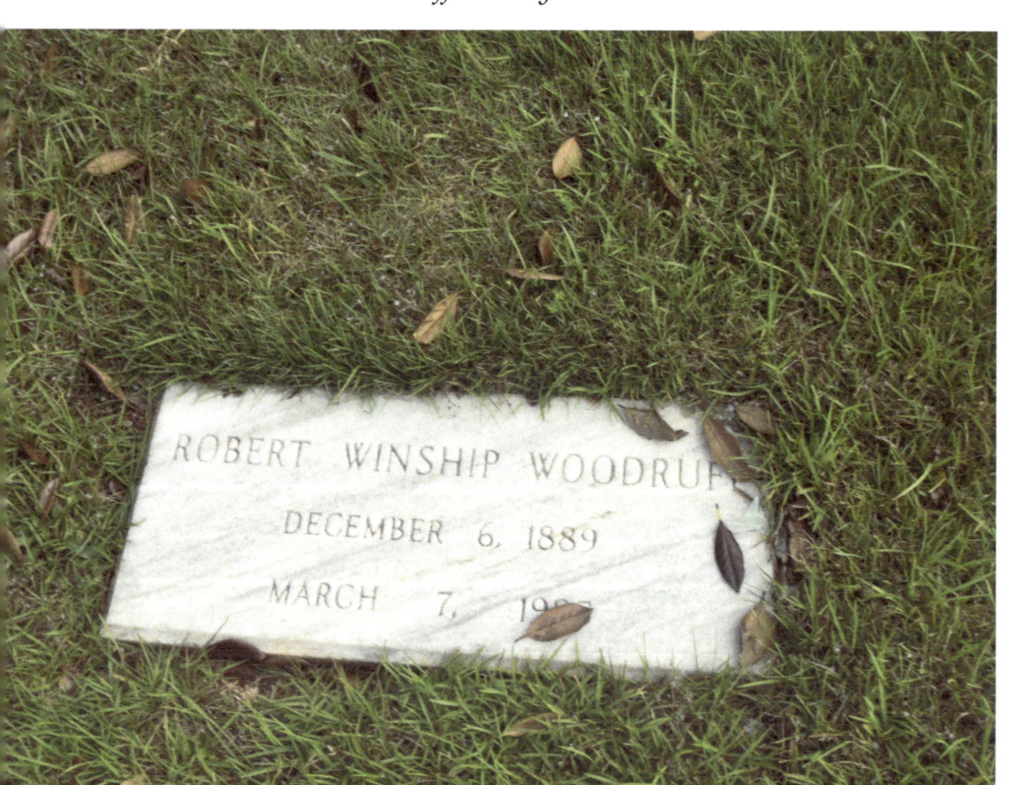

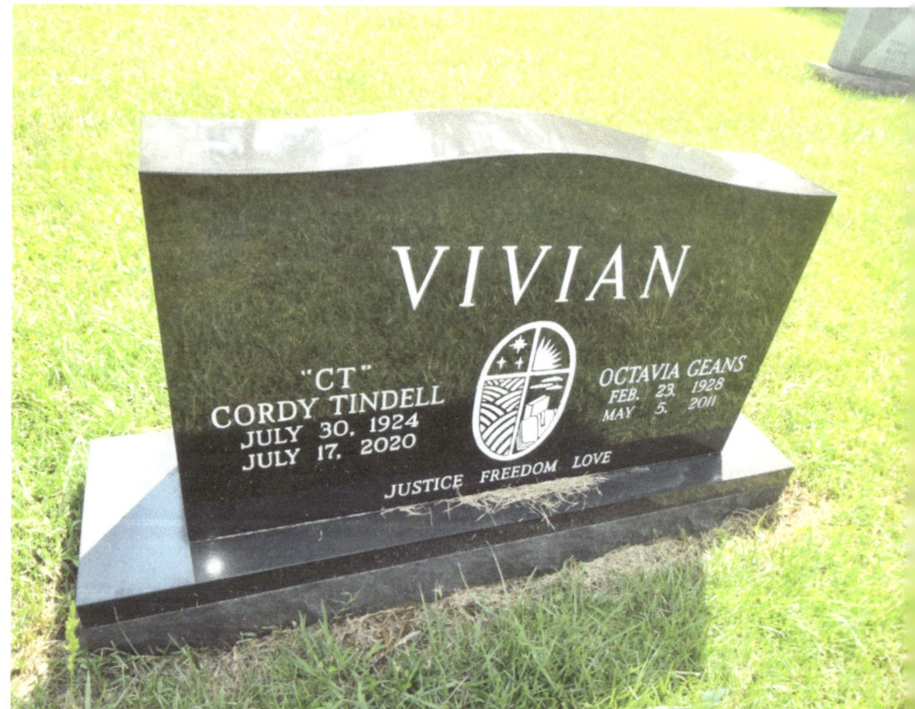

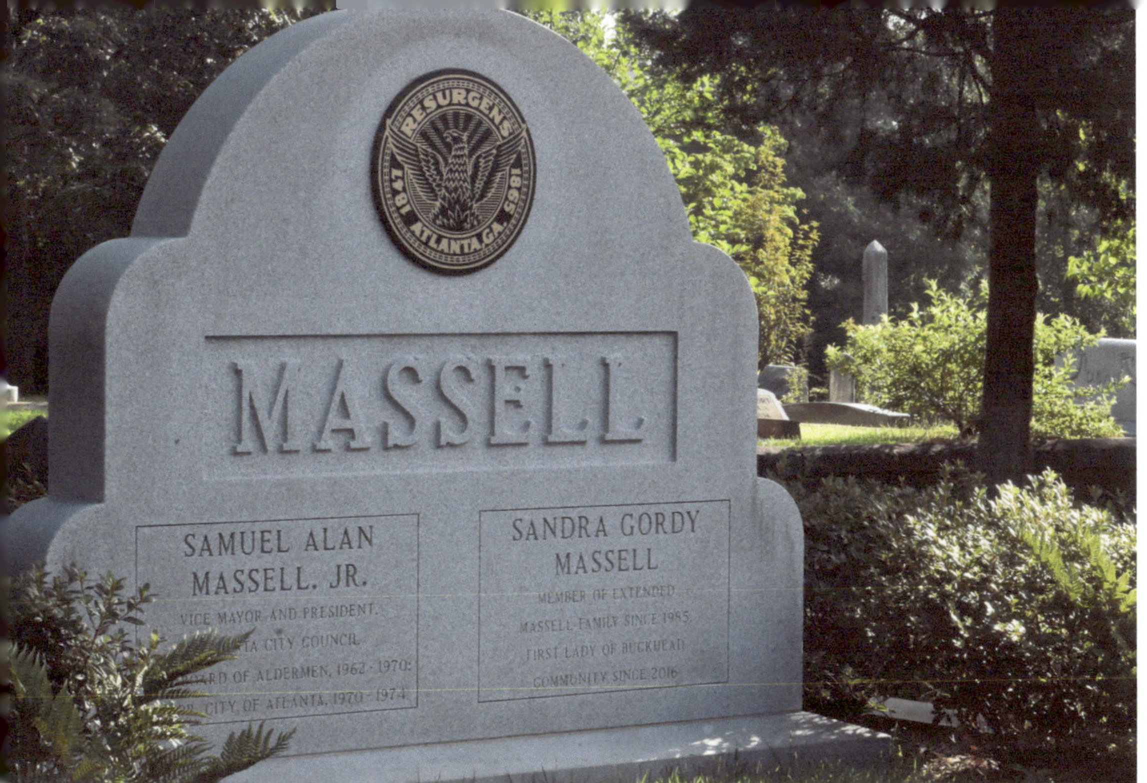

Samuel A. Massell

Samuel A. Massell was a businessman and politician who served as Atlanta's fifty-third and first Jewish mayor elected in 1969, and notably persuaded voters to support the creation of MARTA, the Omni Coliseum, and Woodruff Park.

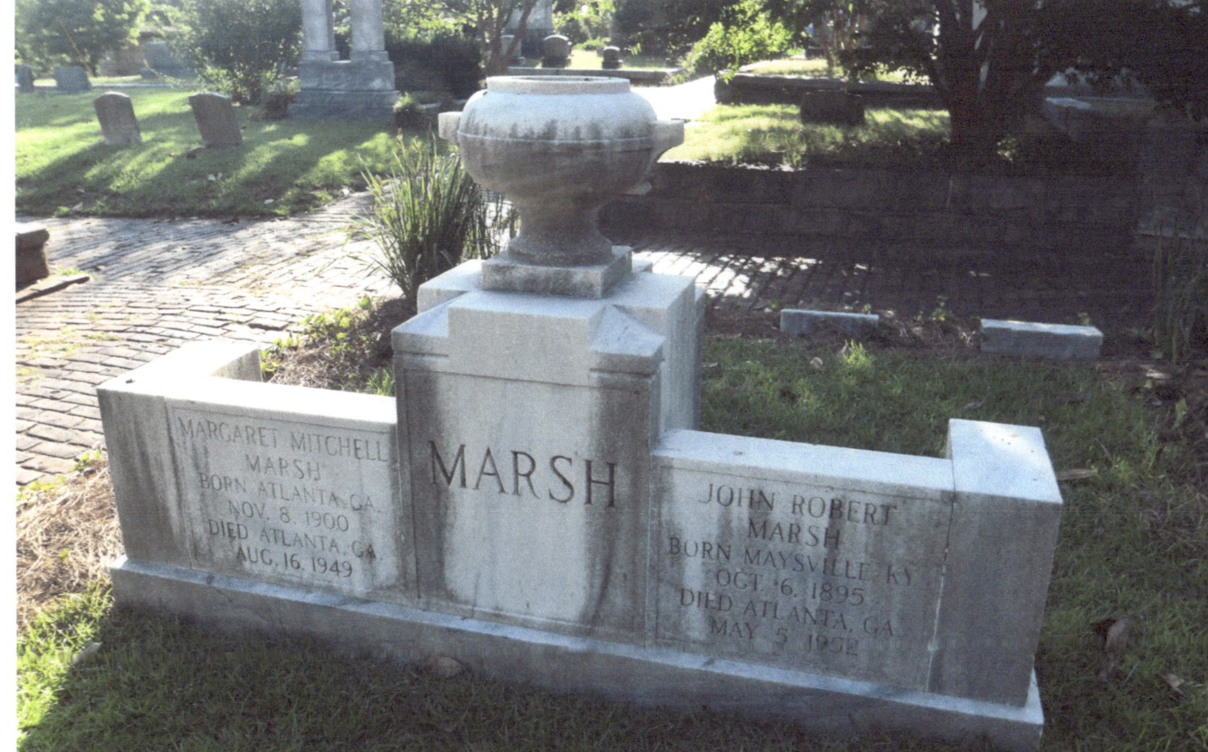

Margaret Mitchell Marsh

Margaret Mitchell Marsh was a feature writer for the Atlanta Journal *who wrote and published one hugely famous novel in her lifetime,* Gone with the Wind.

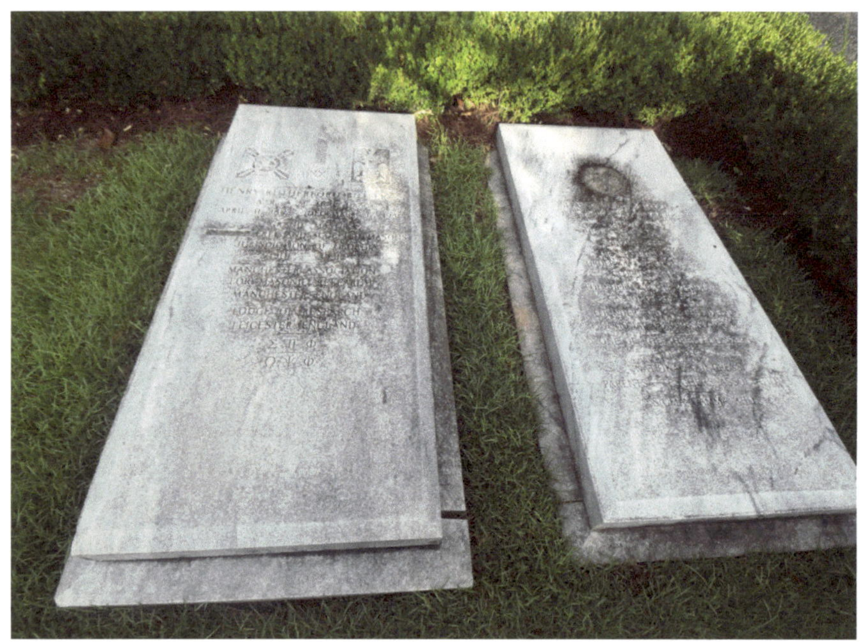

Selena Sloan Butler

Selena Sloan Butler was the founder of and the first president of the National Congress of Colored Parents and Teachers Association.

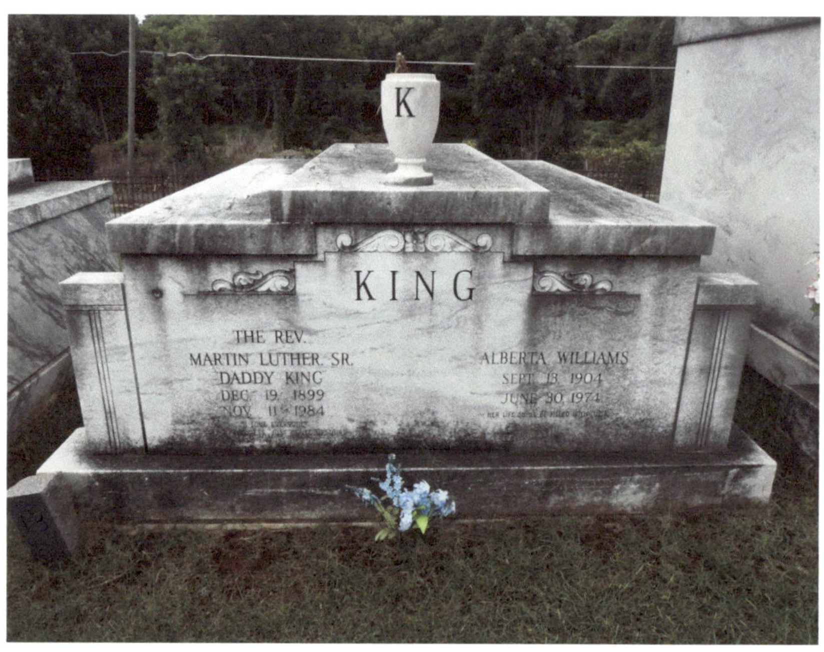

Final Resting Place of Martin Luther King Sr. and Alberta Williams King

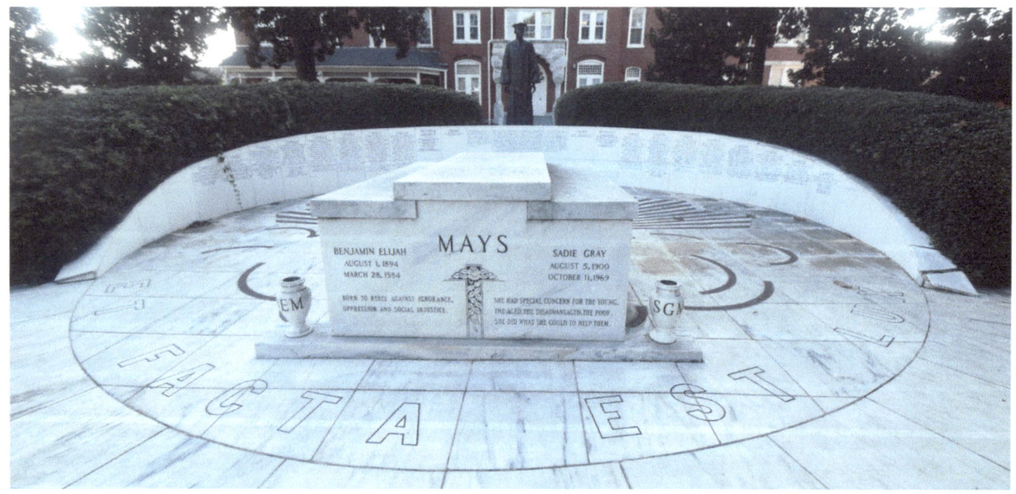

Dr. Benjamin Elijah Mays

Dr. Benjamin Elijah Mays was a distinguished Atlanta educator and Baptist minister who is credited with laying the intellectual foundations of the Civil Rights Movement. Morehouse College is Dr. Mays's final resting place along with his wife, Sadie.

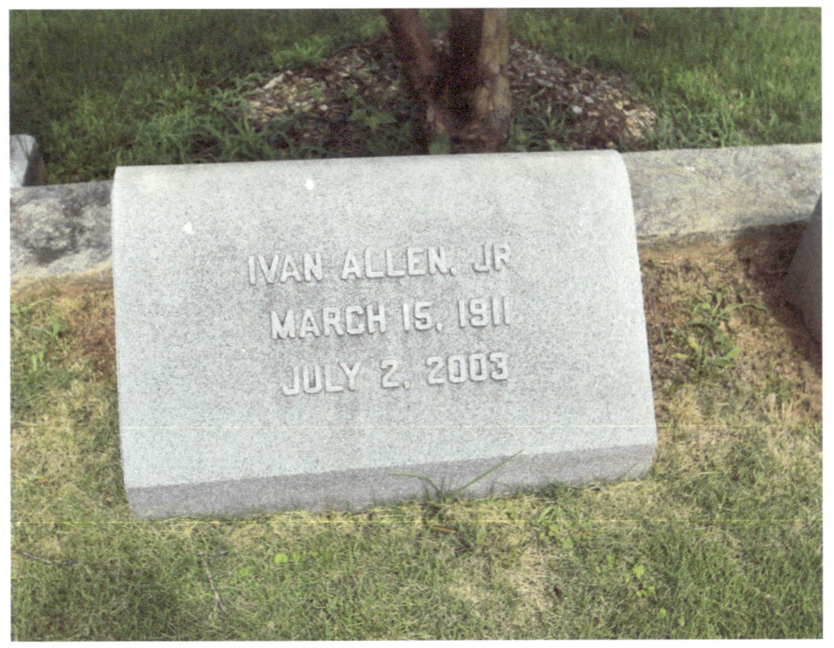

Ivan Allen Jr.

Atlanta's fifty-second mayor served two terms during the Civil Rights movement from 1962–1970.

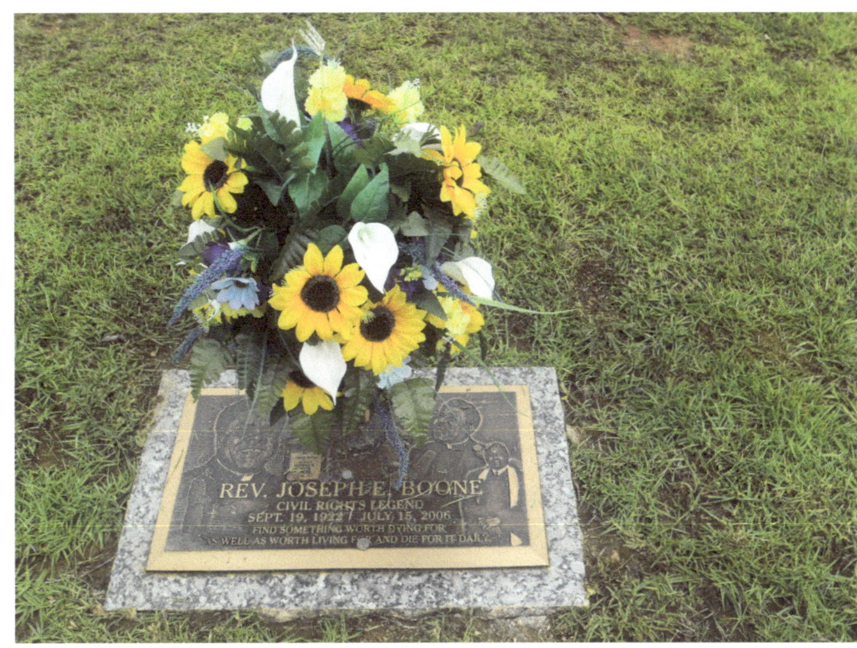

Reverend Joseph E. Boone

Reverend Joseph E. Boone was an activist and Civil Rights legend who marched with Dr. Martin Luther King Jr.

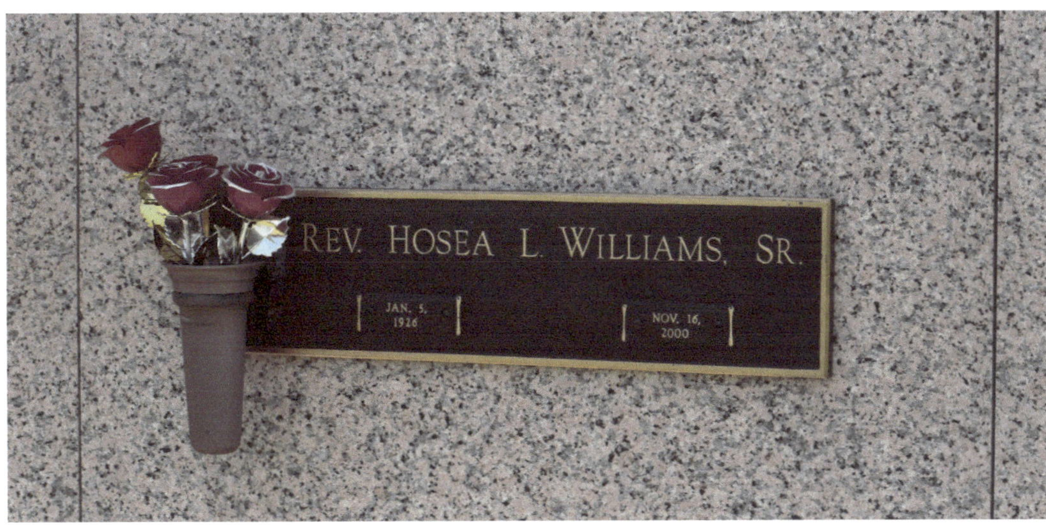

Reverend Hosea L. Williams

Reverend Hosea L. Williams described himself as the "thug" of the Southern Christian Leadership Conference. Martin Luther King Jr. affectionately referred to Williams as his "wild man, his Castro," because he was a skilled protest organizer. He also organized the Thanksgiving and Christmas Feed the Hungry programs, which fed over five thousand of Atlanta's homeless and delivered hot meals to thousands of senior citizens' homes annually.

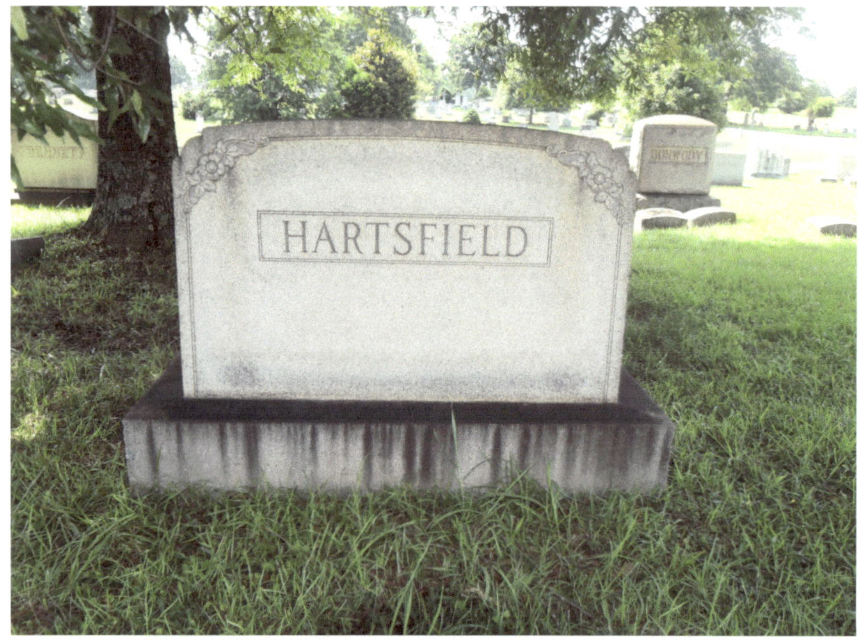

William B. Hartsfield

William B. Hartsfield was the longest-serving mayor of Atlanta. He was also instrumental in opening Atlanta's golf courses to Blacks.

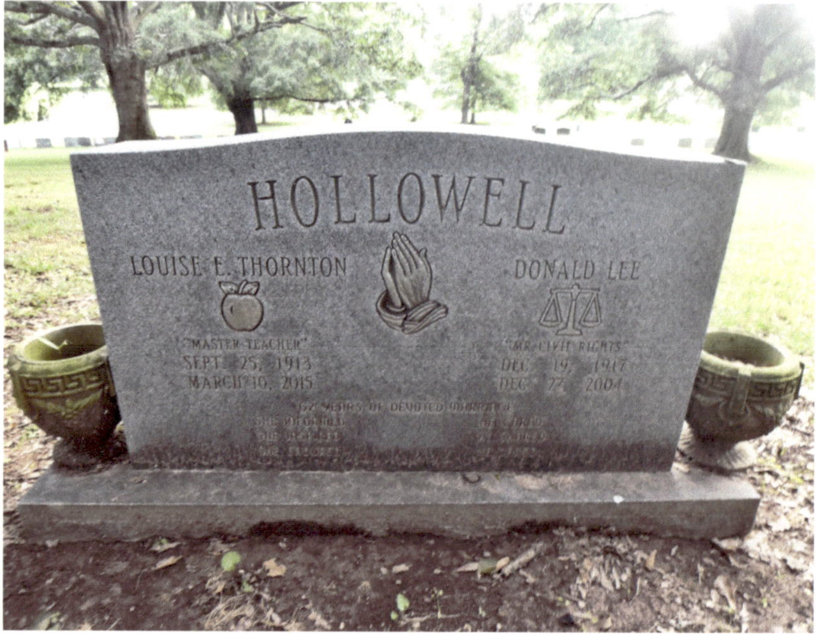

Donald Lee Hollowell

Donald Lee Hollowell was a Civil Rights attorney during the Civil Rights Movement. He was known for successfully integrating Atlanta public schools, colleges, universities, and public transit, and his legal strategies freed Martin Luther King Jr. from prison.

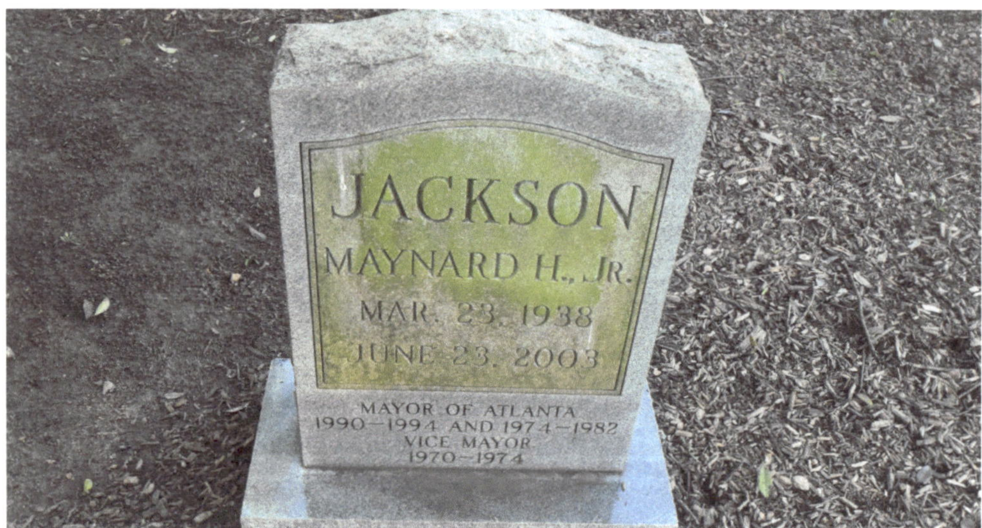

Maynard Holbrook Jackson Jr.

At the age of thirty-four, Maynard Holbrook Jackson Jr. was the first African American mayor of a large city in the Deep South. This began a shift in the United States's political power of African American leaders.

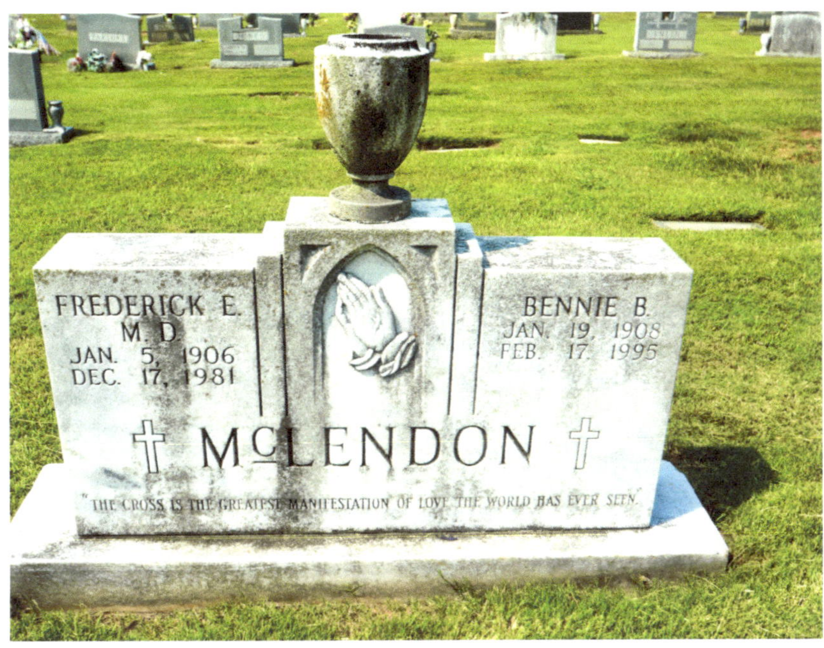

Frederick E. McLendon
Founder of McLendon Hospital.

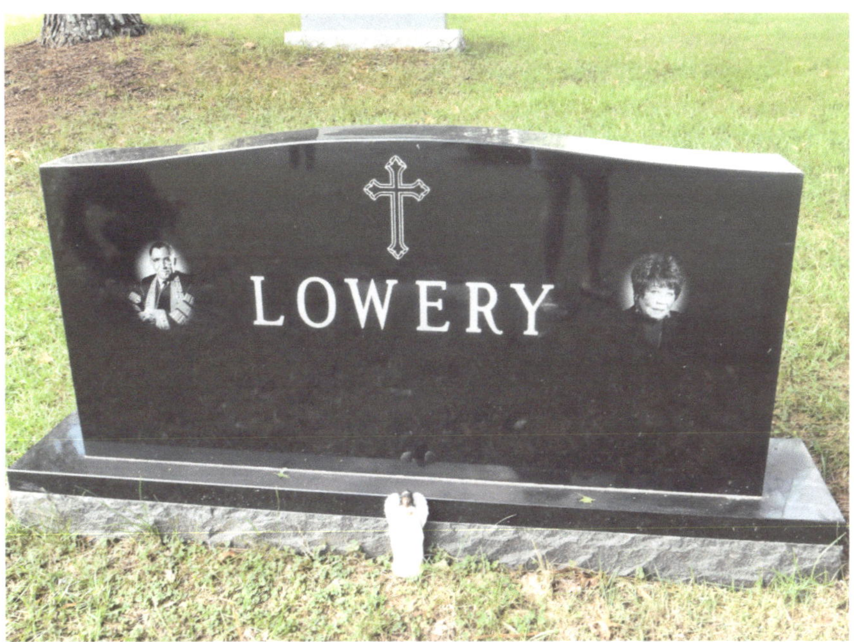

Joseph Echols Lowery
Outspoken Civil Rights activist and founder of the Southern Christian Leadership Conference along with Reverend Dr. Martin Luther King Jr.

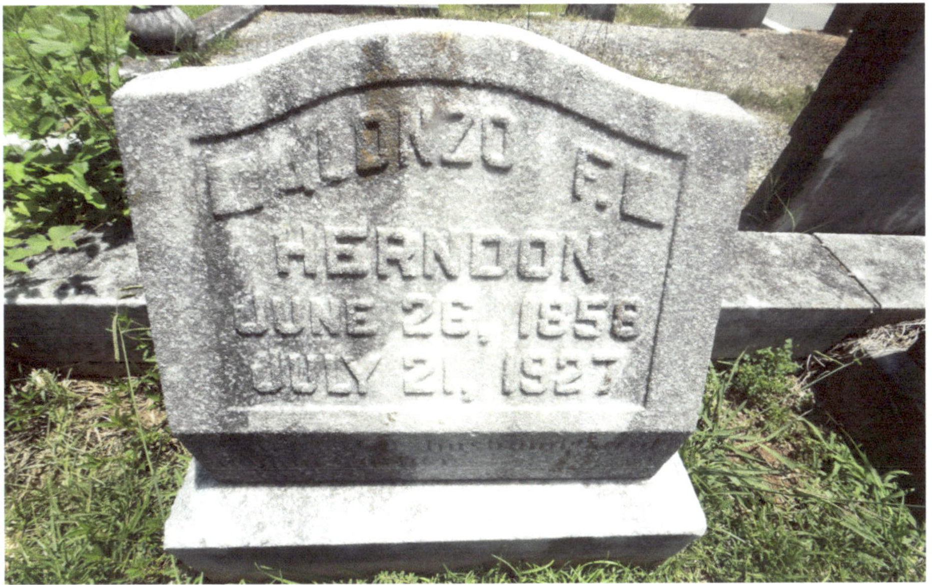

Alonzo Herndon
Born into slavery, Alonzo Herndon became one of the first African American millionaires in the United States.

Beacons of Hope—Our Future

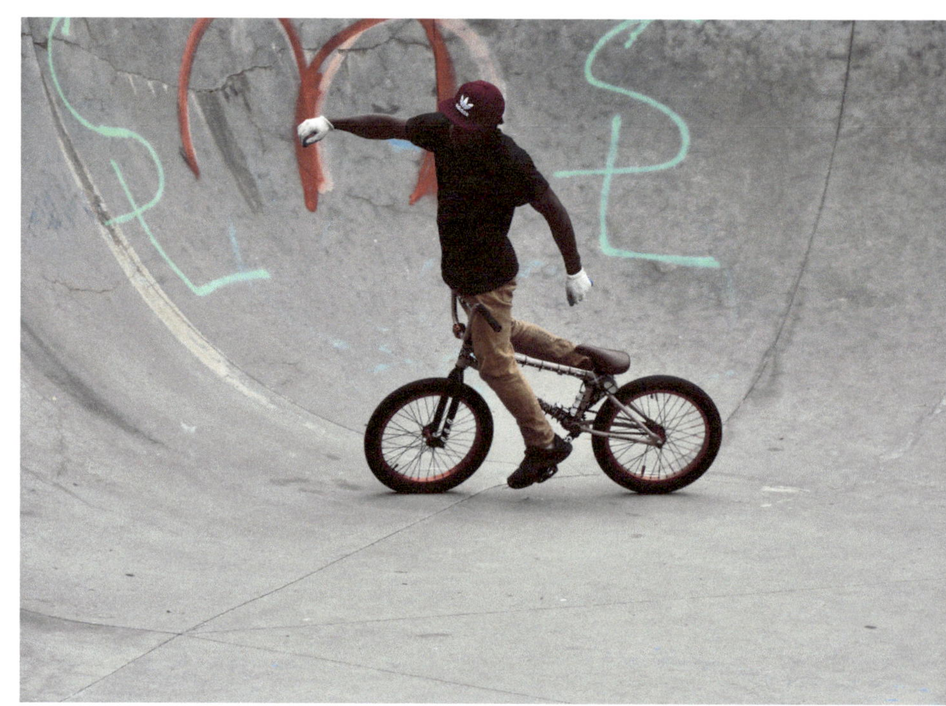

Skate Park (Old Fourth Ward)

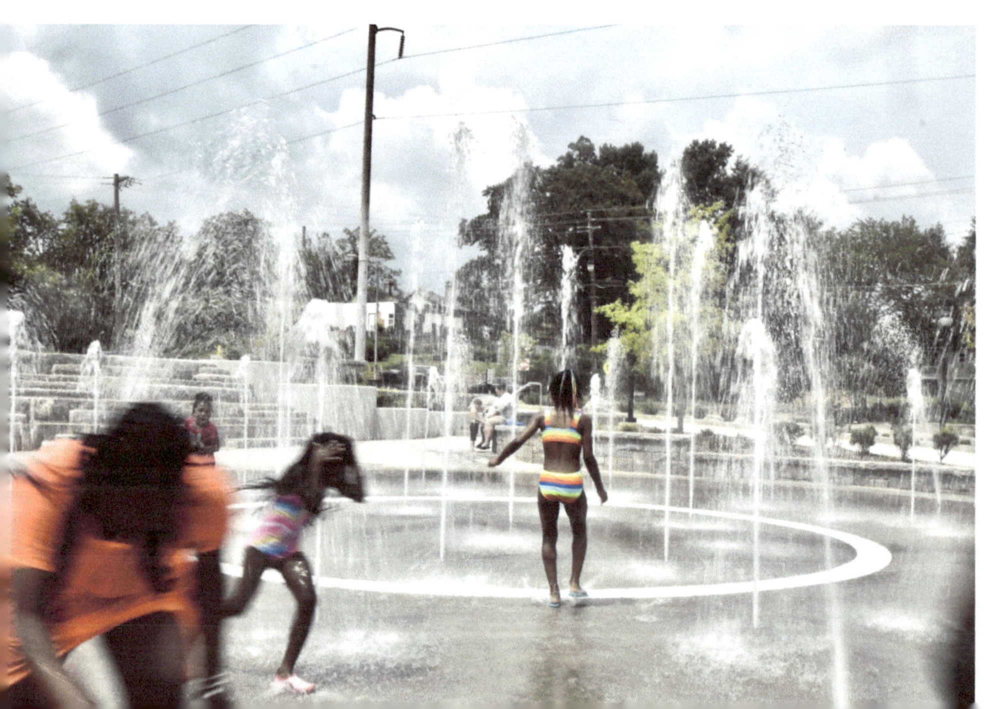

Rodney Cook Sr. Park (Historic Vine City)

Atlanta's Sunset

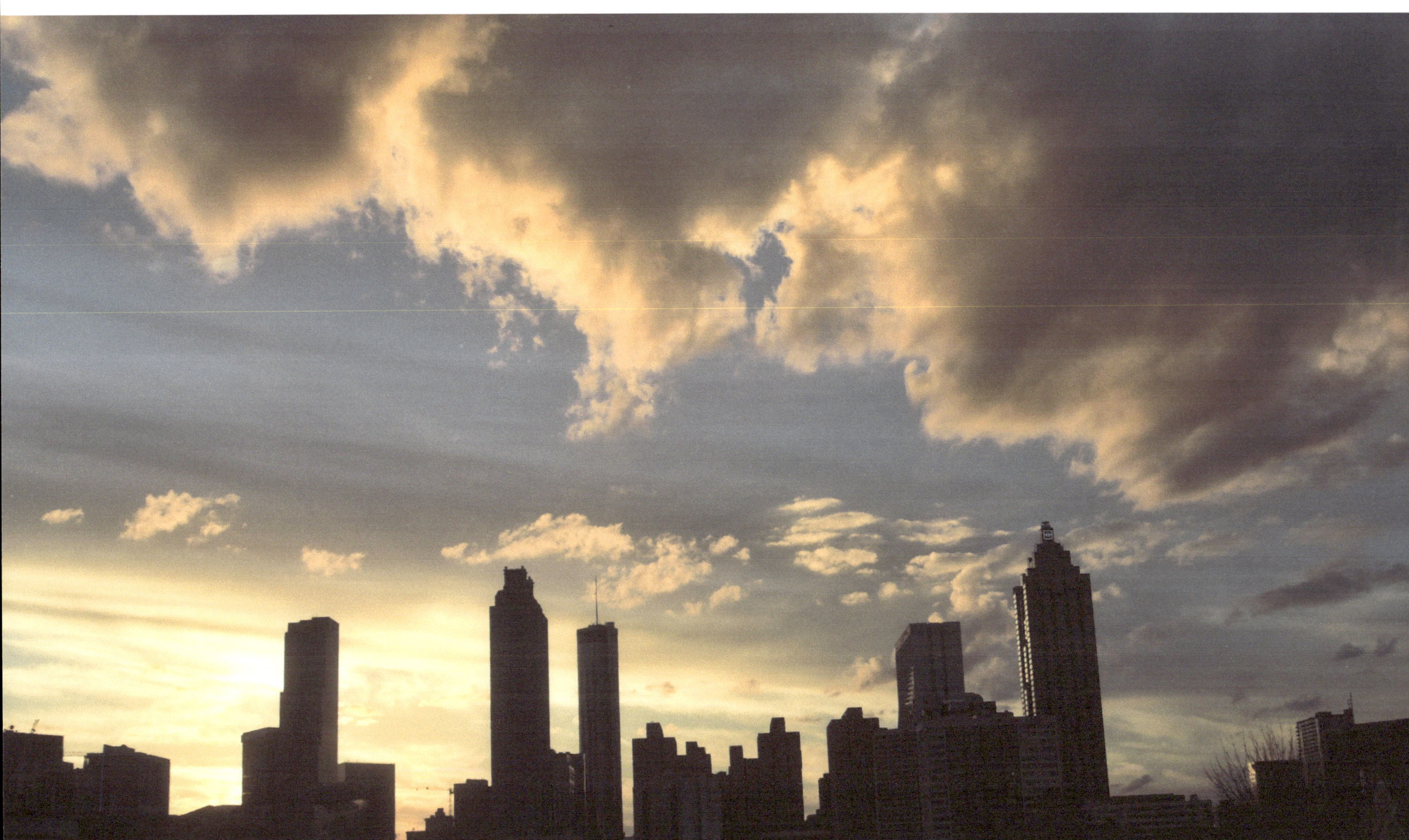

Acknowledgments

I am so very grateful for the creative gifts that God has given me and the blessings I've received and continue to receive that have brought *Angles of Atlanta* to life. Incredible gratitude to my mom, for everything she has done for me throughout my life, whose love is my beacon of hope, whose prayers have carried me through life, and whose wisdom and faith have always been a source of strength to me. Many thanks to Joan Taylor whose words grace the pages of this book, and for the countless hours of work, dedication, and research in the creation of *Angles of Atlanta*. I would also like to extend many thanks to the people who stood by me with so many encouraging words to create this project. Tony Mitchelson, Rosalind "Becky" Beasley George, Lynnette Stovall Clove, Sharon Friday, Wendy Loyd Thomas, Angela Kendrix, Toni Roquemore, Sharontine Bottley, Denise Rhodes-Webb, Rhonda James, Sylvia Donato-Moore, Dwain Evans, Donelle Douroux Johnson, Patrick Rock, Ingrid Kelly, Jamil Zainaldin, Deborah Mitchelson, Pamela Hart, and Viola D. Garris Bey. I truly thank you for believing in me and this project. I also would like to thank Nelson East for giving me the idea for the title of this book. Also thank you to Sid Morrison Washington for creating the footer. Much gratitude especially to Keith Schoeman for your support and generosity. Words cannot express my appreciation.

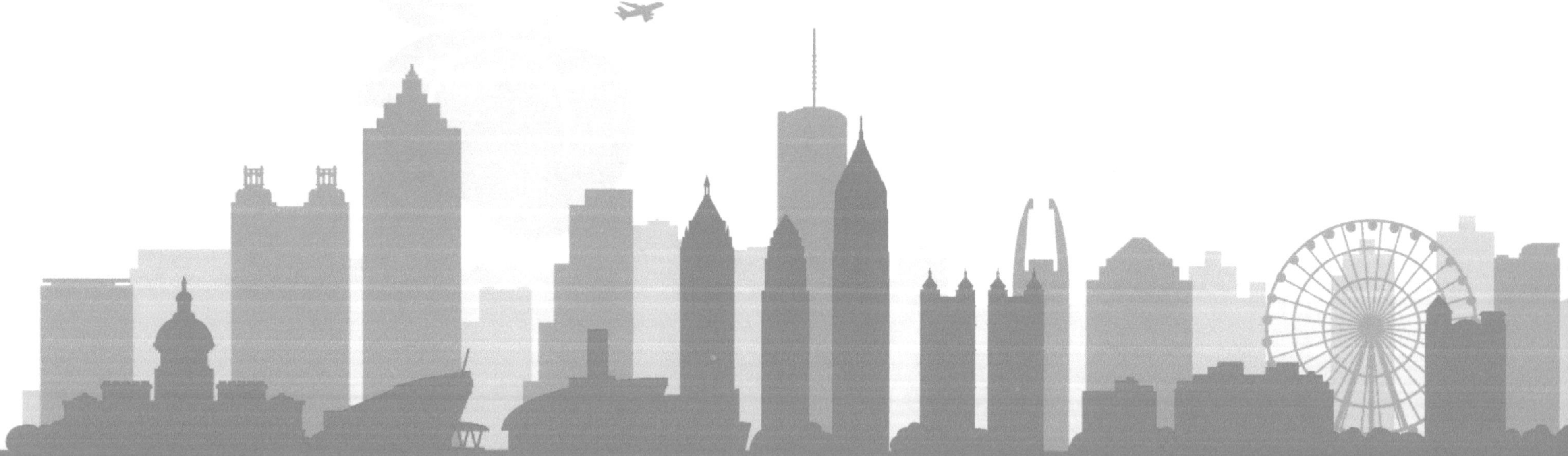

Printed in the USA
CPSIA information can be obtained
at www.ICGtesting.com
LVHW061240221024

794504LV00008B/224